Evolution of the Onondaga Iroquois

Evolution of the Onondaga Iroquois

ACCOMMODATING CHANGE, 1500–1655

James W. Bradley

SYRACUSE UNIVERSITY PRESS

This book is published with generous support from the John Ben Snow Foundation and from the Rochester Museum and Science Center.

The paper used in this publication meets the minimum requirements of American National Standard for Information Sciences—Permanence of Paper for Printed Library Materials, ANSI Z39.48-1984. ∞™

Library of Congress Cataloging-in-Publication Data

Bradley, James W. (James Wesley)
    Evolution of the Onondaga Iroquois.

    (An Iroquois book)
    Bibliography: p.
    Includes index.
    1. Onondaga Indians—Antiquities. 2. Indians
of North America—New York—Antiquities. I. Title.
II. Series.
E99.O58B7   1987   974.7'01   87-1977
ISBN 0-8156-2404-2 (alk. paper)

Manufactured in the United States of America

This book is dedicated to the Onondaga Iroquois,
who were a great and proud people,
and still are.

nya:wẽhah   onõdá'gehe:nǫ ?

JAMES W. BRADLEY is currently Survey Director at the Massachusetts Historical Commission, author of numerous articles and monographs on Native American archaeology, and twice recipient of the Arthur C. Parker Research Fellowship.

Contents

Plates

Figures

Maps

Tables

Preface

During the summer of 1978, I had the opportunity to work on Alaska's North Slope as part of an archaeological field survey. After several years of semi-cloistered life as a graduate student, it was quite a change. At first everything seemed alien and strange—the round-the-clock sun of the arctic summer, the treeless, featureless panorama of the tundra, tussock fields, polygonal frost cracks, pingos. From Anchorage we had flown north to Barrow. Here we made ready to go upriver to Atkasuk (Meade River) where our base camp would be located. Barrow too was strange, still locked in pack ice and glimmering under the June sun. Even more surprising was the seemingly chaotic character of the town, a discordant mix of traditional Eskimo and materialistic Western traits. Barrow was all the smells, sounds, and sights of a culture in transition: the waft of aviation fuel mingling with very ripe whale meat, snow machines whining down the dirt streets followed by howling sled dogs, Evinrude 150-horsepower outboard motors on sealskin umiaks, Eskimo youngsters in designer jeans listening alternately to disco hits and Inupiak gospel songs on their transistor radios.

Beneath this hodgepodge, however, something was naggingly familiar. It took a while, but over the course of the summer I gradually realized that what I was seeing was not very different from what I had been studying. What happens when two very different cultures meet? What are the dynamics of the interaction, and what are the consequences for the participants? For several years I had been trying to answer those questions archaeologically, looking at the Onondaga Iroquois and their increasing contact with Europeans during the sixteenth and early seventeenth centuries. Barrow brought the present into the equation. I came home from Alaska much more certain of two things. One was that the dynamics of cross-cultural change could be very similar even when the particulars were quite different. The other was that these are processes that we need to understand.

I am not talking about some dry academic exercise. The issues involved are essential to understanding cultural stability and survival. They apply as readily to our own technologically sophisticated culture as they do to that of a Third World country or "primitive" band of hunter/gatherers. Perhaps even more so. The differences are in scale, not kind.

I have always believed that good scholarship is, essentially, a cooperative venture. Individuals may do the work and the writing, but the results do not become scholarship until they have been tested and refined by the comments and criticisms of one's peers. In this regard I have been quite fortunate. Of the many people who have assisted in this project, four deserve special thanks. They are George Hamell, New York State Museum; Barry Kent, State Archaeologist for Pennsylvania; James Pendergast, formerly of the National Museum of Man, Ottawa; and Jan Baart, City Archaeologist, Amsterdam. Not only have they put up with me for the past several years, they have often put me up as well. Others who read and critiqued drafts include: Gordon DeAngelo, William Fitzgerald, Robert E. Funk, Paul Huey, Wayne Lenig, Brona Simon, Marvin T. Smith, and William Starna.

Among those who have generously shared data with me or otherwise encouraged my efforts are: William Finlayson, James Herbstritt, Karlis Karklins, Francis P. McManamon, Peter P. Pratt, Jan Piet Puype, James A. Tuck, Stephen S. Webb, and James V. Wright. To all of these individuals, and to those who allowed me access to their collections, I am profoundly grateful.

A few other, particular, acknowledgments are due. Special thanks go to Charles F. Hayes III and the staff of the Research Division at the Rochester Museum and Science Center, for their patient assistance while helping to answer my endless questions. Thanks also to Valerie Talmage, Executive Director of the Massachusetts Historical Commission, whose steady support helped me finish this project. I owe thanks to my friends and colleagues in the New York State Archaeological Association, especially the William Beauchamp and Chenango chapters, for generously sharing information. I also wish to acknowledge my deep gratitude to my good friend, the late Charles F. Wray—thanks, Charlie. Finally, to the members of my own clan, especially Margaret Alice: I hope this book at last explains what it is I've been doing all these years.

I am also pleased to express my thanks to the Arthur C. Parker Fund for financial support in the form of a research fellowship. This fellowship, administered through the Research Division of the Rochester Museum and Science Center, enabled me to complete much additional postdoctoral research.

Several institutions and individuals have been kind enough to allow me to reproduce graphic work or photographs, and I would like to acknowledge them here: Figure 6, "A Specific Model for Iroquoian Tribal Development," is reproduced from Niemczycki (1984:90) with the permission of Mary Ann Niemczycki and the Rochester Museum and Science Center; the photographs used in Plates 1b and c and 12e and f were provided through the courtesy of Peter P. Pratt; the double bird effigy pipe in Plates 4a and b was photographed with permission at the Lorenzo State Historic Site, Cazenovia, New York; the photograph of the sixteenth-century dagger in Plate 7b is reproduced with the permission of the New York Metropolitan Museum of Art; the photographs of the "Amsterdams anderhalf stael" cloth seal, Plates 10b and c, and the majolica and Weserware vessels, Plates 11b and d, are by courtesy of Dienst Openbare Werken Amsterdam/Amsterdams Historisch Museum-Afd. Archeologie (DOW/AHM-Afd. Archeologie); and the photographs of the European ceramic vessels in Plates 11f and h were provided by the Rochester Museum and Science Center.

I also wish to thank the New York State Museum (NYSM), the Rochester Museum and Science Center (RMSC), the Office of Museums and Historical Sites, Onondaga County Department of Parks and Recreation (Onon. Co. Parks Dept.), the Onondaga Historical Association, and several individuals, particularly Dr. A. Gregory Sohrweide and Albert D. LaFrance, for permission to photograph artifacts in their collections for use in this book. As a matter of convention, all illustrated artifacts from museum collections are identified by institution and, wherever possible, catalog number; all artifacts without specific attribution are from private collections. Information on these collections is presented in end notes.

A few important acknowledgments remain. Credit for the maps belongs to Montine Jordan. The majority of the illustrations were executed by Patricia Miller; Gene Mackay and Ed Britt also contributed. Special thanks to Karen Maini, who helped put the graphics in final form. Finally, a particular word of thanks to Margaret Donovan, a meticulous typist, a relentless editor, and a patient friend.

With all this assistance one might think the result would be error-free. Alas, this is unlikely. In spite of my conviction that scholarship is a cooperative venture, at this point the author must stand alone.

James W. Bradley

Charlestown, Massachusetts
May 1987

Evolution of the Onondaga Iroquois

Introduction

Initially, two considerations led to this study. One was the desire to understand more clearly events in northeastern North America during the sixteenth century, that formative yet enigmatic phase of native American-European relations. The first significant contacts occurred then, precedents were established, and the processes of change set in motion. If we are ever to understand the complex, and from a native point of view often cataclysmic, events of the seventeenth century, we must know more about their sixteenth century antecedents.

A second concern was to look more closely at the Iroquois and their League.[1] During the seventeenth and eighteenth centuries, the Iroquois dominated native American affairs in the Northeast, exerting an influence far in excess of their numbers. The recurring question has been: Why were the Iroquois so successful, and to what degree was the Confederacy a factor?

This topic is hardly new. In 1940, William Fenton noted that more ink had been shed over the Iroquois than over almost any other native people in North America (1940:190). The flow of ink has certainly not lessened since then. That, in fact, is part of the problem. There is so much literature on the Iroquois and the Confederacy that the people themselves have become all but lost in the process of attempts to explain them. And yet, for all our scholarship, we still know very little about the Five Nations Iroquois prior to the middle of the seventeenth century, when Europeans began to document interaction with them in greater detail. By then, however, the Iroquois had already experienced over a century of contact. What effect did earlier interaction have, not only on the material aspects of Iroquois culture, but in defining the Iroquois and their institutions?

To a large degree, both of these considerations are components of a broader issue. What happened when native Americans and Europeans came into contact with one another early in the sixteenth century? What subsequently, as exploration and eventually settlement intensified during the later sixteenth and early seventeenth centuries? Clearly this process of contact between autonomous yet radically different cultures resulted in change, change that affected both groups. Contact forced both native Americans and Europeans to respond to unexpected and exotic circumstances. The resulting process of reciprocal though not always equal interaction between differing cultures is what anthropologists term "acculturation."[2]

At this point, the question is: How can we comprehend such large and complex issues, break the processes into their component parts, and reduce them to a manageable and testable size? I intend to do so in two ways. First, to focus on the Onondaga, the central member of the Five Nations and the traditional seat of the Confederacy. My goal is to track the Onondaga and the traits defining their culture from before European contact through the middle of the seventeenth century, to reconstruct their history for the period 1500 to 1655. This information in turn serves as a baseline, a set of reference points, against which the events of the sixteenth and early seventeenth centuries can be plotted and assessed.

The second focus of the study is the process of acculturation, that is, the process of reciprocal interaction which occurs when one autonomous culture comes into contact with another. In spite of the inherent cross-cultural emphasis, our primary concern will be native Americans and how their culture responded to that of the Europeans. The common perception is that they did not fare very well and that, once contact occurred, native culture began to disintegrate. Craft skills disappeared as European materials replaced traditional ones. Diseases, to which native people had no immunity, often escalated into major epidemics, resulting in massive population loss. These and other factors all helped speed the breakdown of traditional native culture and society. In short, as one historian has observed, "Within a generation of the original contact, Indian civilization was on the road to extinction" (Trelease 1960:viii). Lamentably, in some ways this assessment is correct. The St. Lawrence Iroquois, Huron, and Susquehannock no longer exist, at least not as identifiable cultures.

Nonetheless, this view of the acculturative process is profoundly misleading. Native people were not just swept away. In addition to the Five Nations, many other tribal groups still live in the Northeast. More serious is a subtle but fundamental misconception that underlies this interpretation: that native culture was passive, static, and unable to cope with changing conditions. This simply is not true. Native American cultures, like those of Europeans, had been in a state of flux for centuries prior to contact; change did not stop just because Europeans happened to appear. From this perspective, continuity plays as much a role in the process of acculturation as does change.

Acculturation is difficult to address comprehensively in one case study. Therefore, I concentrate on three particular issues to help us see the acculturative process in a more balanced manner:

—To what degree do existing (traditional) cultural patterns and values serve to screen, filter, and even define what is accepted and absorbed from another culture?

—To what extent are there different rates of change within a culture? What elements are most susceptible to influence? Which are most resistant?

—While the acculturative process can have a negative impact, what is its potential for initiating innovation and cross-cultural creativity? What circumstances maximize this potential?

To examine these aspects of the acculturative process, we need a specific system, one in which these dynamics can be traced and explored with some control. Here again, the Onondaga serve well as a test case.

One further point needs to be made. While acculturation is an important process in the reshaping of cultures, it is not the only one. Other external factors, such as a shift in environmental conditions, can play a major role in initiating cultural change. In addition to external factors, cultures also modify themselves in response to internal stimuli. In the case of the Onondaga, several centuries of cultural evolution preceded European contact. If we are ever to see the effects of acculturation in perspective, we must first be able to distinguish the internal factors for change from the external ones.

Before introducing the remaining chapters, two methodological problems need to be addressed briefly. First: Can we reconstruct a history for a preliterate people, that is, people who did not keep written records? If so, how? The most reliable approach is ethnohistoric. This interdisciplinary method uses four basic sources of information: historical documents kept by literate observers; the oral history of the people themselves, including their myths and legends; linguistic analysis of their language; and finally, the archaeological record. By triangulating in from these diverse sources, one can reconstruct a great deal about a culture (Trigger 1976, 2:11–21; 1983).

While ethnohistory has proved to be a powerful methodology for crossing both cultural and temporal boundaries, it does have its limitations. Ethnohistorical analysis often utilizes a technique called "upstreaming," or the "direct historical approach," which starts with known events and then attempts to work back in time or "upstream" from them.[3] Unfortunately, this method cannot be used in reconstructing acculturative change. To track the process of acculturation, we must follow the arrow of causality and chronology; otherwise, we cannot reliably separate cause from effect, continuity from change.

The second problem concerns the archaeological evidence and how it is used. While the other components of the ethnohistorical approach are utilized wherever possible, any reconstruction of Onondaga history for the sixteenth and early seventeenth centuries must rely primarily on archaeological data. This is an excellent basis from which to work, for the archaeological record can be amazingly detailed and instructive. Sometimes, however, the sheer magnitude and potential of this data base obscure an essential caveat: we are not reconstructing historical reality but rather are formulating our best approximation of it. As in quantum mechanics, it may not be possible to know exactly what happened. What we can do is build testable explanations for the patterns we observe in the surviving material record.

Nowhere is the issue of historical reconstruction versus historical reality more apparent than in proposing a site sequence and chronology, that fundamental first step in any archaeological investigation of cultural change. It is the foundation on which all subsequent analysis of the material culture rests. And yet, these are often some of the most ephemeral and arbitrary of archaeological constructs. As working hypotheses, a site sequence and a chronology are always subject to change. The discovery of additional sites, new analytic techniques, and even a change in theoretical approach, can result in a shuffling of the site order or a recalibration of dates.

The site sequence and chronology that underly this study are ones I have tried to test in several ways. One technique has been to use as long a baseline as possible. While the primary concern remains acculturative change during the sixteenth and early seventeenth centuries, the first sites to be considered predate European contact by several hundred years. Sites postdating 1655 will also be briefly discussed. As a result, we can track the Onondaga from the end of the thirteenth century, when their antecedents are first visible archaeologically, through the establishment of the Onondaga Reservation in 1788. Nearly forty sites are considered; all are located in Central New York, and most lie within the boundaries of Onondaga County.

I expand the site sequence for a simple reason. The longer the archaeological baseline, the more reliably we can examine cultural continuity and change, especially in material traits. Material patterns alone will not prove that a sequence is correct. However, the more indices one can seriate, the greater the probability that the sequence is at least internally valid. Then the proposed sequence and chronology can be tested externally against other documented sequences and events.

After establishing a site sequence and chronology, I then examine the specific components of Onondaga culture and identify its broad patterns of settlement, subsistence, and material culture. Settlement patterns focus on site location, physical characteristics and layout of the sites, and on the kinds of structures built for either shelter or defense. Subsistence patterns identify the resource base that supported the population as well as the strategies used to obtain food and raw materials. Material culture patterns include, among others, the artifact forms, raw material preferences, methods of production, and techniques of style and embellishment that characterized the Onondaga and their antecedents.

Emphasis is placed on material culture patterns, which can be extremely sensitive indicators of change within a culture. In the case of the Onondaga, change occurred at three different levels: (1) the ongoing, internal evolution of Onondaga culture itself, (2) the influence of other non-Iroquois groups on Onondaga culture, and (3) the effects of European contact and materials. By carefully examining material culture patterns, we can track each of these processes and their interaction. In addition, we can use the material record as a basis for drawing inferences about other, broader aspects of Onondaga culture.

The remainder of this book is divided into five chapters plus three appendices. Chapter 1 focuses on the evolution of the Onondaga in the centuries prior to European contact. This chapter basically reexamines Tuck's work (1971), which proposed a model for Onondaga evolution from Owasco antecedents. I trace the patterns of settlement, subsistence, and material culture during the four final phases of the Late Woodland stage, using the archaeological record to understand Onondaga culture prior to contact. Other specific topics discussed include models of tribal evolution, the dating of the Onondaga as a discernible tribal entity, and archaeological evidence for the establishment of the Confederacy.

Chapter 2 traces the Onondaga through the sixteenth century, or the protohistoric period. This was a period of indirect contact, when European materials reached Central New York, but not Europeans themselves. As in chapter 1, I trace the patterns of settlement, subsistence, and material culture across a series of sites. I discuss the different factors that combined to produce change within Onondaga culture, including internal processes, the influence of other native people, particularly the St. Lawrence Iroquois and Susquehannock, and, of course, the impact of European materials.

Chapter 3 shifts from the presentation of archaeological evidence to a broader interpretative view of the sixteenth-century Onondaga. I emphasize three issues. The first two are the intertribal dynamics of warfare and trade between the Onondaga and a specific non-League neighbor. The relationship between the Onondaga and the St. Lawrence Iroquois of Jefferson County, New York, illustrates the function of warfare as a means for increasing population through the assimilation of captives. Changing relations between the Onondaga and the Susquehannock provide an opportunity to follow the evolution of a precontact exchange network into a historic trading system. Third, the chapter reviews the Confederacy and how this larger unit of Iroquois culture may have changed as a consequence of European presence.

Chapter 4 traces the Onondaga archaeologically through the middle of the seventeenth century. As in chapters 1 and 2, I examine the patterns of settlement, subsistence, and material culture across several sites. Emphasis is placed on documenting the changing character of Onondaga culture and the impact that the ever-increasing flow of Europeans and their materials had on the Onondaga.

Chapter 5 returns to the question of process. How did the Onondaga fare during the first century or more of contact, and what can their experience tell us about the process of acculturation? Initially I consider material culture and reach three general conclusions: (1) the Onondaga response to contact was active and selective, not passive; (2) continuity marked the acculturative process as much as change did; and (3) many of the changes that did occur were creative and innovative. Finally, I discuss briefly the Confederacy and its response to acculturative pressures, both internal and external, during the second and third quarters of the seventeenth century.

One final comment. This book seeks to understand the process of acculturative change from a native, rather than a European, perspective. Is this possible? Can we as twentieth-century westernized technocrats understand a traditional native-American point of view? Probably not. Then why make the attempt?

The answer, in part, is to understand ourselves better. Native people are integral to our history, just as we are to theirs. As Trigger has observed, without a clear understanding of people's motives, respect for them is impossible (1976, 1:26). Another reason, however, concerns the future rather than the past. Processes of cultural change are on-going. Even though mass media and multinational economics have begun to homogenize the globe's cultures, acculturative dynamics still reshape us. These are processes we need to understand, and not just from the vantage point of the winner, the dominant culture. How does a culture respond to acculturative stress without losing its stability and vitality? How does a culture accommodate change without losing its own identity? These concerns may now seem trivial as we bask in the high noon of our own prosperity and power. But if history teaches us anything, it is to observe and learn, for our time to adjust and cope will certainly come.

The Indigenous Onondaga

The Iroquoian people known as the Onondaga, who emerged as the core of the Five Nations Confederacy during the seventeenth century, were like most other native groups in the Northeast the result of a long and localized evolution.

Human occupation in northeastern North America can be traced back at least 10,000 years when small, mobile bands of hunters and foragers began to occupy the lands earlier scoured by glaciers. For the next nine millennia, human populations of many different cultural traditions coexisted in the Northeast, adapting to its gradually changing environment and periodic climatic fluctuations. Each of these cultural traditions was characterized by a particular survival strategy, by which means the essential needs of shelter, subsistence, and security were provided. There was often considerable continuity in survival strategies as one tradition succeeded another; yet improvement of existing technologies or the development of entirely new ones frequently marked the transition. Although the flow was not always smooth or direct, such cultural changes over the millennia were marked by a broad evolutionary pattern, one that pointed in a particular direction. That direction was toward coalescence: an increase in population size, cohesion, and identity.

In the central portion of what is now New York State, this trend became particularly evident around A.D. 1000, or at the beginning of what has been termed the Late Woodland stage. Coalescence was manifest in several ways. One was an increased tendency toward sedentism, or the year-round occupation of a specific site. Growing sedentism correlates with changes in the size and organization of habitation sites; over time, these became larger and better defined. Another hallmark in this process was an increase in community-based exploitation of locally available food resources, particularly anadromous fish along the major rivers and fresh-

9

water species around the large interior lakes. It was also at about this time that cultigens were introduced into the Northeast. Maize horticulture appears to have reinforced the tendency toward larger, more complex, and sedentary groups. Whatever the causes, this process of coalescence is one of real importance for archaeologists, for it allows discrete and trackable communities to emerge from the archaeological record for the first time.

Coalescence did not, of course, proceed uniformly. By the beginning of the Late Woodland stage there was already some evidence of the differentiation into the two basic linguistic/cultural groups indigenous to the Northeast—the Iroquoians and the Algonquians.[1]

The centripetal forces that characterize the beginning of the Late Woodland stage were particularly evident among Iroquoian antecedents. These proto-Iroquoians were inland people, living primarily along the upper portions and headwaters of the major rivers. Known by several names, which reflect different regional sequences, these people are best known as Owasco, a term first defined by William Ritchie (1936:4; 1969:272–73) and later used to describe the antecedents of the Five Nations Iroquois in Central New York State. The precursors of the Ontario Iroquois (Huron, Neutral, and Petun) have been termed Glen Meyer and Pickering by J. V. Wright (1966). Equivalent ancestral antecedents for the other two major Iroquoian groups, the St. Lawrence Iroquois and the Susquehannocks, have not been clearly identified.[2]

The general process by which the Onondaga evolved from Owasco forebears has been outlined by Tuck (1971) and supplemented by Ritchie and Funk (1973). Together these studies provide a detailed basis for tracing the Owasco-to-Iroquois transition in Central New York. They also allow us to focus on one set of discrete communities that emerged during the beginning of the Late Woodland stage, and to track it over the next four centuries of its growth and development. At first, the trail is somewhat spotty; significant gaps do remain. Increasingly, however, as we move through the later phases of Iroquois development the archaeological record fills out. More sites are known and the relationships among them are often clearer.

Our focus now is the evolution of the Onondaga between about A.D. 1200, the final Owasco phase, and 1500, immediately prior to European contact. Four major cultural phases merit discussion, including their settlement and subsistence patterns, and how these are reflected in the material culture, or artifact, record.

Tuck's model of Onondaga development, in light of additional information now available, is especially useful. More important, a clear view of Onondaga prehistory is the necessary point of departure if we wish to learn how Onondaga culture responded to Europeans, their exotic material wealth and novel ways of thinking. Only then can the continuities be separated from the changes and the changes themselves be seen in context.

Environmental Setting/Owasco Antecedents

The transition from Owasco to Iroquois is not characterized by sudden or dramatic change. Rather, it reflects an interpretative distinction, the somewhat arbitrary division of a developmental continuum into cultural phases. This is an important point. Owasco people did not wake up one morning and suddenly find themselves Iroquoian. The distinction between Owasco and Iroquois, like the earlier division between Middle Woodland (Point Peninsula) and Late Woodland (Owasco), reflects the archaeologist's need to subdivide complex evolutionary processes into more manageable units.

The evolution of the Onondaga took place within a particular regional setting, near the geographical center of New York State, primarily within the current boundaries of Onondaga County (Map 1). The major topographic feature of this area is a limestone escarpment that outcrops west-east across the central portion of the county. This escarpment literally divides the county in half and serves as the demarcation line between two distinctly different topographical and ecological zones to the north and south. It was along this physiographic boundary, where the resources of both ecological zones could be easily exploited, that the Owasco-to-Iroquois transition took place.

South of the Onondaga Escarpment the land rises, forming the northern edge of the Appalachian Uplands. Here drainage is primarily to the south into tributaries of the Susquehanna River, and eventually into Chesapeake Bay. The land is rolling and often rugged, its contours shaped primarily by glaciation. Deep, U-shaped valleys and old outwash channels furrow the plateau. Some of these valleys have remained flooded, forming Central New York's well known Finger Lakes; others drained, producing broad expanses of fertile bottomland. The soils, like the land forms, reflect their glacial heritage. Derived from the underlying Silurian and Devonian bedrock, they tend to be both well drained and fairly high in lime content. As a result these soils, especially those of the Honeoye and Lima association, are well suited for agriculture (Hutton and Rice 1977:1–5, 228–29).

The northern half of Onondaga County, although also shaped by glacial action, is markedly different. Here the land is lower and flatter, the soils sandier. During the last glacial retreat this was the bed of a large shallow lake, Lake Iroquois, the precursor of Lake Ontario. While it is now part

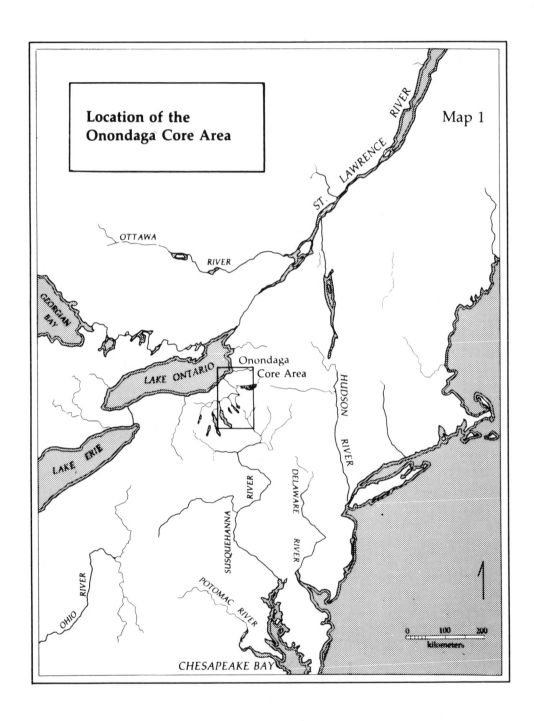

Location of the
Onondaga Core Area

Map 1

of the Erie-Ontario Lowland, evidence of its lacustrine past remains in the form of Oneida Lake and in large expanses of marsh and peaty bogs. Drainage in this part of the county is to the north by two major rivers, the Oneida, flowing west from Oneida Lake, and the Seneca, which flows east and drains the Finger Lakes. These two rivers mark the northern boundary of Onondaga County. They meet to form the Oswego River, which flows north to Lake Ontario and the St. Lawrence River.

The physical differences between the northern and southern portions of the county are also reflected in climatic and ecological terms. In general, Central New York has a humid continental climate partially modified by its proximity to Lake Ontario. Summer temperatures in the uplands average 65° to 70° F. The winters are long and cold, temperatures averaging below 20° F (ibid.:227; Alexander 1976:17–18). This results in an upland growing season of about 150 frost-free days between late May and early October. The combination of shallower soils and a more severe climate produces a mixed hardwood and conifer forest cover, the major species being sugar maple, beech, and hemlock.

North of the Onondaga Escarpment, the climatic conditions are slightly more moderate, largely due to Lake Ontario's proximity. On the lake plain the growing season can be up to twenty-five days longer than on the uplands (Hutton and Rice 1977:227; Alexander 1976:17–18). Here the sandy to gravelly soils and more moderate temperatures produce a hardwood forest dominated by oak, hickory, and chestnut. In addition, other species more typically central or even south Appalachian in character such as tulip tree, black tupelo, dogwood, and sassafras occasionally occur (Storey 1977:41–42). Pollen studies, although far from conclusive, indicate that the current ecological patterns are quite similar to those at the beginning of the Late Woodland stage.[3]

This ecological variation supported a diverse wildlife population. White-tailed deer is the only big game species which has survived in the area. Prior to extensive settlement during the early nineteenth century, other species including elk, black bear, wolf, and wild turkey were also common. The extensive lakes, waterways, and marshes of the county supported large and varied populations of shellfish, fish, amphibians, reptiles, birds, and small mammals. Located within the eastern flyway, these wetlands also served as a major resting and feeding stop for migratory waterfowl.

In addition to the diversity of plants and animals, two other important resources, chert and clay, were locally available. Lenses of chert, a flintlike crypto-crystalline silicate, occur throughout the Onondaga Limestone (Wray 1948:40–41). Pieces could easily be quarried from along the face of the escarpment and then worked into projectile points and other implements. Finely washed clay, used for making pottery and pipes, was also available either in stream beds or along old glacial outwash channels.

In sum, all the resources necessary to support a human population were readily, albeit seasonally, available. Although a variety of cultural groups exploited its ecological diversity for several millennia prior to A.D.

1000, this environmental setting was particularly well suited to the larger, more sedentary groups of the Late Woodland. With their larger, better organized populations they could more efficiently fish and farm, harvesting sufficient quantities of food to support a stable, even growing, population.

The ecological diversity of Central New York was an important factor in the evolution of Onondaga culture in another way. There was a wide range of potential resources, but any specific resource might be available only at a particular, and usually for a limited, time. As a result, both Owasco and Onondaga cultures were characterized by flexibility and adaptiveness. This ability to exploit a wide range of resources and to utilize effectively whatever came to hand was a tradition which stood the Onondaga in good stead when confronted by the stresses of acculturative change.

The Castle Creek Phase: Convergence

The known Owasco sites tend to cluster in the western part of the county just north of the Onondaga Escarpment. The number of sites, while not large, is sufficient to document Owasco cultural patterns in general and those of the late, or Castle Creek, phase in particular.

The settlement data indicate the presence of small but cohesive communities (100–250 people) living in semi-permanent villages of modest size, usually about two acres in extent. While these villages were probably occupied year-round, there was undoubtedly movement back and forth to smaller seasonally occupied camps used for fishing or other specialized purposes.

Only one large Castle Creek phase site is known from Tuck's excavations—the Chamberlin site (A.D. 1290 ± 60) (1971:23–34). This large village site suggests several of the ongoing changes characterizing late Owasco settlement patterns. One is a shift in location preference away from the riverine lowlands favored by earlier Middle Woodland populations and toward hilltop locations usually some distance from major bodies of water. Several reasons for this shift have been proposed, among them greater defensibility and access to soils and microclimates more favorable for agriculture. At present the evidence does not clearly support any explanation. Another characteristic is an increasing tendency to define village boundaries with either a palisade, a ditch, or both. Although duration of occupation is difficult to estimate, the rebuilding of houses and overlapping of palisade lines and features suggest a reasonably lengthy stay. While villages probably moved with some regularity, not enough sites are currently known to reconstruct the process in any detail.

Not only the villages but the houses within them become better defined on large Castle Creek phase sites. As opposed to the small round or oblong structures found on earlier Owasco sites, the houses at Chamberlin are rectangular with rounded ends, side entrances, and hearths along one wall (ibid.:29–30). While these structures presage Iroquoian longhouses in their overall shape, they still retain an Owasco floorplan.

Surprisingly, little or no evidence of food storage facilities has been found on these large sites. The cylindrical or bell-shaped pits, used for storage of both wild and cultivated plants and frequently found on Castle Creek phase sites elsewhere in New York, have not been found in Central New York (Ritchie and Funk 1973:166–67). Even food preparation features, such as large cooking pits and stone roasting platforms, have only occasionally been discovered.

In contrast with the single known large village site, several small campsites are known though poorly documented (Map 2). Five small sites have been reported in the Central New York area and only two of these, the O'Neil site and the Cabin site, have been described in any detail.[4]

Four of these small sites are multicomponent and probably represent short-term use over a long period of time within which the late Owasco is included. In addition to these four, other small sites have been reported along both the Seneca and Oneida rivers as well as around Onondaga Lake.[5] None has been verified archaeologically. These small sites share a set of traits different from the large village sites. Besides being smaller, usually a half acre or less, they are located close to major waterways, often at a confluence or adjacent to a large rift or shallow.[6] None of these small sites has provided any evidence of house structures. The presence of stone roasting platforms and storage pits suggests that the sites were important for collecting and processing fish and other food resources. The Cabin site is an exception to the pattern. Like the larger Chamberlin site, it is located on an upland hilltop away from major waterways. In spite of its small size (less than one-half acre), Tuck estimates that the site was occupied for a period of fifty or more years (1971:37).

Tuck observed that the Owasco subsistence pattern was a mixed one, based on the cultivation of corn (maize), beans, and squash, but strongly supplemented by fishing, hunting, and gathering (1978:324–25). This diversity is reflected by the archaeological evidence. Cultigens have been recovered from both the Chamberlin and Cabin sites, although not in large quantities. Fish remains have also been found on both sites.[7] While fishing was undoubtedly an important component in the Castle Creek phase subsistence pattern, the Cabin site emphasizes hunting. Of the wide range of large and small game species included in the Cabin site sample, white-tailed deer (Odocoileus virginianus) was clearly the most important (Tuck 1971:44). The Castle Creek phase sites also show some of the wide range

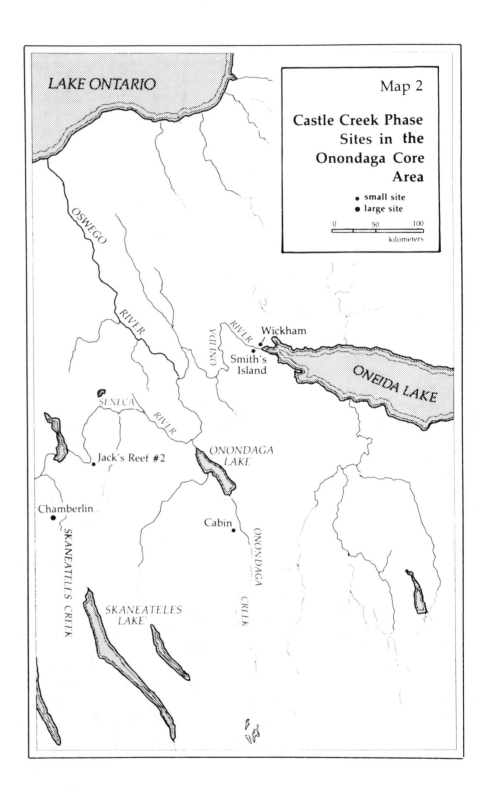

Map 2

Castle Creek Phase Sites in the Onondaga Core Area

- • small site
- • large site

0   50   100
kilometers

LAKE ONTARIO

OSWEGO RIVER

ONEIDA RIVER

Wickham

Smith's Island

ONEIDA LAKE

SENECA RIVER

Jack's Reef #2

ONONDAGA LAKE

Chamberlin

Cabin

ONONDAGA CREEK

SKANEATELES CREEK

SKANEATELES LAKE

of flora and fauna gathered by Owasco people. For example, all the sites produce freshwater mussel shell and evidence of plums, nuts, or other edible wild plants.

It is not surprising that the material culture from the Castle Creek phase sites reflects many of the characteristics visible in the settlement and subsistence patterns. Pottery, for example, is the most frequent and diagnostic class of artifacts. Like house patterns and the village sites themselves, ceramic vessels become increasingly well defined throughout the various Owasco phases. By Castle Creek times, vessels had evolved from an elongated conoidal form with an everted lip to a globular-shaped body with a clearly defined collar (Figure 1a). In terms of decoration, there is a shift from cord-wrapped stick impressions over most of the vessel's exterior surface to a more restricted use of cord impressions, primarily on the collar face. On late Castle Creek sites like the Cabin site, new decorative techniques such as linear stamping and incising begin to be used. Reconstructing this ceramic evolution, both in vessel form and method of decoration, has been one of the foundations on which interpretation of Middle and Late Woodland stage cultures has been built. In fact, the differentiation of the Owasco tradition into separate phases has been based largely on ceramic criteria (Ritchie and MacNeish 1949; Ritchie and Funk 1973:165).

Ceramic smoking pipes also undergo an evolutionary process, although the stages are less clear. In general, pipes become less straight over time with a more distinct angle between the stem and bowl. The bowl itself takes on more distinctive forms. On the Castle Creek phase sites, the most common bowl forms are barrel shaped and bulbous (Figure 2). Decoration on these pipes includes finely executed patterns of cord impressions or pointillé work, and occasionally, modelled effigies.

A second major class of artifacts is lithic, made by flaking or by a combination of pecking and abrasion. Again, the material remains reflect the broader patterns of the culture. Here, lithic preference parallels the overall subsistence pattern, organized around the intensive use of local resources. For example, ground stone tools were made from cobbles picked out of the glacial drift; chipped implements were made exclusively from the local Onondaga chert. The exotic raw materials frequently included in the lithic assemblages on Early and Middle Woodland sites are gone. The most common lithic artifact is a broad triangular projectile point probably made to tip an arrow shaft. Usually equilateral in form, these large points have been given the type name Levanna by Ritchie (1961:31–32). In addition, a wide range of bifacial scraping, cutting, and perforating tools also occurs. Ground stone tools include implements used in food preparation such as mortars, mullers, and occasionally, pestles. Hammerstones occur, both pebble and cobble sized, as well as anvil stones. Both

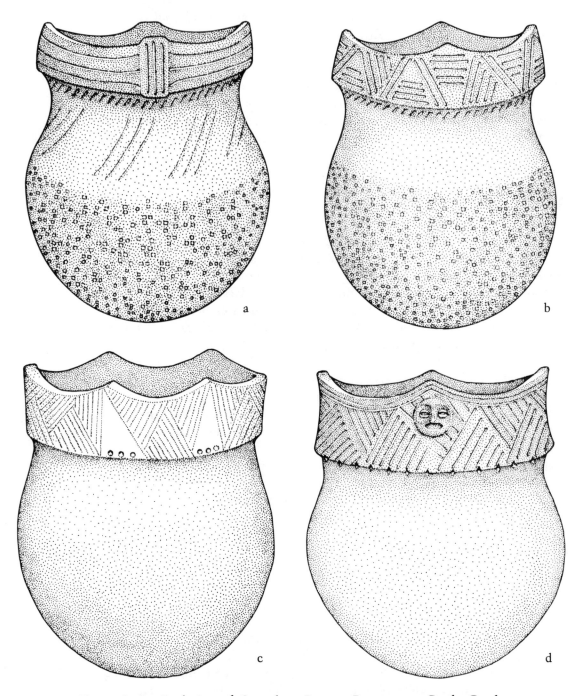

Figure 1. An Evolution of Onondaga Pottery Forms. a. a Castle Creek
phase pot with a low channelled collar profile, neck decoration, and check-
stamped body; b. an Oak Hill phase pot with a Chance round collar
profile, no neck decoration, and check-stamped body; c. a Chance phase
pot with a Chance straight collar profile, no neck decoration, and smooth
body; d. a Garoga phase pot with a biconcave collar profile, notched
collar base, and smooth body.

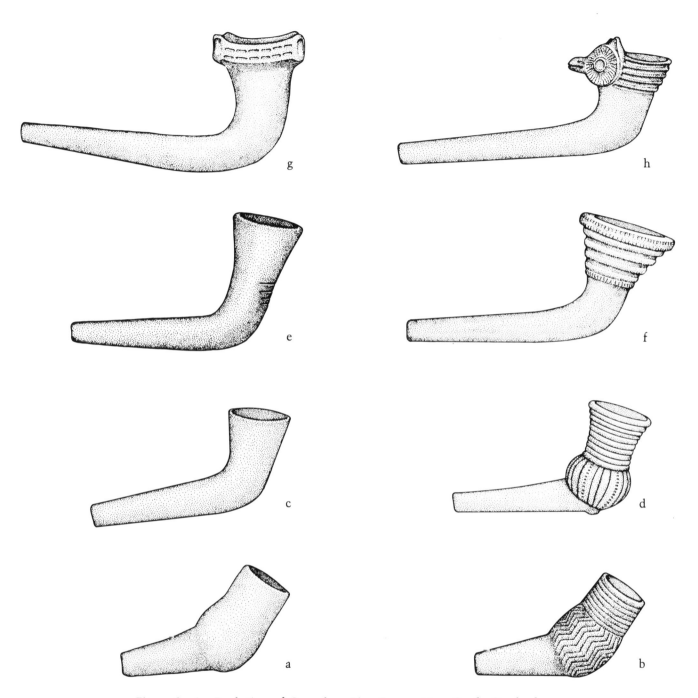

Figure 2. An Evolution of Onondaga Pipe Forms. Two Castle Creek phase
pipes: a. an undecorated barrel-shaped bowl, b. a barrel-shaped bowl decorated with fine cord-wrapped impressions (after Tuck 1971:38, #8); two
Oak Hill phase pipes: c. an undecorated proto trumpet, d. a pipe with a
finely incised vasiform bowl of the "Willow Point" style (after Ritchie
and Funk 1973:272); two Chance phase pipes: e. a plain trumpet, f. a
ringed trumpet; two Garoga phase pipes: g. a coronet trumpet, h. a ringed
trumpet with bird effigy.

celts and adzes served as woodworking tools.[8] Another distinctive group of lithic artifacts is bifacially chipped discs which range between 5 and 15cm in diameter. Different functions have been assigned to these discs, most notably as hoes (Ritchie 1969:279–80), yet it seems much more likely that they were related to fishing and probably served as bottom weights for seines.[9] In contrast to this array of stone implements, the non-utilitarian use of stone appears quite limited. An occasional pendant and, rarely, a stone pipe or effigy, are the only evidence for its ornamental or ritual use.

The third major class of artifacts is from animal bone, antler, or teeth. Animal bone was an available and adaptable medium for making a variety of implements. Most common are awls, multipurpose perforators, usually of split long bone. Beamers for de-hairing hides, and flat, often centrally perforated needles, occur frequently as well. Fishing implements are one particularly distinctive group of bone artifacts. These include multiply barbed bilateral harpoons, and fish hooks, both barbed and unbarbed.[10] Antler seems to have been used primarily for lithic reduction tools, including billets for direct percussion and tines for final pressure flaking. Antler was occasionally used for hafting cutting tools as well. Rodent incisors, especially from beaver, were frequently hafted and used for carving.

Although ornamentation does not appear to have been central to Castle Creek material culture, most of our knowledge of it is based on surviving remains of this third class of material. Most ornaments were quite simple— perforated or grooved canine teeth from dog or bear, tubular beads made from the long bones of small mammals or birds, modified deer phalanges. Occasionally, human bone was used to make simple ornaments as well. More complex ornaments, such as hair combs and bone pins with elaborately carved tops, are rare. Other infrequently found artifacts, such as turtle shell rattles and bone whistles or flutes, suggest ritual or ceremonial use.

Ceramic, lithic, and bone artifacts dominate the excavated assemblages from Castle Creek sites in the Central New York area. Other material categories are also important even though their archaeological visibility is much lower. For example, organic materials rarely survive in the ground. But fortuitous conditions at the Castle Creek site in Broome County, New York, permitted the preservation of fragments of basketry, cordage, textiles, and fishing equipment. A similar extensive use of wood and fiber undoubtedly occurred on the Castle Creek phase sites in Central New York. On the other hand, objects of marine shell and native copper probably were used as infrequently as their occurrence in the archaeological record suggests. Like exotic lithic materials, shell and copper were substances highly valued by Late Archaic to Middle Woodland cultures in the Northeast. By the beginning of the Late Woodland stage, however, these materials virtually disappear from the archaeological record. No artifacts of marine shell or native copper have been recovered from Owasco sites in the Central New York area. Their rare appearance on other Owasco sites demonstrates that although perhaps out of fashion, these materials still remained a part of Owasco material culture.[11]

In summary, examination of Owasco culture in general and the Castle Creek phase in particular provides a starting point for tracing the evolution of the Onondaga. Sometime prior to about A.D. 1200, a stable culture had emerged around the regular seasonal exploitation of locally available resources. Traditional hunting and gathering took place as well as fishing and agriculture. As Cleland has pointed out, these last two pursuits were labor intensive ones and "undoubtedly . . . community enterprise[s]" (1982:775). The effectiveness of this subsistence strategy appears to have had a centripetal effect. Site size, definition, and complexity increase over time, reflecting larger, more cohesive, and distinct populations. Initially there appears to have been little competition or conflict among these emerging groups. However, this situation would change.

The Oak Hill Phase: Coalescence

Oak Hill is the name given to the first phase of the Iroquois cultural tradition.[12] As discussed above, the shift from Owasco to Iroquois is largely a matter of definition and does not indicate a break in the developmental continuum. To the contrary, a pattern of both continuity and gradual change is evident in settlement and subsistence systems as well as in the material culture.

Settlement data for this period indicate the presence of somewhat larger village populations, numbering perhaps between 300 and 350 people.[13] In addition, discrete communities are identifiable and for the first time can be traced from one site to another. At present, three large Oak Hill phase sites are known:

Name	Date (C[14])	Estimated Size	Source
Furnace Brook	1300 ± 60 1370 ± 60	2.5 acres	Tuck 1971:48–71
Howlett Hill	1380 ± 60	unknown	Tuck 1971:77–90
Kelso	1390 ± 100	two overlapping villages; 2 acres each	Ritchie and Funk 1973: 253–75

One small Oak Hill phase site, Coye II, has been tentatively identified (Tuck 1971:90).

These sites indicate a continued tendency to move away from lowland areas into the hills south of the Onondaga Escarpment. Defense may have been the reason for the shift. The village sites certainly reflect a greater concern for definition if not defense. Furnace Brook had a single, and occasionally double, palisade. Each of the villages at Kelso had a double, and in places triple, palisade.

Not only is palisading more evident on these sites, the overall pattern of settlement is more clearly defined. Examples of longhouses occur for the first time, although structures in the earlier oblong style continue to occur as well. Some longhouses show evidence of rebuilding and expansion; however, the longest one (at Howlett Hill) was apparently built to an original length of 334 feet.[14] Details of other settlement features remain vague. For example, food processing and storage features are not common. As on the Castle Creek phase sites, only a few large stone roasting platforms, and rarely a cylindrical pit, are known. The lack of storage pits characteristic of these proto-Onondaga groups suggests that some other means of storage, such as above-ground granaries, may have been used.

In general, these sites appear to have been occupied for a fairly long period of time. The evidence of rebuilding and the expansion of houses and palisades certainly argues for an occupation of some duration. Tuck estimates that Furnace Brook was occupied between eighty and one hundred years (1971:58).

What does begin to show clearly for the first time on sites of the Oak Hill phase is some sense of discrete communities, enabling us to trace their movement through a series of sites. Tuck identifies two such communities and suggests that a third also may have existed. The first was located in the Skaneateles Creek drainage and included the Castle Creek phase Chamberlin site and its likely successor, the Oak Hill phase Kelso site. The second community was in the Onondaga Creek drainage. This included the Castle Creek phase Cabin site and the Oak Hill phase Furnace Brook and Howlett Hill sites. A rather tentative third community was located in the Butternut Creek drainage based on the Coye II site (Map 3). These communities were identified not only by geographical proximity but also by material culture preferences, or "microtraditions," which could be traced from site to site (ibid.:92).

While changes occurred in settlement patterns, subsistence patterns appear to have remained much the same as in the Owasco period. The only apparent variation is a somewhat greater emphasis on cultigens. Corn was recovered from all three sites, and beans appear at both Furnace Brook and Howlett Hill. Agriculture played a greater role in the Oak Hill subsistence system, but fishing, hunting, and gathering were major components. Fish remains are found on all three sites, with the largest and most reliable sample at Furnace Brook. Of a faunal sample of over 2600 pieces,

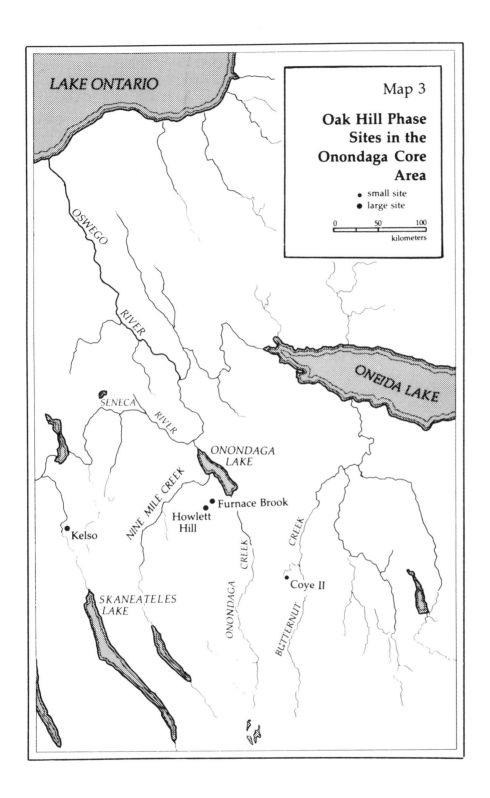

the majority (56 percent) of the remains are fish.[15] This suggests that the strong emphasis on fishing during the Owasco continued into the Oak Hill phase. The faunal sample from Furnace Brook also indicates the diversity of other species either hunted or collected. White-tailed deer dominate the mammalian species (32 percent), although many other large and small mammals are represented. Birds (5 percent) include both upland game and migratory species. Freshwater mussels and small amphibians are also present (ibid.:70).

Oak Hill phase material culture, like its settlement and subsistence systems, shows both a strong continuity with the patterns of the preceding Castle Creek phase and the results of gradual change. As Lenig observed, pottery styles are the most sensitive and useful indicators of cultural change (1965:5). Oak Hill phase pots tend to have a globular body with a long neck and fairly well defined collar, usually of low height (10–20mm) (Figure 1b). Collars are decorated primarily in patterns of horizontal and oblique cord-impressed lines that become increasingly complex. In addition to corded decoration, other techniques such as stamping and incising are occasionally used, especially on the neck of the vessel. During the Oak Hill phase there also appears a strong tendency to mark the body of the pot with check stamping.[16]

Smoking pipe styles show an even more marked evolution from their Owasco antecedents. Increasingly, the bowl and stem are set at a right angle instead of an oblique one (Figure 2). Pipe bowls also exhibit greater regularity in form. The most common forms are proto trumpet, barrel shaped, and vasiform or collared (see Appendix A for definitions). Decoration of these forms ranges from nonexistent to elaborate. Most have fine plats combining lines and dots, motifs usually created by incising supplemented with punctates. Corded decoration still occurs but with decreasing frequency. One distinctive trait on the pipes from these proto-Onondaga sites is the use of small, finely modelled effigies, particularly frogs and salamanders, on either the bowl or stem.[17]

In contrast to the increased elaboration of pottery and pipes, the other components of Oak Hill phase material culture appear to change only in minor ways if at all. Triangular projectile points, still common, are increasingly isosceles and less equilateral in form.[18] Other lithic implements include bifacial scrapers and ovate knives as well as a few unifacial blades and utilized flakes. All are made from locally available Onondaga chert.

Larger stone tools, such as hammers, celts, and food processing utensils are basically unchanged from those described for the Owasco. The presence of chipped stone discs on all three Oak Hill phase sites again appears to reflect the importance of fishing.

As on the late Owasco sites, ornamental or ritual stonework is extremely limited. A single lozenge-shaped pendant from Furnace Brook is the sole example from the three sites (Tuck 1971:69).

Bone implements also show a strong correspondence to Castle Creek phase forms. Most common are split bone awls, flat centrally perforated needles, and antler flakers. One notable change is the diminished presence of harpoons, fish hooks, and other fishing gear in the overall assemblages. This may indicate a greater emphasis on net fishing or may simply be a function of sampling and preservation biases.

The ornamental use of bone, as with stone, appears to have been quite restricted. A few small tubular beads and a perforated bear canine are the only occurrences. One other possible ornament is a piece of cut and polished human cranium from the Kelso site (ibid.:76).

Oak Hill phase sites in Central New York, like those of the late Owasco, show little if any evidence of trade or contact with outside areas. In fact, the Oak Hill phase seems to represent the termination of extended exchange systems characterizing the Early and Middle Woodland stages. What typifies Oak Hill phase sites is a profound localism. One has the impression that there was little movement beyond the prescribed annual rounds of subsistence and that those activities did not take people very far afield. The reasons for this localism remain unclear. Certainly the local environmental setting was diverse and rich enough to support a stable, even growing, population. Larger villages and a dramatic increase in house size suggest favorable conditions. At present, however, not enough is known about the environmental and climatic conditions of the period to build a convincing argument.

If optimal environmental conditions did encourage a more intense exploitation of locally available resources resulting in increased group size, then it is likely that competition between groups increased as well. This would be the case especially for groups in close proximity to each other. The signs of competition and nascent hostility are slight but suggestive. Most notable is the tendency to fortify villages, by both selecting less accessible site locations and constructing increasingly elaborate palisades.

Tuck identified three separate communities of probable Onondaga antecedents within the Central New York area. Each appears centered within a particular drainage. There are, however, other drainages equally as attractive in terms of environmental setting that have yet to be tested systematically. It may be that some of these also were inhabited by distinct Oak Hill phase populations.

As long as environmental conditions remained favorable, these groups may have been able to coexist peacefully. If conditions became more adverse, however, competition certainly would have intensified.[19] If severe enough, environmental pressure could have resulted either in hostilities or, conversely, in a cooperative solution. During the succeeding Chance phase, both alternatives apparently were tried. The result was the emergence of the Onondaga.

The Chance Phase: Consolidation

The Chance phase of Iroquois development, like its predecessors, begins at a somewhat arbitrary point. Even the name reflects the random quality of demarcation (Ritchie 1952:6). The important point is that the developmental process traced from the Castle Creek through the Oak Hill phases continues.

The settlement data, although not as complete as for the Oak Hill phase, indicate a continued pattern of community movement in an easterly direction. At present seven Chance phase sites are known, five of them large and two small.[20] In estimated chronological order, the large sites are:

Name	Date (C^{14})	Estimated Size	Source
Schoff	1400 ± 80	2 acres	Tuck 1971:94–104.
Keough	undated	2 acres	Tuck 1971:119–22.
Christopher	undated	2.5 acres	A. D. LaFrance 1984
Carley II	undated	unknown	LaFrance and LaFrance 1976
Burke	1480 ± 80[21]	a double village, 2–4 acres[22]	Tuck 1971:125–36; A. D. LaFrance n.d.

All five large sites are located in the uplands south of the Onondaga Escarpment and most reflect a continued preference for hilltop locations. One site, Keough, is located on a lower elevation terrace and does not conform to this pattern.

Defense considerations are usually cited as the primary explanation of these rather exposed locations. To a degree this is supported by evidence of fortification, the clearest indication being found at the Burke site where Tuck's excavations revealed two intersecting palisade lines. One consisted of three parallel rows of posts, the other, four (Tuck 1971:126). While only a small section of these palisades was exposed, it is an unusually strong stockade compared with other examples from the Central New York area. Traces of a palisade have been reported from both Keough and Carley II, and Tuck suggests that the Schoff and Christopher sites may have been fortified as well.[23]

At present, no large-scale excavation of the settlement pattern, that is, the palisade and the number of longhouses, has been attempted on these Chance phase sites. Therefore less is known about the internal organization of these villages than of comparable Castle Creek or Oak Hill phase sites. Nonetheless, they appear to have been well defined, containing from three to five longhouses as well as other smaller structures. Tuck's excavations exposed two longhouses, one at each of the Schoff and Burke sites. They were large houses, 400 feet and at least 240 feet in length, respectively. Subsequent work revealed a second longhouse at the Burke site. This had burned; its remains lay roughly parallel to the first, approximately 100 feet to the southwest.[24] Aside from a few hearths and small roasting pits, further information about features within the large Chance phase sites is scarce.[25]

The length of occupation of these sites is difficult to determine. If the overlapping palisade lines at the Burke site do indicate a double village (the rebuilding of the village in place), then a stay of some duration, perhaps fifty years, was likely. In general, however, the impression is that Chance phase sites had a shorter period of occupation than those of the preceding phases. This was probably a result of larger population size and, therefore, a greater demand on resources.

The known Chance phase sites of small size, one-half acre or less, fall into two distinct categories and help clarify both subsistence and settlement patterns. One category, camps for seasonal fishing, hunting, or gathering, is exemplified by the Conway site. Located on the edge of a low glacial moraine along the south shore of Oneida Lake and about one-half acre in size, the site produced no evidence of a palisade or of houses. It did have five large stone roasting or drying platforms and clearly served as a seasonal camp for collecting and processing food and other raw materials. The artifacts from the site also support this conclusion and are very similar to the materials from the larger, late Chance phase sites like Burke (Weinman and Weinman 1982:7–15).

The second category of small sites suggests a different and perhaps new function—a way station for the assimilation of smaller populations. These sites appear to have been small satellite villages or hamlets located in the uplands in close proximity to the large villages. The Bloody Hill site is an example. Like the nearby large sites, Bloody Hill is also situated on an exposed hilltop. Tuck's excavations indicate the site is less than half an acre in extent and apparently was unpalisaded. Evidence for only one small, irregularly shaped house was found. One unusual feature on the site was a large, rock-filled roasting pit containing fragmentary human bones as well as refuse. The material culture from the Bloody Hill site, as well as its C[14] date of 1420 ± 80, place it well within the Chance phase (Tuck 1971:104–19).

These Chance phase sites were crucial to the process of coalescence and fusion that produced the Onondaga. At the end of the Oak Hill phase, there were at least three proto-Onondaga communities; by the end of the Chance phase, only one, or possibly two, remained. While the details of this consolidation are incomplete, the broad outline of the process can be drawn. Of the three Oak Hill phase communities, the western one, including the Chamberlin and Kelso sites, essentially disappears from the archaeological record.[26] The middle community, which includes Furnace Brook and Howlett Hill, continues into the Chance phase as the Schoff site and then seems to vanish abruptly as well. The eastern community, rather weakly represented by the Coye II site during the Oak Hill phase, becomes the center of activity during the Chance phase (Map 4).

Two changes occurred within this eastern community. First, the village sites continued to move steadily eastward from the Butternut Creek to the Limestone Creek drainage. The sites occupied include Keough, Bloody Hill, and Christopher. The distances between them are fairly short (averaging about 2.5km). Second, Tuck has argued that sometime during this period another community appeared in the Pompey Hills and settled at the Burke site. Analyzing settlement traits and material culture microtraditions, he concludes that this is the same community which abandoned the Onondaga Creek drainage after the Schoff site. He interprets this population shift as evidence of the establishment of the Onondaga as a tribal entity (1971:214–16).[27]

While Tuck has identified two of the key components of the centripetal process that produced the Onondaga, major questions remain. For example, the Schoff site is an early Chance site, while the Burke site represents the end of the phase. The cultural and chronological distance between them suggests strongly that other, intermediate, sites exist. Clearly, some key sites are missing; several others are poorly documented. In addition, there are still many sites to be integrated into the sequence.[28] Equally important, we need to understand better the sites already known. What was the function of hamlets like Bloody Hill? Were they a vehicle for the assimilation of smaller groups as they apparently were during the historic period? Was the rebuilding and perhaps expansion of the Burke site related to the merging of previously separate communities? Not enough field work has been done to answer these questions satisfactorily.

While social and settlement patterns during the Chance phase were dynamic, subsistence remained fundamentally unchanged. The evidence indicates the traditional Iroquoian mix of horticulture, hunting, fishing, and gathering. All the excavated assemblages include cultigens, particularly corn and beans. It should be noted, moreover, that the Burke site is the first Onondaga site where beans have been recovered in quantity (Tuck 1971:135). Fish bones were also present in all the faunal samples and indicate a predominance of freshwater species, such as sheepshead, rather than anadromous ones. Unfortunately, soil conditions at the Conway site did not permit the preservation of identifiable species, although fragments of fish bone and mussel shell were present.

The material culture on Chance phase sites reflects many of the trends seen in their settlement pattern, especially in the case of ceramics. Like the sites on which they are found, Chance phase pots are more clearly

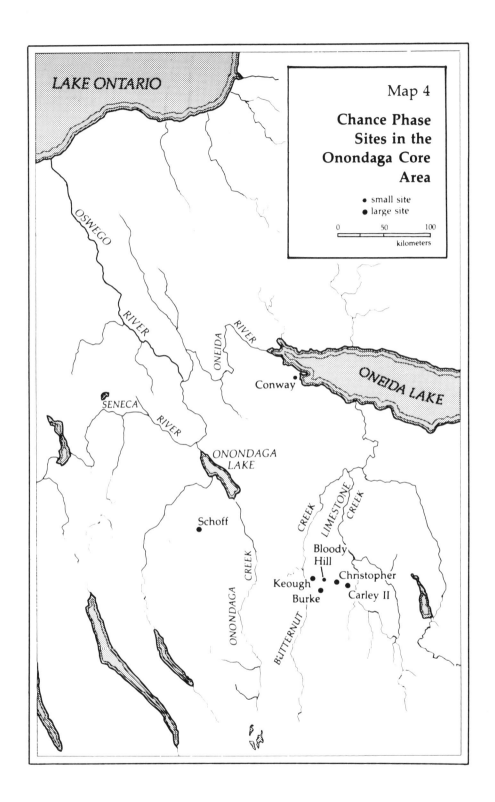

Map 4

**Chance Phase
Sites in the
Onondaga Core
Area**

• small site
• large site

0   50   100

kilometers

LAKE ONTARIO

OSWEGO

RIVER

ONEIDA   RIVER

ONEIDA LAKE

Conway

SENECA

RIVER

ONONDAGA
LAKE

Schoff

CREEK

LIMESTONE

CREEK

Bloody
Hill

Keough   Christopher

Burke   Carley II

ONONDAGA   CREEK

BUTTERNUT

defined than their Oak Hill phase antecedents. The most common vessel form has a globular body, a constricted neck, and a well-defined collar, usually of medium height (20–30mm) (Figure 1c). Three traits differentiate these vessels from their predecessors. First, the collar is more clearly articulated, its form more standardized. This is best seen in the profile of the collar. The most commonly occurring profile forms have been called "Chance rounded" and "Chance straight" by Tuck (see Appendix A for technical definitions and illustrations of these terms). During the Chance phase, a third collar profile evolved from the first two. While the new "biconcave" profile remained a minority form during the Chance phase, it achieved dominance during the subsequent Garoga phase. A reliable means for arranging sites in chronological order is to seriate the percentage rates at which these profiles occur on each site. These percentages, as well as those of other selected material traits, are summarized in Table 1.

The second characteristic of these collared pots is that incising replaces corded stick impressions as the technique for decorating the collar face. Decorative motifs also become more elaborate and stylized, encouraging some researchers to state that Chance phase ceramics represent the zenith of Iroquois pottery making (Ritchie 1969:313).

The third trait concerns the body finish of the vessel. During the Chance phase, the check stamping that typified Oak Hill phase pots disappeared and pots were left generally with a smooth finish. This occurs both on collared pots, usually 70–80 percent of all vessels, and on the remaining 20–30 percent which were made without collars.

Smoking pipes also continued to evolve into more elaborate, yet standardized, forms. Most notable is the development of the full trumpet pipe as well as several distinctive subvarieties. Among these are ringed-bowl trumpets and square or coronet trumpets (Figure 2). An additional characteristic of Chance phase pipes is the occasional use of large, finely detailed effigies on the pipe bowl[29] (Figure 3 and Plate 1b and c).

Other aspects of Chance phase material culture change in modest ways, if at all. Lithic projectile points, for example, continue toward a more isosceles shape. While the reasons for this tendency remain unclear, the average length-to-width ratio of points provides one more artifact basis for seriating sites (Table 1). Like the projectile points, other lithic implements, such as ovate knives and utilized flakes, are all made of local chert. The array of larger stone tools is essentially unchanged with the possible exception of chipped discs. While none has been found on the upland sites, several discs were recovered from the Conway site, reinforcing the idea that these artifacts relate to fishing.

At present there is no evidence for the non-utilitarian use of lithic material. No stone pipes, beads, pendants, or other related forms have been recovered from any of the Chance phase sites.

Table 1
Selected Artifact Attributes from Chance Phase Onondaga Sites

Pottery

Rim Profile

Site	Total Rims	Collarless (%)	Chance Round (%)	Chance Straight (%)	Biconcave (%)	Other* (%)
Schoff	14	21.4	71.4	7.2	0	0
Keough	19	0	79.0	10.5	0	10.5
Christopher	115	27.8	59.1	12.2	0.9	0
Carley II	398	20.9	39.4	31.9	7.8	0
Burke	50	13.0	18.0	9.0	7.0	3.0
Bloody Hill II	76	36.8	46.1	9.2	0	7.9
Conway	71	—	50.0	36.0	14.0	0

	Neck Decoration				Body Treatment			
Site	No.	Decorated (%)	Plain (%)		No.	Check Stamped (%)	Plain (%)	Other† (%)
Schoff	70	12.9	87.1		134	77.6	7.5	14.9
Keough	65	30.8	69.2		178	43.3	52.2	4.5
Christopher	263	31.2	68.8		4295	8.1	91.9	—
Carley II	—	—	—		5632	3.9	96.1	—
Burke	420	8.6	91.4		3320	2.8	95.8	1.4
Bloody Hill II	685	35.3	64.7		3387	50.3	44.4	5.3
Conway	—	—	—		1984	3.6	96.4	—

Projectile Points

Site	No.	Length-to-Width Ratio
Schoff	6	1.71:1
Keough	6	1.51:1
Christopher	9	1.76:1
Carley II	1	2.05:1
Burke	24	1.80:1
Bloody Hill II	23	1.61:1
Conway	—	—

* channelled low collar or incipient collar
† smoothed-over check stamp, or corded
0 means trait not present.
— means trait not reported.
Sources: See Tuck 1971; A. D. LaFrance 1984; LaFrance and LaFrance 1976; LaFrance n.d.

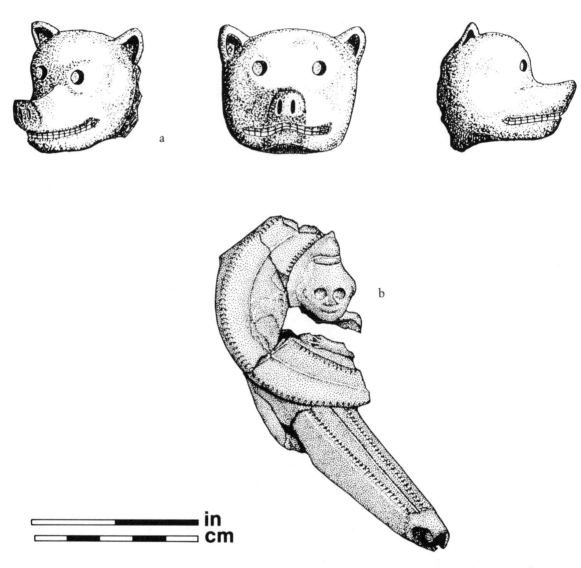

Figure 3. Effigy Pipes from the Burke Site. a. three views of a bear effigy probably from a trumpet pipe; b. a "moon" pipe (RMSC 11000/ 251).

Bone artifacts are not particularly well represented in the existing collections; however, the same basic utilitarian assemblage appears to have been used. This includes split bone perforators, flat needles, and antler flaking tools. Bone, like lithics, seems to have been used rarely for non-utilitarian purposes. Aside from the Burke site effigy, only two beads and one possible pendant have been reported from these sites.[30]

INCH

CM

a

b

c

Plate 1. Chance Phase Effigies from Onondaga Sites. a. an effigy made from a human patella, Burke site; b. and c. an effigy pipe, Christopher site (photograph courtesy of Peter P. Pratt).

33

Apart from stylistic intricacies of pottery decoration and the occasional flamboyance of pipes, Chance phase material culture presents a rather austere and utilitarian appearance. No marine shell or exotic lithics occur. The localism and simplicity of material culture during the Oak Hill phase remain strong during the Chance phase as well.

In summary, the Chance phase represents the consolidation of at least two antecedent communities into the tribe known historically as the Onondaga. To some extent, this fusion appears to have occurred in a peaceful manner; at least the available evidence suggests assimilation rather than annihilation as the mechanism. All the same, the emphasis on defensible site locations and the human bone from the Bloody Hill site suggest that the process was not always a cooperative one. While the basic outline of this consolidation seems reasonably clear, many aspects remain frustratingly vague or incomplete. Cooperative solutions to the problems of environmental stress, and resulting intergroup competition, are rare in the ethnographic literature. It seems well worth the effort to more fully document this apparent example.

The Garoga Phase: Crystallization

The final phase of Iroquois development prior to European contact has been termed Garoga. Like the preceding Oak Hill and Chance phases, the name comes from a specific site in eastern New York and has been adapted to a more general use (Tuck 1971:140).

Although not very complete, settlement data for sites of this phase indicate continued stability and growth. Five Garoga phase sites are currently known; all appear to be large although their sizes vary considerably. None has been C[14] dated. In estimated chronological order, they are:

Name	Estimated Size	Source
Indian Hill II	2–3 acres	F. LaFrance 1977[31]
Cemetery	1–2 acres	Tuck 1969:274–89
Nursery	2–3 acres	Tuck 1971:146–49
McNab	5–6 acres	T. Weinman, personal communication
Barnes	6–8 acres	Gibson 1968; Tuck 1971:149–60; Bradley 1979:49–77

At present, the pattern of these sites suggests one large village which moved periodically in an easterly direction.

Once again, small sites are less understood than the large ones. No well documented small site of this phase has been reported, although the Cemetery site is a possible candidate. Likewise, no Garoga phase fishing camps are known, even though they certainly existed.[32]

Continuities with the preceding Chance phase are quite strong; however, there are intriguing variations. One is an increase in site size. If the estimates are correct, late Garoga sites like McNab and Barnes represent villages of an unprecedented size. Another and probably related change is a subtle shift in location preference. While all of these sites are still situated in the uplands south of the Onondaga Escarpment, the exposed hilltop locations favored during the Chance phase give way to secondary elevations such as plateaus, ridges, or the promontories that flank the broad glacial valleys. In one instance, at the Nursery site, a low rise in the midst of creekside bottomland was selected (Map 5).

This shift in location preference parallels another in settlement pattern. While only limited evidence is available, there seems to have been less palisading on Garoga phase sites than on those of previous phases. At the Barnes site, for example, several sections of the palisade were traced. It was composed of a single row of posts averaging four inches in diameter and spaced about fourteen inches apart. Despite considerable testing, no evidence of other palisade lines was found (Gibson 1968:9). While palisade lines have been noted on the other Garoga phase sites, none has been recorded in detail. Perhaps the Barnes site is atypical. Nonetheless, there appears to have been a tendency away from the massive and complex fortifications seen at the Chance phase Burke site. This, in tandem with the shift in location preference, suggests a lessening of the hostilities that appear to have characterized the Chance phase. It is tempting to see this as archaeological evidence of the "Great Peace" which, according to Iroquois tradition, followed the establishment of the Five Nations Confederacy.

While villages appear to increase markedly in size during the Garoga phase, little can be said about their internal configuration. At least one longhouse has been reported and partially traced at both the Indian Hill II and McNab sites, and it is likely that a combination of both long and small houses was used on all five sites. Despite extensive testing, no house pattern was defined at the Barnes site. Data on other Garoga phase settlement features is also very limited.

The duration of occupation for these villages is also difficult to estimate. Most sites, if not all, are characterized by a series of extensive middens (trash deposits) around the margins as well as by a thin mantle of refuse in the occupied areas. This accumulation suggests a stay of some duration, perhaps twenty to twenty-five years. The length of site occupation has been the subject of considerable scholarly discussion, as has the reason for

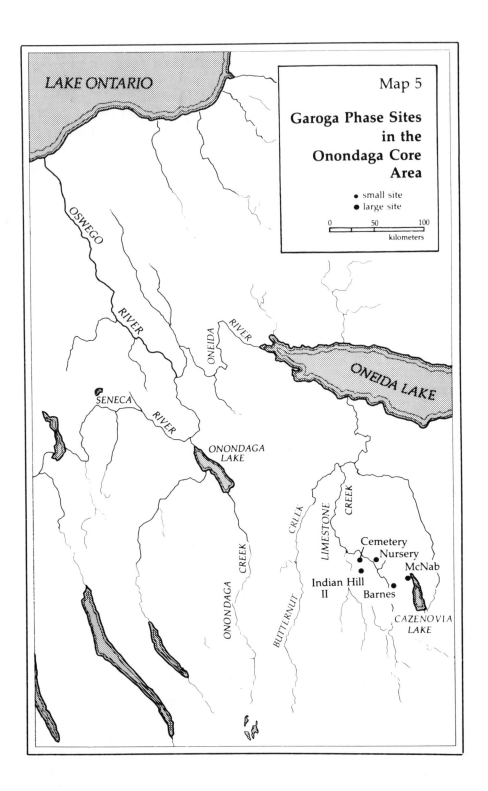

Map 5

**Garoga Phase Sites
in the
Onondaga Core
Area**

• small site
• large site

0   50   100
kilometers

LAKE ONTARIO

OSWEGO

RIVER

ONEIDA RIVER

ONEIDA LAKE

SENECA

RIVER

ONONDAGA
LAKE

ONONDAGA CREEK

BUTTERNUT CREEK

LIMESTONE CREEK

Cemetery
Nursery
McNab
Indian Hill
II
Barnes
CAZENOVIA
LAKE

removal to another location. Some reasons for site relocation are known from the documentary record and include a decrease in soil productivity (due to Iroquoian slash-and-burn farming practices) and the depletion of readily available supplies of firewood (Pratt 1976:16–17; Thwaites 1896–1901, 62:55–57). Certainly other factors were also important.[33] The matter is of interest because if villages did move on some regular basis, then archaeologists have a means not only for organizing sites in proper sequence, but also for estimating how long they were occupied. At present, however, estimates of site occupation dates remain based more on intuitive assessment than hard data.

As he did for the Chance phase sites, Tuck (1971:210, 216) proposed a series of large site-small site pairs and a pattern of sequential removals for the Garoga phase. Although the general patterning he proposed may be correct, the specific site pairings and movements are conjectural. There is simply not enough currently known to reconstruct these details of Garoga phase settlement.

In contrast to the changes in settlement pattern, Garoga subsistence patterns remain much the same as in the Chance phase. Only three of the sites (Cemetery, McNab, and Barnes) have produced floral/faunal assemblages, and these reflect the typically broad spectrum of resources utilized by the Onondaga. Cultigen remains (corn, beans, and squash) are present, along with a mixed variety of wild flora such as plum and hackberry. Faunal remains still consist primarily of white-tailed deer although elk, bear, and several species of smaller mammal and birds are also present. Fish remains include pike, pickerel, and bullhead; freshwater mussels also occur.

One important change is the presence of human bone in small quantities from refuse deposits at the Barnes site.[34] This suggests that ritual cannibalism which Tuck found at the Chance phase Bloody Hill site was practiced during the Garoga phase as well. It is important to note, however, that this was a ritual, not a subsistence activity, for deer and bear were sufficiently plentiful to provide an adequate supply of protein. The human bone from these Garoga phase sites is evidence of aboriginal warfare in the Northeast. Traditionally it had two aims—the adoption of captives to swell the population, and vendetta killing. The latter included ritual torture and cannibalism.[35]

A fairly detailed material culture record is available for the Garoga phase, and helps fill out and amplify some of the changes suggested by the settlement data. The material record indicates two dynamics at work. First is the continued, gradual evolution of Onondaga material culture, especially its utilitarian aspects. Bone and lithic implements change little if at all; ceramic pots and pipes continue to evolve in a predictable manner from Chance phase forms. Second, and in counterpoint to continuity, is an undercurrent of change evident in two ways. One is a shift in the overall character of the material assemblage. In contrast to the almost exclusively practical and austerely utilitarian quality of Oak Hill and Chance phase artifacts, Garoga assemblages reflect a more frequent occurrence of ornamental and ritual objects. Also evident is an increased concern for embellishment and detail. At the same time, there is a reversal in the longstanding pattern of localism and a reactivation of the moribund exchange networks. For the first time in several centuries, exotic materials such as marine shell, native copper, and lithics from non-local sources are again part of the material culture.

Pottery is still the most common artifact, providing evidence for both continuity and change. In general, pots retain the same basic form—a globular body, constricted neck, and a well-defined lip or collar. Collarless pots continue as a distinct minority form, little different from those of the Chance phase. Collared pots, usually about 70 percent of the sample, more consistently reflect the continuing evolution of vessel form, most noticeable in the shape of the collar (Figure 1d). Collar height, for example, increases throughout the period. At the Barnes site over 70 percent of all measurable rims were from high-collared vessels. The form of the collar changes as well as its height. Preference shifts away from the earlier Chance round and Chance straight profiles in favor of the biconcave and new concave profiles (Table 2).

Decoration on the exterior of these large collars is almost exclusively incised, the motifs less varied than during the Chance phase.[36] Most frequent are opposed triangles (composed of oblique parallel lines) or simply oblique parallel lines beneath horizontal lines.[37] Despite this stylization of collar motifs, Garoga phase pottery gradually becomes embellished with other kinds of detail. Most dramatic is the use of effigy faces, usually beneath a castellation. The large, often striking or grotesque faces found on pottery from the Barnes and McNab sites represent a strong departure from the previous ceramic tradition (Figure 4). In addition to effigies, small applied beads or fillets of clay are occasionally used to ornament collars.

Other Garoga phase ceramic traits continue trends of earlier phases. For example, there is little decoration on either the neck or shoulder portions of vessels. The check-stamped finish used on the body of the pot during the Oak Hill phase and infrequent in the Chance phase essentially vanishes during the Garoga (Table 2).

Pipes, like pottery, reflect both continuity and innovation. While the same basic styles continue in use, there is a shift among those which predominate. Trumpet-shaped bowls remain most common, square bowl varieties outnumbering other forms. Effigy pipes occur more frequently and still reflect a high level of technical and artistic skill. One specific

Table 2

Selected Artifact Attributes from Garoga Phase Onondaga Sites

Pottery

			Rim Profile				
Site	Total Rims	Collarless (%)	Chance Round (%)	Chance Straight (%)	Biconcave (%)	Concave (%)	Other* (%)
Indian Hill II	32	28.1	9.4	40.6	21.9	0	0
Cemetery	65	37.0	1.5	20.0	40.0	0	1.5
Nursery	6	16.7	0	0	83.3	0	0
McNab	16	12.5	18.8	18.8	37.4	12.5	0
Barnes	241	30.7	14.5	14.5	31.5	8.8	0

		Body Treatment		
Site	No.	Check Stamped (%)	Plain (%)	Other[†] (%)
Indian Hill II	394	1.0	99.0	0
Cemetery	6000+	0	99.9	>0.01
Nursery	11	0	0	0
NcNab	107	0	0	0
Barnes	1724	>0.01	97.0	2.9

Projectile Points

Site	No.	Length-to-Width Ratio
Indian Hill II	6	1.87:1
Cemetery	11	1.90:1
Nursery	5	2.13:1
McNab	22	1.70:1
Barnes	71	1.90:1

* inverted lip
† cord impressed
Sources: See F. LaFrance 1977; Tuck 1969; Tuck 1971; T. Weinman personal communication; Gibson 1968; Bradley 1979.

trait deserving mention is the tendency to incise rings around the stem of the pipe. Up to one-third of the pipe stems at the Barnes site have incised rings, and many of these stems are multiply incised. Despite

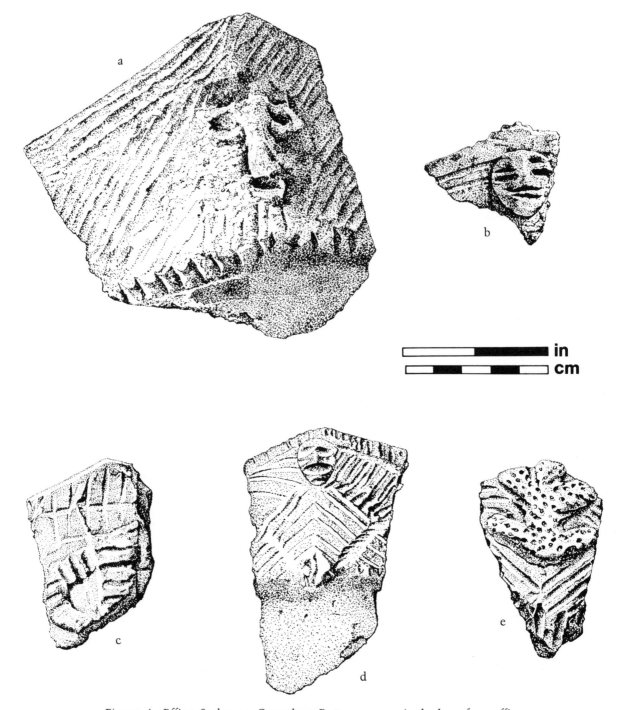

Figure 4. Effigy Styles on Onondaga Pottery. a. a pinched-up face effigy, Barnes site; b. an applied face effigy, Atwell site; c. an applied figure effigy, Chase site (RMSC CZA5-3/1069); d. an incised figure effigy, Pompey Center site; e. an applied animal effigy, Atwell site (RMSC 19315).

speculations that this was a means for reworking broken pipe stems into beads (Tuck 1971:152), the function of this microtradition remains unclear.[38]

In general, lithic implements change little or, like ceramic pottery, in predictable ways. Projectile points are increasingly isosceles in form and reach a maximum length-to-width ratio by the end of the phase (Table 2). Points also seem to occur much more frequently on Garoga than on Chance phase sites. The reason for this is not known. A variety of other bifacial tools, including haftable knives and scrapers, remains present, as do some unifacial scrapers and utilized flakes. The frequency of large, rough stone implements such as hammers, mullers, and an occasional chipped disc also changes little from that of earlier phase sites. Finally, pecked and polished celts are common and occur in what appears to be a fairly standardized form—rectanguloid in plan, thick and generally oval in section. The significant change in lithic implements is not one of function; rather, it is in the reappearance of exotic materials on the later Garoga sites.[39] In terms of frequency, the change is small; as a departure from the tradition seen on all the sites previously discussed, it is more significant.

The other change in lithic artifacts is an increase in the occurrence of ornamental/ritual objects. Prior to the late Garoga phase sites, non-utilitarian use of lithics was restricted to a rare pipe, pendant, or occasional bead. The difference on late Garoga sites is not overwhelming, but it is noticeable. The Barnes site, for example, has produced one stone effigy pipe and a half-dozen pendants and beads. While admittedly not a large number, this is more than occurred on all previous sites combined. In addition, there is another lithic form which seems to be particular to Garoga phase sites. This is a small disc, most commonly of red or grey slate, and usually centrally perforated.[40] These discs appear on nearly all the Garoga phase sites, with the largest sample on the Barnes site. If their function remains unclear, their presence indicates another traceable microtradition characteristic of the Onondaga Garoga phase.

Trends in the use of bone and antler parallel those of the lithic assemblages. A wide range of traditional tools occurs, including split bone awls, flat centrally perforated needles, antler billets, and diverse fishing implements. Among the latter are unilaterally and bilaterally barbed harpoons, fish hooks, leister points, and gorges. This is basically the same assemblage found on late Owasco sites, one which changed little over the course of Onondaga evolution.

The ornamental use of bone and antler, however, is radically different. Here the evidence of change is even more dramatic than it was with lithic ornaments. Bone beads, previously scarce, are fairly common. This is true of perforated teeth as well, most frequently the canines of either black bear or members of the *Canidae* family (dog, wolf, and fox). A variety of other forms also occurs, among them: pendants made from the epiphyseal cap of bear femurs, asymmetrically ground bear molars (occasionally finished to resemble a human foot), and modified deer phalanges.[41] In addition to these fairly simple artifacts, several more complex forms are present. Antler hair-combs reappear for the first time in the archaeological record since the Middle Woodland stage,[42] as do turtle-shell rattles.[43] Finally, face effigies occur in bone and antler as well as on ceramic pots and pipes.

Evidence of external contacts highlights these internal changes in Onondaga material culture. As noted above, exotic lithics reappear on late Garoga sites for the first time in several centuries. So do other imported materials— marine shell and native copper. Several forms of shell ornaments appear at the Barnes site, including a dozen beads predominantly discoidal or tubular in shape, and a pendant.[44] Two native copper artifacts have also been recovered from the Barnes site. One is a small, irregular blade-shaped piece; the other is a small, centrally perforated disc similar in shape to the stone discs described above[45] (Plate 6).

The exotic materials are of particular interest for several reasons. First, all come from fairly distant and quite diverse sources, ranging from the Upper Great Lakes to the mid-Atlantic coast. Juxtaposed against the evolution of the Onondaga Iroquois traced as an intensively localized process, the reappearance of foreign materials is significant. The change is especially notable since, as a group, exotic lithics, marine shell, and copper have been absent from archaeological assemblages for a long time. These materials occur occasionally on sites of the Late Archaic stage (ca. 2000–1000 B.C.), particularly shell and copper, and most often in mortuary contexts. The pattern continues through the Early Woodland stage (ca. 1000–0 B.C.). However, by the end of the Middle Woodland stage (ca. A.D. 0–1000), they have ceased to be part of the archaeological record in Central New York.[46] Moreover, exotic lithics, shell, and copper are of interest because literally and symbolically they represented wealth and power. Generally in Great Lakes Indian cosmology these substances were gifts from the Under(water) World Grandfathers, powerful man-beings able to change their shape into serpents or panthers. When consecrated to ritual use, exotic materials could bring success in hunting or war, ensure physical and spiritual well being, and even renew life itself.[47] Clearly, whatever changing within Onondaga culture had implications beyond Central New York.

If the challenge for the archaeologist is first to reconstruct, and next to interpret, the material record a people leave behind, then the Garoga phase Onondaga sites present an intriguing puzzle. On the one hand there is considerable evidence of continuity from the preceding phases. Many aspects of Garoga phase settlement, subsistence pattern, and material culture are straightforward extensions of Oak Hill and Chance phase traits. On the other hand, there are marked deviations. These include a massing of population and apparently not for just defensive purposes, a dramatically more elaborate material culture, and the revival of long-distance exchange for exotic materials. Clearly, something happened during the late Garoga, something that had an impact on Onondaga culture both internally and externally.

The establishment of the Iroquois Confederacy is a plausible explanation of these events. Despite the vast amount of information available on the Confederacy during the historic period, there is little documentary evidence of how and when it was formed. According to native oral tradition, the Peace Maker ended a period of warfare and blood feuding among the Iroquois and established the Great Peace under which the Five Nations confederated (Fenton 1975). Tooker has argued that both in conception and form the Confederacy was indigenous and not a hybrid of native and European ideas. A considerable amount of scholarly research and debate has attempted to establish a date for the Confederacy's founding. Although no clear consensus has emerged, a mid- to late fifteenth-century date is not implausible (Tooker 1981:5; 1978:418–22).

The establishment of the Confederacy explains the continuities and changes characterizing the late Garoga phase Onondaga sites. Founded on a mutual non-agression agreement, the Confederacy would have reduced intertribal tensions. One tangible result may have been a lessened need for defense. Such an agreement also could have served as a catalyst accelerating the tendency toward nucleation and the crystallization of tribal identities. Larger villages would have been a likely consequence. One could reasonably expect to see some material culture evidence for so significant a change as the establishment of the Confederacy: for example, an increase in ritual or symbolically related artifacts expressed in both locally available and exotic materials. One might also predict that such changes would be especially noticeable at the geographical center of the Confederacy where the most intensive interactions would occur. It was at Onondaga, of course, that the Confederacy was established and where the Council fire traditionally burned.

The convergence of archaeological data, oral tradition, and gleanings from the historical record is suggestive as to when the Confederacy was founded. It is far from conclusive. Yet two points are clear. First, the establishment of the Confederacy provides a reasonable explanation for the observed changes on late Garoga phase Onondaga sites. Second, the weight of evidence strongly suggests that the Confederacy existed in some form prior to European contact. Whatever its original structure and function, the Confederacy, like every other aspect of native culture, changed as a result of that contact. How those changes occurred, and to what end, are the central issues in the following chapters.

Concluding Comments

This review gives us a sense of Onondaga cultural definition prior to European contact, and enables us approximately to determine when the Onondaga became an identifiable tribal entity and what traits mark that transition. Although generally following the model of Onondaga prehistory proposed by Tuck (1971), it is useful to supplement his model with more recent findings.

Tuck's model can be summarized in three main points: (1) the presence of increasingly larger and more discrete communities across Central New York at the beginning of the Late Woodland stage; (2) a pattern of eastward movement in some of these communities during the Castle Creek and Oak Hill phases; and (3) the convergence or merger of two of these communities in the Pompey Hills during the Chance phase, signalling the formation of the Onondaga "Nation" (ibid.:139, 207–16). Many of the specifics of this process are subject to revision and clarification; still, we can confirm the general model of *in situ* development that Tuck proposed.

Nonetheless, several problems remain unsolved. One is chronology. There is a serious lack of fit between the "absolute" chronology for the Onondaga sequence, based on C^{14} dating, and the "relative" chronology implied by the seriation of settlement and artifact data. Figure 5 illustrates the problem. If we assume that the C^{14} dates are accurate, then the A.D. 1480 date for the Burke site advances all the Garoga phase sites into the sixteenth century. But as we will soon see, the sixteenth century is already crowded. In fact, the seriation data from protohistoric sites argue that all Garoga phase sites should predate 1500. Clearly there is a contradiction here. Until more dates are available, especially for Garoga phase sites, or some other means is found to resolve this discrepancy, a fundamental aspect of Onondaga tribal evolution—its chronology—will remain ambiguous.

Other unresolved issues also cloud our understanding of Onondaga tribal evolution. The term "tribal evolution" is itself a slippery one. Tuck avoided using it and thus did not have to worry about defining it. In her recent study of the origin and development of the Seneca and Cayuga Iroquois, Mary Ann Niemczycki addresses directly this problem of definition (1984). After examining the semantic difficulties that surround use of the term "tribe," Niemczycki proposes a general model for tribal evolution and expected patterns of settlement (84–86). In order to test and refine her model, she uses Tuck's Onondaga sequence. The outcome is a specific model for Iroquoian tribal development (Figure 6). Niemczycki's model adds considerable theoretical vigor to Tuck's sequence. It also provides a more precise understanding of *how* the process of tribal

Figure 5
A Summary of Pre-contact Onondaga Tribal Development (by drainage)

	Skaneateles Creek	Onondaga Creek	Butternut Creek	Limestone Creek	Chittenango Creek
1500				Barnes	
					McNab
				Nursery	
				Cemetery	
				Indian Hill II	
				Burke (A.D. 1480)	
				Carley II	
				Fietta ?	
				Sperry ?	
1450				Christopher	
			Bloody Hill II (A.D. 1420)		
		Schoff (A.D. 1410)	Keough		
1400	Kelso (A.D. 1390)	Howlett Hill (A.D. 1380)	Coye II?		
1350		Furnace Brook (A.D. 1300–1370)			
1300	Chamberlin (A.D. 1290)	Cabin			
1250					
1200					
1150					
1100	Maxon-Derby (A.D. 1100)				

evolution may have taken place. However, this model does not clarify two other fundamental aspects of the process—the *rate* at which tribal evolution occurred, or *why* it occurred at all.

Our view of Onondaga origins suggests a steady process of change. Phase follows phase in a neat, progressive order. It is likely, however, that this implied uniformity is more apparent than real. While change may have been incremental, it was probably also episodic, periods of relative stability and modest adjustment punctuated by bursts of coalescence and experimentation. The Chance phase, with its community mergers and elaborated ceramics, appears to have been one such episodic burst, resulting in the emergence of the Onondaga as a tribal entity.

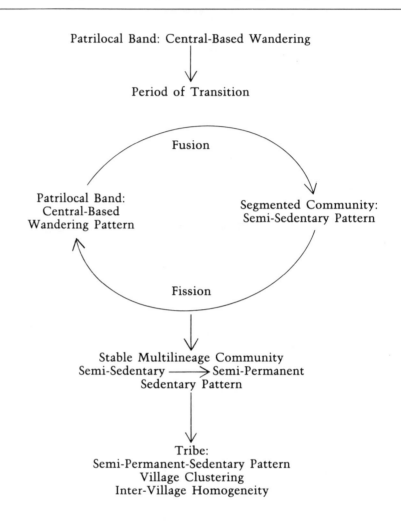

Figure 6
A Specific Model of Iroquois Tribal Development
(after Niemczycki 1984:90, Figure 25)

Patrilocal Band: Central-Based Wandering

Period of Transition

Fusion

Patrilocal Band:
Central-Based
Wandering Pattern

Segmented Community:
Semi-Sedentary Pattern

Fission

Stable Multilineage Community
Semi-Sedentary ⟶ Semi-Permanent
Sedentary Pattern

Tribe:
Semi-Permanent-Sedentary Pattern
Village Clustering
Inter-Village Homogeneity

Still we must ask: What caused the change? What were the factors that first initiated, then continued to drive, the process of tribal evolution? The most commonly accepted explanation for Late Woodland stage coalescence is the introduction of maize and its ever more prominent role in subsistence patterns (Ritchie 1969:312; Tuck 1971:223; Ritchie and Funk 1973:364–66; Noble 1975). There is certainly a strong correlation between the occurrence of cultigens and evidence of an increasingly large and nucleated population. However, it is difficult to determine which is the cause and which the effect.

Other factors that may have induced centripetal tendencies include an increase in internecine warfare (hence the need to aggregate for defense) and environmental change which altered traditional subsistence patterns in favor of more community-based efforts. However, as Hasenstab has observed, both these explanations lead back to the agriculture/nucleation problem without clarifying which came first (1985). Hasenstab's own response to this circular argument is to look for external causes, especially in the direction of the large Mississippian cultures of the continental interior. Although provocative, Hasenstab's thesis remains to be tested. Thus, the identification of forces driving the process of Iroquoian tribal evolution remains incomplete.

To conclude, while many aspects of Onondaga evolution are yet to be clarified, we can define several of the salient characteristics of Onondaga culture prior to European contact:

—Onondaga culture was dynamic, not static.

—Different components of the culture changed at different rates. For example, ceramic styles changed more rapidly than utilitarian implements.

—The culture was flexible and thus able to take maximum advantage of a wide range of resources.

—The definition of the culture changed over time as the process of coalescence integrated new people and traits.

On this basis one might predict that, initially, the Onondaga viewed European materials as just another set of exotic elements to be integrated into their culture and used in traditional ways.

2

The Protohistoric Onondaga
1500-1600

Superficially, the sixteenth-century Onondaga seem a reclusive, almost isolated people. Nearly all their sites are tucked along the margins of the Appalachian Uplands in a tightly concentrated core area away from major waterways. This preference for the hills has provided fertile ground for misinterpretation. For George Hunt, these sites were evidence that the Onondaga were "a beaten people . . . on the defensive deep in their own forests" (1940:24, 161). Allen Trelease echoes this assessment, claiming that when Europeans first arrived to trade, the Onondaga and other Iroquois nations were "beset on all sides" by their enemies (1960:23). The Iroquois remained in this beleaguered condition, the argument continues, until the effects of European contact launched them into a frenzy of conquest.

This view of the sixteenth-century Onondaga as a small and unobtrusive people radically altered by the effects of European contact was based primarily on a migration theory of Iroquois origins. According to this explanation, the Onondaga originated in the St. Lawrence River Valley and were driven from their ancestral homeland at about the time of European contact. Retreating south, the Onondaga finally took refuge in the Pompey Hills. This interpretation drew archaeological support from artifact similarities between prehistoric Iroquoian sites in northern New York and known Onondaga sites in the Pompey area.[1]

Research during the past two decades has all but demolished this view of the sixteenth-century Onondaga. It is now clear that the Onondaga evolved through a process of *in situ* development within Central New York and did not migrate from elsewhere in the Northeast. Far from being a weak and defeated people, the Onondaga were populous and prosperous when the first European materials reached them during the second quarter of the sixteenth century.

This chapter examines the protohistoric Onondaga sites in order to trace two dynamics. First, it follows the continued evolution of the Onondaga as a discrete tribal entity. Second, it examines the major role played by external factors in shaping Onondaga culture during the protohistoric period. External factors include the influence of other native groups as well as that of European contact. Our primary goal is to trace the material evidence of these processes.

Before discussing specifics, however, a few words need to be said about the archaeological information upon which the chapter is built. The archaeological work on protohistoric Onondaga sites differs in an important way from that done on the prehistoric sites. Much of the prehistoric data has come from excavations by professional archaeologists; nearly all the data on protohistoric sites has come from avocational archaeologists.

Digging for artifacts has been a popular pastime in central New York since the mid-nineteenth century. As early as 1849, a local antiquarian noted that many sites and burying grounds had already been dug through in order to "adorn the cabinets of the curious" (Clark 1849, 2:267–68). In the 130-odd years since Clark's observation, extensive excavations have occurred on nearly all the protohistoric Onondaga sites. While much of this digging has been little more than looting, some has been quite good, especially when judged against the standards of the day. In fact, it is in these existing collections and the accompanying notes that most of the information on the protohistoric Onondaga has survived.[2]

Settlement and Subsistence Patterns

At present, eight protohistoric Onondaga sites are known; three are large sites. Listed in order of their estimated dates of occupation, these large sites are:

Name	Estimated Dates	Estimated Size	Source[3]
Temperance House	1525–1550	4–5 acres	Ricklis 1966
Quirk	1550–1575	4–5 acres	Ibid.
Chase	1575–1600	4–5 acres	Ibid.; A. D. LaFrance 1977

In general, these sites are very similar to their Garoga phase predecessors. All are located in the uplands south of the Onondaga Escarpment. Until the sixteenth century, site movement had been in an eastward direction. This changes during the protohistoric period as the Onondaga begin to shift their villages in a southerly direction following the east branch of

Limestone Creek (Map 6). The location preference for villages continues to follow the late Garoga pattern favoring terraces and promontories along the broad, steep-sided glacial valleys. Generally, these village sites overlook the valley floor and favor locations sheltered from the prevailing winds. With some additional fortification, access to these villages would have been quite restricted and surprise attack difficult.

Since little settlement pattern excavation has been done, site size is difficult to determine accurately. Nonetheless, these large villages do not seem to have changed appreciably in size over the course of the sixteenth century, a fact suggesting population stability during the protohistoric period. While settlement pattern data are limited, the large sites appear to follow Garoga phase precedents. All three were fortified, although excavated data are available only for Temperance House. In contrast to the rather insubstantial single palisade at the Barnes site, Temperance House had a substantial palisade composed of a double row of irregularly spaced posts ranging from 3 to 7 inches in diameter. Temperance House is also the only large site where a house pattern has been exposed. Ricklis' excavations uncovered the southern end of a typical longhouse eighteen feet in width (1966:3). Information on other settlement features or the internal configuration of these large sites is lacking.[4]

The five small sixteenth-century Onondaga sites are:

Name	Estimated Dates	Estimated Size	Source
Atwell	1525–1550	3 acres	Ricklis 1963, 1966, 1967
Pickering	1525–1550	2 acres	
Sheldon	1550–1575	2–3 acres	
Dwyer	1575–1600	2–3 acres	
Brewerton	1575–1600	unknown	

These small sites, like their predecessors during the earlier phases of Onondaga development, appear to fall into two distinct groups. The first are lowland sites, seasonal fishing and gathering camps on the major waterways of the Great Lakes plain. A small site in Brewerton on the south side of the Oneida Lake outlet is the only such site known from the protohistoric period.[5] All the other known small sites are located in the uplands. These sites appear to have been small villages or hamlets, contemporary with the large villages, and located in fairly close proximity to them (between 1.5 and 3.5km).

Generally, the small sites parallel the larger ones in location preference and other settlement traits. All four apparently were palisaded. The best-documented example is at the Atwell site, which had an irregular palisade similar to that of the neighboring Temperance House site. The exterior line was composed of large blunt-ended posts up to 14 inches in diameter with an average of about 10 inches. The interior line was of smaller,

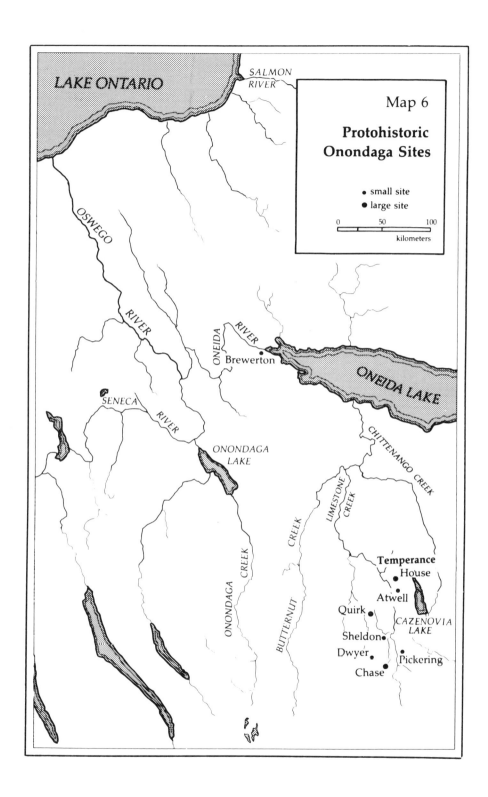

SALMON RIVER

LAKE ONTARIO

Map 6

**Protohistoric
Onondaga Sites**

• small site
• large site

0   50   100
kilometers

OSWEGO

RIVER

ONEIDA
RIVER

Brewerton

ONEIDA LAKE

SENECA

RIVER

ONONDAGA
LAKE

CHITTENANGO CREEK

ONONDAGA CREEK

BUTTERNUT CREEK

LIMESTONE CREEK

Temperance
House
•

Atwell
•

Quirk •

CAZENOVIA
LAKE

Sheldon•

Dwyer •

Chase •

Pickering
•

pointed posts averaging about 4 inches in diameter.[6] Palisades have also been documented at the Sheldon and Dwyer sites.

Information about other settlement features on these small sites is scarce. The only well-documented structure is a small, rectangular house excavated at the Atwell site (Ricklis 1967). In both size and configuration, the house resembles examples from earlier small sites such as Bloody Hill, as well as large sites like Howlett Hill and Furnace Brook. This suggests that the building of small structures as well as longhouses was a long-standing tradition among the Onondaga.

Dating these protohistoric sites is somewhat problematic. As with the Garoga phase sites, no C^{14} dates or other "absolute" measures of chronology are available for the eight known protohistoric sites. With neither firm dates nor detailed information on settlement patterns, it is also difficult to estimate how long each of these sites was inhabited. Current estimates for dates and duration of site occupation are based primarily on the seriation of artifact traits. Although seriation is an effective means for organizing artifact data, and a good basis on which to estimate site order and chronology, it is important to remember that the dates are only "best guess" estimates and not historical facts.

Many of the considerations described above also bear on the question of site patterning. Tuck has argued that a two-village pattern (one large and one small) emerged during the Chance phase and continued to characterize the Onondaga throughout the protohistoric and historic periods (Tuck 1971:210, 216–17). Certainly both large and small sites are present; however, the pattern of relationship is not as clear-cut as Tuck's reconstruction suggests.

Interestingly enough, a relationship between large and small sites appears most clearly during the protohistoric period. Most of the sixteenth-century Onondaga sites can be matched into large site–small site pairs. Once again, it is the seriation of artifact traits which allows us to trace this pattern. While several artifact indicators were used, ceramic coefficients of agreement were particularly helpful (ibid.:198–99) (Table 3). These were calculated on the basis of four attributes: rim profile for collared vessels, lip decoration preference for collared vessels, collar height, and collar base marking. The proposed site pairs are:

Temperance House (large)	Atwell (small)
Quirk (large)	Pickering (small)/Sheldon (small)
Chase (large)	Dwyer (small)

While these sites do seem to match well in terms of both artifact traits and locations, the likelihood that additional sites will be discovered cautions against simplistic patterning.

To summarize, prehistoric settlement patterns do not seem to change significantly during the protohistoric period. Site size, location, and other general characteristics follow prehistoric precedents rather than deviate from them. This continuity is underscored by the observations of previous researchers who classified some of these sites, Temperance House and Atwell in particular, as prehistoric. Only the subsequent recovery of European materials from these sites has permitted us to shift them from prehistoric to protohistoric.[7]

As with settlement, the basic pattern of subsistence does not appear to have changed significantly during the protohistoric period. The mixed economy of horticulture, hunting, fishing, and gathering that characterized the prehistoric Onondaga appears to continue throughout the sixteenth century as well.

Only small samples of faunal and floral remains are available for most of the sixteenth-century sites and few of these have been evaluated in a detailed manner. The one faunal assemblage analyzed is from the late sixteenth-century Dwyer site. In many ways this sample provided the expected results. The predominant species was white-tailed deer (*Odocoileus virginianus*, 69 percent of the identifiable remains). Also present were black bear (*Ursus americanus*, 6 percent), and smaller percentages of elk, moose, several species of smaller mammals, birds, fish, and fresh-

Table 3

Ceramic Coefficients of Agreement for Protohistoric and Early Historic Onondaga Sites
(based on four attributes)

	McNab	Barnes	Temperance House	Atwell	Pickering	Quirk	Sheldon	Chase	Dwyer	Pompey Center	Shurtleff
McNab		187	183	176	180	180	170	164	154	154	136
Barnes			186	167	172	178	160	145	137	128	107
Temperance House				181	177	182	171	155	147	137	117
Atwell					172	177	171	175	165	155	135
Pickering						178	173	156	147	140	115
Quirk							176	166	157	147	127
Sheldon								174	168	158	135
Chase									183	178	150
Dwyer										178	164
Pompey Center											164
Shurtleff											

Source: Bradley 1979.

water mussels. In two other ways, however, this sample was unusual. First, the presence of human bone (6 percent of the sample) is an indication that the ritual torture and possible cannibalism, noted at prehistoric Onondaga sites, continued also during the sixteenth century.[8] The second notable sample difference was the high percentage of beaver (*Castor canadensis*) present, 14 percent of the total. This is much higher than on prehistoric Onondaga sites and is undoubtedly a reflection of increased hunting for the fur trade.[9]

Material Culture: Native Materials

As on Garoga phase sites, pottery is the most commonly occurring artifact. In general, pots retain the form of the late prehistoric period— a globular body with constricted neck and well-defined collar. Collared vessels continue to predominate and are usually 70 percent to 80 percent of the ceramic assemblage. In terms of vessel form and decoration pottery is the most sensitive indicator of change, whether that change reflects internal Onondaga development or the influence of other native ceramic traditions.

The primary change in Onondaga ceramics during the sixteenth century was a gradual breakdown of the rather formalized ceramic tradition developed during the Garoga phase. This shift toward heterogeneity appears in the structural as well as decorative aspects of protohistoric Onondaga pottery. Among the structural changes is a gradual decrease in collar height, reversing the trend seen during the Garoga phase. On early protohistoric sites such as Temperance House, the percentage of high collar vessels is nearly the same as on late prehistoric sites like Barnes, at least 70 percent. The percentages of low and medium collar vessels are correspondingly small. By the end of the century, however, the frequency of high collar vessels has dropped to below 50 percent, while low and medium collar vessels have increased dramatically (Table 4).

A second and probably related change occurred in collar shape. Throughout the period, vessel collars were made in increasingly diverse ways. The older Chance round and Chance straight profiles, as well as the biconcave profile which dominated the Garoga phase, continue to occur but in ever-decreasing quantities. At the same time, the newer concave and frilled profiles become more common (Table 4). To some degree, the preference for these newer profiles, as with the shift toward lower collars, seems to reflect the ongoing, internal evolution of Onondaga ceramics. This is especially so for the concave profile, a logical outgrowth of the

Table 4
Selected Artifact Attributes from Protohistoric Onondaga Sites

| | Pottery | | | | | | | | | | Projectile Points | |
| | Rim Profile | | | | | | | Collar Height | | | | |
Site	Total Rims	Collarless (%)	Chance Round (%)	Chance Straight (%)	Biconcave (%)	Concave (%)	Frilled (%)	High (%)	Medium (%)	Low (%)	No.	Length-to-Width Ratio
Barnes	241	30.7	14.5	14.5	31.5	8.8	0	72.6	16.4	11.0	71	1.90:1
Temperance House	146	32.3	14.5	10.5	28.2	14.5	0	73.8	14.7	11.5	37	1.58:1
Atwell	260	31.9	4.7	7.4	32.8	23.2	0	62.7	15.9	21.4	19	1.64:1
Pickering	44	22.7	4.6	4.6	31.8	36.3	0	83.9	9.7	6.4	—	—
Quirk	64	15.6	6.2	9.4	34.4	31.3	3.1	68.6	14.3	17.1	6	1.40:1
Sheldon	30	13.3	10.0	3.3	23.4	50.0	0	70.0	10.0	20.0	8	1.46:1
Chase	274	30.3	4.4	6.9	19.7	36.1	2.6	45.7	27.7	26.6	9	1.25:1
Dwyer	72	19.5	8.3	6.9	22.2	38.9	4.2	42.9	14.2	42.9	8	1.37:1
Pompey Center	252	21.8	7.1	3.2	15.1	38.1	14.7	33.3	38.1	28.6	100	1.30:1

0 means trait not present.
— means specific data not available.
Source: See note 2.

earlier biconcave profile. At the same time, however, these changes increased and accelerated under the influence of other native ceramic traditions (discussed below).

The third change is a noticeable increase in the variety and complexity of collar decoration. Some of this stylistic diversity seems tied to the structural changes. As collars grew shorter, motifs tended to become busier and more compressed. In addition, a wider repertoire of motifs was used for decoration, and in less conventional ways. As with the changes in collar height and rim profile, some of the decorative aspects of Onondaga pottery seem to undergo an evolutionary drift. The use of effigies, for example, continues throughout the period, but on a changing basis. The large, often grotesque faces found on late Garoga phase pottery give way to smaller, more stylized faces on the early protohistoric vessels. These is turn become full figure effigies by the end of the sixteenth century as bodies were either applied or incised beneath the faces (Figure 4).

It is in this heterogeneous quality, however, that the influence of other ceramic traditions on the Onondaga is most evident. Exotic influences fall into two broad categories. The first is from north of Onondaga and includes ceramic traits of both the St. Lawrence Iroquois and the Huron. Each of these Iroquoian peoples had its own distinctive ceramic traditions. For our purposes, however, both form the general category of "northern" influence.[10]

In many instances this northern influence on Onondaga ceramics is easily recognized. Huron ceramics, for example, are quite different from those of the Onondaga. As a result, the occasional pieces of typical Huron pottery which turn up on Onondaga sites are hard to miss (Plate 2a and b). In general, however, the truly exotic pieces are uncommon. More frequent is the incorporation of one or two northern traits onto an otherwise typical Onondaga vessel. Among these traits are atypical structural features as well as unusual motifs and techniques for finishing and decorating the vessel. Structural features include the use of carinated shoulders, handles, or specific castellation styles.[11] Decorative motifs which reflect a Huron and/or St. Lawrence Iroquois influence include the use of crisscrossed lines, horizontal lines, blank triangles and rectangles, rows of punctates, and ladder plaiting.[12] Unusual techniques in this category include the use of cord impressions, dentate stamping, or large circular punctates to decorate the vessel's collar, and the use of either check stamping or cord malleation to finish the body of the pot.[13] Examples of ceramic miscegeny, Onondaga rimsherds with one or more of these northern traits, are illustrated in Plate 2.

While this northern influence on Onondaga ceramics is present throughout the protohistoric period, the frequency and pattern of its occurrence vary. On earlier sites, such as Temperance House and Atwell, the pattern is very similar to that on late Garoga phase sites like Barnes. Exotic examples occur more often than miscegenetic ones, but neither is common. Rarely do these traits occur on more than 1 or 2 percent (certainly less than 5 percent) of the total ceramic assemblage. In spite of their rarity, the exotic and miscegenetic traits which do occur on the earlier sites tend to stand out against the rather uniform backdrop of mainstream Onondaga ceramics.

On later protohistoric sites such as Chase, northern traits are more common, occurring on 5 percent or more of the pottery. The majority of these are miscegenetic examples, though some exotic examples continue to occur as well. Although more common, the overall visibility of these pieces has diminished, in large part because Onondaga ceramics have become more diverse. By the end of the protohistoric period, many of the traits which initially stood out as exotic now fall within the boundaries of the Onondaga ceramic tradition.

What does all this mean? At present there are two interpretations for what exotic and miscegenetic ceramics imply about cultural relationships. Both rest on the assumption that women made the pots. On the basis of

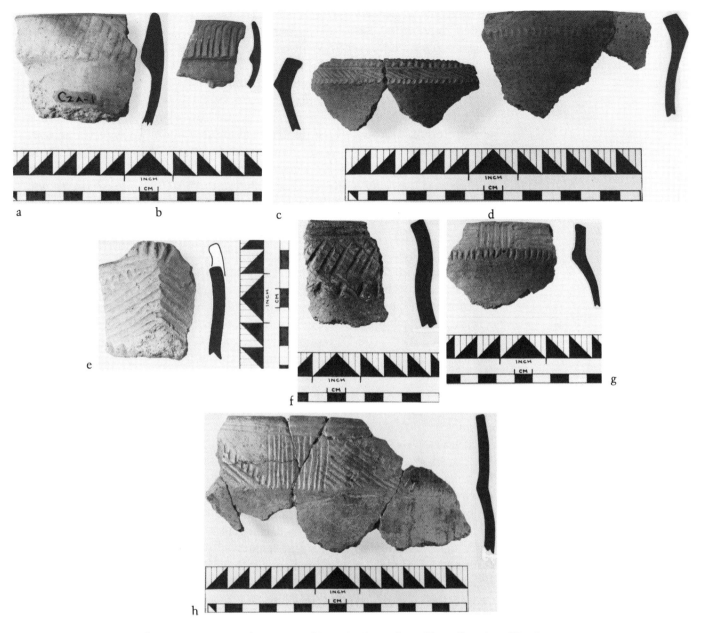

Plate 2. Ceramics from Protohistoric Onondaga Sites Showing Northern Influence. a. and b. two examples of Huron pottery (Huron Incised), Atwell site; c. and d. two examples of St. Lawrence Iroquois pottery (Roebuck low collar), Chase site (RMSC CZA5–3/1090 and 1087); four examples of ceramic miscegenation: e. a broad castellation on a high-collar, biconcave profile rim with an opposed triangle motif, Atwell site; f. a medium collar, concave profile rim with a criss-crossed motif (Lanorie Crossed), Pompey Center site; g. a low collar, biconcave profile rim with a horizontal/vertical motif (Copeland Incised), Chase site (RMSC CZA5–3/1076); h. a medium collar, concave profile rim with a blank triangle motif and no collar base notching, Chase site.

57

his analysis of pottery from the Five Nations Iroquois, Engelbrecht concluded that "female trading activities" provided the best explanation for the patterns he observed.[14] Women who visited neighboring tribes to trade would be exposed to different ceramic styles and techniques. Upon returning home, they easily could have incorporated some new ideas into their own ceramic tradition (Engelbrecht 1972:8).

A second interpretation sees exotic and miscegenetic pottery from a very different perspective, as material evidence of one of intertribal warfare's primary functions—increasing population through assimilation. From this viewpoint, women who were captured and adopted by a neighboring tribe would initially continue to make pottery according to their own ceramic tradition. However, over time, this tradition would break down as the women, or their daughters, adapted to the ceramic tradition of the dominant group. Along the way, of course, various degrees of mixing could occur between the two traditions. Pendergast has documented different stages in this process in his analysis of St. Lawrence Iroquois and Huron sites of the late prehistoric period (Pendergast 1981a). This latter interpretation provides the best explanation for the presence of northern ceramic traits on protohistoric Onondaga pottery.[15] Over the course of the sixteenth century, the Onondaga appear to have assimilated small groups, remnants perhaps, of the St. Lawrence Iroquois from Jefferson County (for a fuller discussion of assimilation see chapter 3).

Not all the external influence helping to shape the protohistoric Onondaga came from the north. To the south of Onondaga were the Susquehannock, another Iroquoian group exercising a profound impact on Onondaga development during the last half of the sixteenth century.

The clearest indication of this southern influence is the presence of Susquehannock pottery on Onondaga sites. Most distinctive is a type known as Schultz Incised, which differs sharply from other Iroquoian ceramics both in structure and decoration. The major attributes of this ware include the use of shell rather than grit tempering, a weakly defined collar base, and a medium to high collar decorated with triangular or trapezoidal plats and filled with a combination of incised lines and linear punctates (Witthoft and Kinsey 1959:68–69, 76–77; Kent 1984:113–16). A Schultz Incised vessel is illustrated in Plate 3a. The earliest known examples of this ware, found on small Susquehannock sites located in southern New York and northern Pennsylvania, appear to date to the mid-sixteenth century.[16] During the last half of the century Schultz Incised becomes the most common ceramic type on Susquehannock sites. While this exotic ware never becomes common on Onondaga sites, it is present in small quantities throughout the protohistoric period (Plate 3b and c).

Closely related to Schultz Incised is a similar ceramic type which MacNeish termed Ithaca Linear (MacNeish 1952:49). In form and deco-

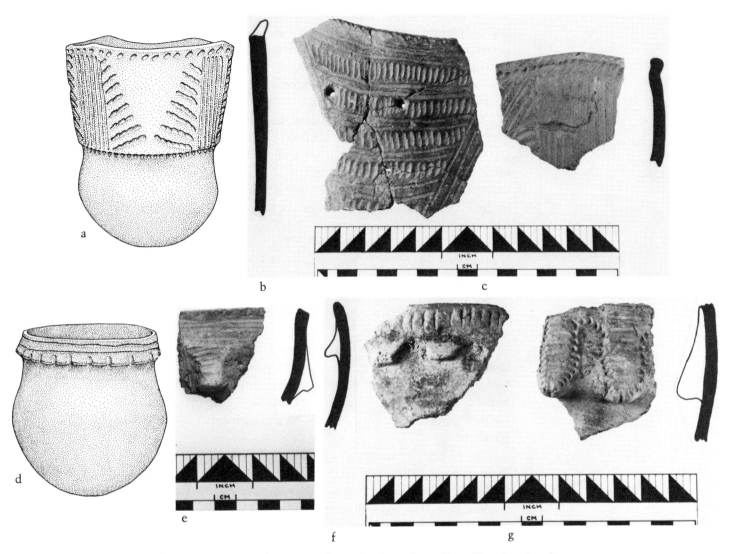

Plate 3. Ceramics from Protohistoric Onondaga Sites Showing Southern Influence. a. a schematic drawing of a Shultz Incised vessel; b. an Early Schultz Incised rim, Atwell site (RMSC CZA1–1/219); c. a Schultz Incised rim, Chase site (RMSC CZA5–3/1094); d. a schematic drawing of a frilled vessel; e. a frilled rim, Chase site; f. and g. two frilled rims, Pompey Center site.

ration this ware is virtually identical to shell-tempered Schultz Incised; the only significant difference is that Ithaca Linear is grit tempered. The ancestry of both these ceramic forms remains unclear as does the relationship between them. At present, it seems most accurate to describe Ithaca Linear as a Susquehannock ceramic concept expressed in an Iroquois medium.[17]

This is not the only instance in which an apparent Susquehannock ceramic concept was adapted or replicated by the Onondaga. During the last half of the sixteenth century a second Susquehannock vessel form not only appears on Onondaga sites, but becomes an established part of the Onondaga ceramic tradition. This form is characterized by a small globular bodied vessel, a low to medium collar, and exaggerated notching along the collar base (Plate 3d). As a Susquehannock form, this ware has been described as Blue Rock Valanced (Heisey and Witmer 1962:111–13). The Iroquois counterpart has been termed Genoa Frilled.[18] Here too, the only significant difference between these two wares is the tempering agent.

In order to avoid confusion, the examples of this ware from Onondaga sites (all of which are grit tempered) have simply been called "frilled," as defined in Appendix A. On Onondaga sites, frilled pottery first appears sometime after the mid-sixteenth century, gradually becoming more common throughout the rest of the protohistoric period. By the early seventeenth century, frilled vessels are an important, though minority, component of Onondaga ceramics (Table 4). The occurrence of Blue Rock Valanced pottery on Susquehannock sites appears to follow a similar pattern (Kent 1980).

In contrast to northern ceramic traits, there appears to have been very little miscegenation between Onondaga and Susquehannock pottery.[19] Virtually no Onondaga pottery has been recovered from protohistoric Susquehannock sites. The few examples of Schultz Incised found in Onondaga are typically Susquehannock, not a hybrid product of the two ceramic traditions. To state it differently, whatever mixing did occur between Onondaga and Susquehannock ceramics took place at a much broader or more fundamental cultural level.

What all this means about cultural process, intertribal relationships, or any of the other more interesting aspects of the sixteenth century, remains unclear. Some things, however, can be factored out. Without more evidence of Onondaga-Susquehannock miscegenation, the assimilation of captives does not provide a satisfactory explanation. On the other hand, there are other artifact groups whose pattern of occurrence does correlate with the increase in Susquehannock-related ceramic traits. These groups are marine shell and European materials. It may be that the increase in Susquehannock ceramic traits on protohistoric Onondaga pottery reflects an increasing participation in exchange networks. If this is the case, perhaps Engelbrecht's model bears reexamination.

Smoking pipes are another material culture indicator of changes in Onondaga during the protohistoric period. Two major changes occur. The first is a much broader range of pipe styles than in the prehistoric periods. In addition to the usual trumpet, square trumpet, and effigy forms, bulbous and barrel-shaped bowl varieties occur. Effigy pipes in particular are both more common and more diverse.

As with ceramics, some of these pipe styles reflect the influence of other Iroquoian traditions. Several styles indicate an influence from the north. One example is what Mathews has called "boat-shaped pipes": a specific style associated with the St. Lawrence Iroquois, particularly those in Jefferson County, New York (1982:51). At least three examples of this form are known from Onondaga[20] (Plate 4c and d). A second instance of pipe style in a St. Lawrence Iroquois tradition is represented by a large double bird effigy pipe from Temperance House (Plate 4a and b). This pipe is nearly identical both in conception and execution to an example from the Morse site, the terminal St. Lawrence Iroquois site in Jefferson County.[21] One additional indication of northern influence on protohistoric Onondaga pipes is the continued occurrence of one or more incised rings on pipe stems. This microtradition, present only on late Garoga phase and early protohistoric period sites, appears to be related to a similar tradition among the St. Lawrence Iroquois, particularly in Jefferson County. The occurrence of incised rings on pipes from Onondaga sites is summarized in Table 5.

The second change in smoking pipes is that, over the course of the protohistoric period, ceramic pipes occur with decreasing frequency. At first, this seems troublesome. Even correcting for sample bias, it is clear that clay pipes have nearly disappeared from Onondaga sites by the end of the sixteenth century. Why does an indigenous tradition that has evolved over several centuries seem to end abruptly? The most satisfying answer is that, rather than ceasing, pipe makers switch from clay to a new medium—wood. The catalyst was metal tools. Wray observed that the decrease in ceramic pipes during the protohistoric period is inversely proportional to the occurrence of metal tools (Wray 1973:13). Hamell's reexamination of both the archaeological and historical evidence suggests that wooden pipes were used extensively by the Seneca during both the sixteenth and seventeenth centuries (Hamell n.d.). The pattern among the Onondaga appears to have been similar.

The apparent disappearance of clay pipes provides a useful cautionary example. During the protohistoric period, European material did begin to have an effect on traditional Onondaga material culture; however, that effect was not necessarily negative.

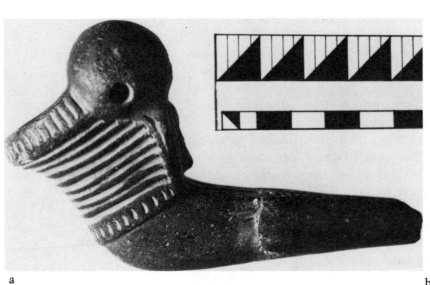

a

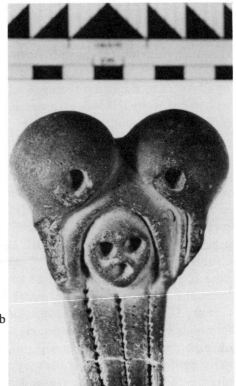

b

c

d

Plate 4. Pipes from Protohistoric Onondaga Sites Showing Northern Influence. a. and b. a double effigy pipe, Temperance House site (courtesy Lorenzo State Historic Site); c. a boat effigy pipe, Oak Orchard (NYSM BX31914); d. a fragment of a boat effigy pipe, Atwell site (NYSM BX31866).

Table 5

*Occurrence of Incised Rings on Late Garoga Phase and Protohistoric
Onondaga Clay Pipe Stems*

Site	Stems with Incised Rings		Total Number of Round Pipe Stems	
	No.	%	No.	%
Nursery	1	33	3	100
Barnes	14	33	42	100
Temperance House	3	27	11	100
Atwell	3	13	24	100
Pickering	1	33	3	100
Quirk	1	11	9	100

Source: Bradley 1979:329.

The use of lithics on protohistoric sites follows much the same pattern as that on late Garoga phase sites. From a utilitarian perspective, the basic tool kit shows little change. Triangular projectile points, ovate knives, and a variety of scraping tools continue to be the most common flaked implements. Mullers, hammers, celts, and occasionally adzes typify the pecked and ground stone tools. All of these forms occur throughout the protohistoric period.

Against this pattern of continuity, two slight changes are discernable. The first is in the shape of triangular projectile points. After growing progressively more isosceles over the course of the Chance and Garoga phases, the trend reverses. During the protohistoric period, points become less isosceles and increasingly equilateral in shape (Table 4). The reason for this is unclear. Perhaps it is just another example of internal stylistic drift, like the shift in preference from high collar pots to ones with a lower collar, or, to take a more contemporary example, hemlines. Whatever its meaning, the changing length-to-width ratio of projectile points provides one more material basis for placing sites in sequential order.

The second change is a slight decrease in the overall frequency with which lithic implements occur. It is hard to be precise about this, much less statistical, given the sample problems; however, it seems clear that the use of lithic tools, especially cutting and scraping blades, diminishes somewhat during the period. It is no coincidence that the use of metal tools increases at about the same rate as lithic blades wane.

The non-utilitarian use of lithics also follows the late Garoga pattern. Ornamental/ritual objects, though not abundant, are present on most of the protohistoric sites. Most notable are small stone discs. This late Garoga microtradition remains strong on early protohistoric sites and provides one more indication of St. Lawrence Iroquois influence on Onondaga material culture (Table 6). While not common, a few more elaborate stone artifacts such as smoking pipes and face effigy pendants are also present.

The patterns for bone and antler artifacts parallel lithics in several ways. As with lithic tools, implements of bone and antler continue to be a strong component of Onondaga material culture. All the traditional forms—awls, perforators, lithic reduction tools, fishing gear—occur throughout the period without any noticeable decrease. However, even in this very stable component of Onondaga material culture there is evidence of St. Lawrence Iroquois influence. Specifically, one finds the occasional use of conical projectile points made from antler or bone, and the decoration of harpoons and awls with notching or incising[22] (Plate 5e). Scant as this evidence is, it provides one more indication of Onondaga assimilation of St. Lawrence Iroquois, men as well as women, during the protohistoric period.

In terms of ornamental use, bone and antler artifacts follow the late Garoga phase pattern and occur with regularity throughout the period. This is especially the case for perforated teeth and modified deer phalanges. Tubular bone beads and simple pendants are common on the earlier protohistoric sites, but like lithic blades seem to diminish in frequency toward the end of the period. Here again, the decrease correlates closely with the increased occurrence of copper beads and pendants. Other more elaborate bone and antler artifacts become more prevalent during the protohistoric period. These include hair combs, gorgets made from human cranial bone,[23] and effigies, usually in the form of pendants or occasionally as handles[24] (Plate 5).

Table 6

Occurrence of Stone Discs on Late Garoga Phase and Protohistoric Onondaga Sites

Site	Perforated Discs		Unperforated Discs		Total	
	No.	*%*	*No.*	*%*	*No.*	*%*
Barnes	31	82	7	18	38	100
Temperance House	11	23	36	77	47	100
Atwell	9	26	25	74	34	100
Pickering	2	67	1	33	3	100

Source: Bradley 1979:330.

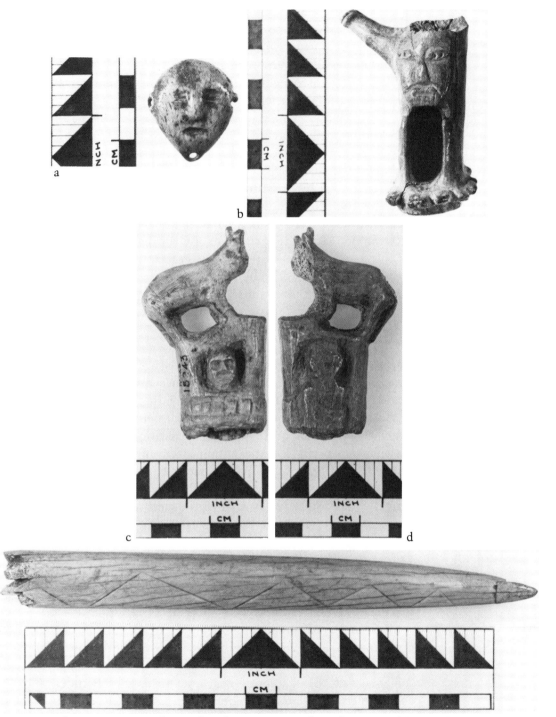

Plate 5. Bone, Antler, and Walrus Ivory Artifacts from Protohistoric Onondaga Sites. a. a bone effigy, Atwell site (RMSC AR19278); b. an antler tube with effigies, Temperance House site (RMSC 72.34.764); c. and d. an antler handle with effigies, Madison County (NYSM 15143); e. an incised walrus ivory dagger, Atwell site.

65

One of the major changes to take place at the end of the Garoga phase and apparently prior to European contact was the reestablishment of long-distance exchange networks and the resulting recurrence of exotic materials on Onondaga sites. While some of these materials may have been acquired for utilitarian or ornamental reasons, the emphasis was on symbolically charged substances—native copper, marine shell and non-local lithics.

Exactly how this pre-contact exchange network functioned and how such symbolically charged materials were distributed among the Onondaga is not known at present. Theoretical models which predict how both exchange and distribution systems work do exist. However, most of these are hierarchical in structure and focus on a chief or headman who controls access to the trade and redistributes the resulting material wealth. In most cases, these models posit a system in which exchange occurs primarily between societal elites, the bulk of the population having been left out of the process (Wells 1980:5–8; Potter 1984). It is questionable how applicable these models are to the Onondaga and other Iroquoian groups. While there were undoubtedly restrictions on who could engage in trade, both Iroquois culture and society were structured along lines more egalitarian than ranked.

Whatever the structure, initial contact with Europeans must have sent a profound shock wave through the existing exchange networks, one which quite quickly reached even inland tribes like the Onondaga. In large part, this shock wave resulted not because Europeans were perceived as bizarre or outlandish, but rather because Europeans and their "otherworldly" material wealth fit quite well into traditional native cosmology. From a native perspective, Europeans appeared as returning culture heroes, otherworldly man-beings who rose from beneath the water on "floating islands," bringing with them a wealth of Under(water) World substances. Hamell has pointed out that Europeans could not have chosen more appropriate materials to bring with them. To European eyes, the brass rings, glass beads, and other trifles and baubles brought for trade had little value. To native Americans, however, the materials which these strange man-beings offered were analogs to the traditional substances of life-enhancing and life-restoring power. The forms may have been novel, but the meaning was crystal clear (Hamell 1983, 1985).

Equating traditional symbolically charged substances (native copper and crystal) with European materials (copper/copper alloys and glass) appears to have characterized the native response to Europeans at first contact and for much of the sixteenth century. Although attitudes and perceptions certainly changed later, the point here is an important one: In the beginning, native Americans viewed European materials as a part of their own world, not someone else's.

The archaeological evidence also supports the idea of fusion between traditional symbolically charged substances and European materials. For an event of such import, the first indications of European materials on Onondaga sites are inconspicuous at best.[25] In fact, it is continuity as much as change which characterizes the first protohistoric assemblages. The small brass and smelted copper ornaments from Temperance House and Atwell are superficially indistinguishable from their native copper predecessors (Plate 6). Only with spectrographic testing or other analytical procedures can the differences be observed.

Before discussing the patterns of occurrence for European materials in more detail, it is important to review briefly the use of traditional exotic materials—shell, non-local lithics, and native copper—during the protohistoric period. Throughout the sixteenth century, Onondaga was an active node in the exchange networks that criss-crossed northeastern North America. Exotic materials appear to have come primarily from two directions. From the north of Onondaga (the Great Lakes and St. Lawrence River valley) came native copper and other exotics such as walrus ivory. To the south of Onondaga (the mid-Atlantic coast reached via the Delaware and Susquehanna River corridors) lay the sources of marine shell and certain desirable lithics. Exchange took place in both directions during the protohistoric period. During the last half of the sixteenth century, however, the emphasis on the southern exchange route grew, virtually eclipsing trade to the north.

In terms of the materials exchanged along these routes, marine shell appears as one of the most important, occurring in steadily increasing quantities throughout the period. As on the late Garoga phase sites, shell occurs in two basic forms—simple pendants and beads. Pendants made of quahog (Mercenaria mercenaria) range in shape from round to oval to irregular. A single perforation for suspension was placed either in the center or along the margin. The degree of finishing was as variable as the shape, and occasionally the polished surface was embellished with a pattern of finely drilled holes. The presence of incomplete examples, as well as blank discs of shell, indicates that at least some of the work was done in Onondaga (Plate 6).

While shell beads occur in a variety of forms, two are dominant. The most common are discoidal. In general, these beads are small, only 5–8mm in diameter and 1–2mm thick. The vast majority is of white shell; however, a few black examples also occur.[26] The other common form is tubular: These are also small beads, generally 4–5mm in diameter and from 5–10mm in length. Most could easily be considered "wampum."[27] While shell beads occasionally occur in other shapes—round, barrel-shaped—the other important group of shell ornaments are small complete shells, unmodified except where perforated for suspension. At least two species are known

Plate 6. Metal and Marine Shell Artifacts from Late Prehistoric and Protohistoric Onondaga Sites. a. a native copper disc, Barnes site; b. a native copper blade (?), Barnes site; c. a brass disc, Atwell site; d. a brass bead, Atwell site; e. a brass bead or ring, Temperance House site; f. an unfinished *Mercenaria* pendant and three beads, a modified marginella, a tubular *Busycon*, and a discoidal bead, Barnes site; g. a partially drilled *Mercenaria* pendant, Temperance House site (RMSC 72.34.381); h. and i. two pendants, Brewerton (RMSC AR39901).

to have been used: the marsh or gulf periwinkle *(Littorina irrorata)* and the common marginella *(Prunum apicinum)*. Both species inhabit the mid-Atlantic coast; in the case of marginella, North Carolina is the northern limit (Morris 1975:130, 232).

The occurrence of other traditional exotic materials appears to be limited, although this may be a reflection of sampling rather than reality. Only a few examples of non-local lithics are known from protohistoric Onondaga sites; they were used primarily for ornaments (stone discs) or for smoking pipes. At present the only identifiable material is a dark grey soapstone, possibly from a Maryland source.[28] Another extremely unusual material is walrus ivory. An ivory dagger or large awl from the Atwell site is illustrated on Plate 5.[29] Although native copper was used for both implements and ornaments elsewhere in the Northeast during the proto-historic period, no examples from Onondaga sites are known.

Material Culture: European Materials

Three categories of European materials are found on protohistoric Onondaga sites: smelted copper and various copper alloys, iron, and glass. Of these, copper is not only the first to occur but is by far the most common.

Virtually all the copper is in the form of a fairly thin-gauge sheet and appears to have come primarily from kettles (see Appendix B for more information on the terminology and background of these kettles). Spec-trographic analysis shows considerable variety in these copper alloys. Of the eleven pieces tested, six were smelted copper, four were brass, and one a low-grade bronze.[30]

The earliest occurrences of European copper in Onondaga are at the Temperance House site (one piece) and at its smaller neighbor, the Atwell site (two pieces). All three pieces were recovered from midden contexts and are illustrated in Plate 6. Artifacts of European copper occur at a slowly increasing rate during the rest of the protohistoric period, with a dramatic rise during the last decades of the sixteenth century. All copper artifacts from early in the period are ornamental in form. By the end of the period, however, pieces of copper have been adapted for utilitarian purposes.

While a wide range of copper ornaments occurs on protohistoric Onon-daga sites, five basic shapes emerge as the most important. The two earliest forms are simple tubular beads and small disc-shaped pendants. Initially the beads are small, ranging from 5–20mm in length and 3–10mm in diameter. The quality of construction, that is, the degree of precision and control in handling the metal, also varies considerably, but with a clear improvement over time (Figure 7a–c). One distinct subgroup of these small tubular beads is characterized by a short length and a relatively large diameter, usually between 10–15mm for each dimension. While these may have been used as beads, it is also possible that they were worn as rings (Figure 7d).

Disc-shaped pendants are the other form in which European copper first occurs. The earliest example is a small flat disc, approximately 15mm in diameter, and apparently perforated along one margin. Later in the period these discs become larger (25–35mm in diameter), convex/concave rather than flat, and are often multiply perforated (Figure 7e). During the last decades of the sixteenth century, there is also more variation in the form of these pendants. In addition to the traditional disc, irregular and zoomorphic shapes appear.

By the last half of the sixteenth century, three additional forms of copper ornament became popular among the Onondaga. The first of these is the large tubular bead. While copper beads appear generally to increase in size as metal became more available, this group is exceptional. Well made and consistently 5–7mm in diameter, the beads usually range between 60–120mm in length. One example exceeds 140mm (Figure 7f). This particular form of copper bead occurs throughout much of northeastern North America and appears to serve as a horizon marker for the last half of the sixteenth century.[31]

The other two ornament forms are more complex and appear to have been made using a similar technique. In each case, a long rectangular strip of very thin gauge metal was rolled into a tube which was then either coiled into a spiral or flattened and formed into a hoop (Figure 7g–i). These are usually large ornaments: Spirals range up to 50mm in diameter and the single example of a copper hoop from Onondaga is just over 60mm across. As with large tubular beads, these forms seem to be horizon markers for the protohistoric period among several native groups in the Northeast.[32]

While these five basic forms account for most of the protohistoric copper ornaments found in Onondaga, a few additional forms begin to occur toward the end of the period. Among these are bracelets and conical bangles. The occurrence of these as well as the other more common forms of ornament is summarized in Table 7.

Increasingly during the last half of the sixteenth century, European copper was adapted for utilitarian as well as ornamental purposes. Edged tools designed for either cutting or scraping were the most commonly made implements. At present, the earliest known examples are from the

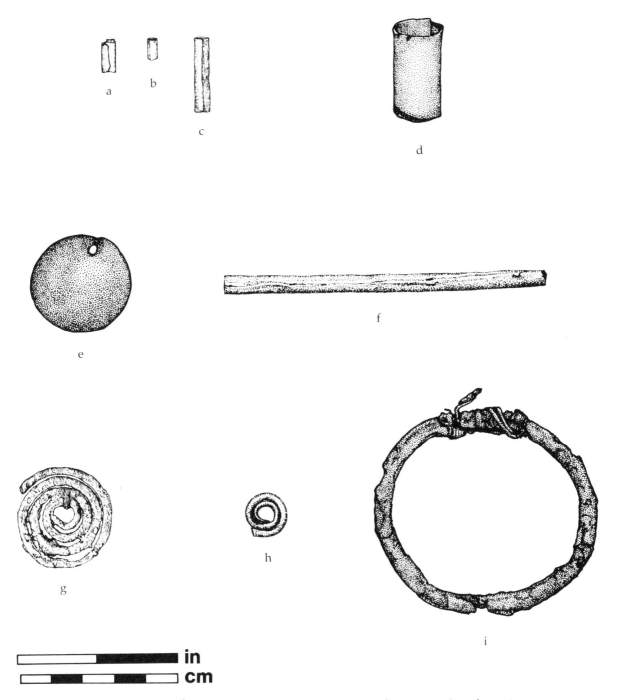

in

cm

Figure 7. Protohistoric Copper Ornament Forms. Three examples of simple tubular beads: a. and b. Dwyer site (RMSC 10002/221), c. Quirk site (RMSC CZA21-1/983); d. a large diameter bead or ring (reconstructed), Temperance House site; e. a disc-shaped pendant, Dwyer site; f. a large tubular bead, Dwyer site; two examples of spiral ornaments: g. Dwyer site; h. Dwyer site (RMSC 10001/221); i. a hoop, Brewerton (RMSC AR39901).

Table 7

Copper Artifacts from Protohistoric Onondaga Sites

Site	Ornaments						Implements			Scrap	
	Tubular Beads	Disc Pendants	Long Tubular Beads	Spirals	Hoops	Other	Formalized Blades	Unformalized Blades	Other		Total
Temperance House	1	0	0	0	0	0	0	0	0	0	1
Atwell	1	1	0	0	0	0	0	0	0	0	2
Quirk	3	0	0	0	0	0	0	0	0	0	3
Sheldon	0	0	0	0	0	0	0	0	3	0	3
Chase	4	1	2	0	0	1	1	2	1	8	20
Dwyer*	75	2	3	3	0	2	2	1	0	3	91
Brewerton*	10	0	1	0	1	0	0	0	0	0	12
Total	94	4	6	3	1	3	3	3	4	11	132

* Sample includes some material from burial contexts.
0 means trait not present.
Source: See note 2.

late protohistoric Chase and Dwyer sites; however, copper blades may also have been used on some of the earlier sites as well.

Copper edged tools can be divided into two distinct categories. The first is composed of blades with a formalized, that is, deliberate, shape. While these shapes do vary—at least three different types are known—they all share the trait of planned design. The most common type is rectangular and frequently has perforations in the center or along the margin opposite the cutting edge which allowed for the attachment of a handle (Figure 8c). A second is teardrop-shaped, replicating in copper one of the traditional forms of hafted lithic blades.[33] A third type of formalized copper blade appears to mimic the shape of a European iron knife. It should be noted that these blades are often made from a thicker gauge metal (1–2mm) and usually show evidence of careful and deliberate craftsmanship (Figure 8d).

The other category of blades contains those without a formalized shape. These are small, irregular pieces of sheet copper sharpened on one or more sides. Basically these are pickup tools, the protohistoric equivalent of the utilized flakes on pre-contact sites. Despite their casual appearance, they were highly useful implements and would have been very efficient skinning or fleshing blades (Figure 8b). While nearly all of the protohistoric copper

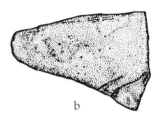

a

b

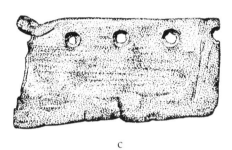

c

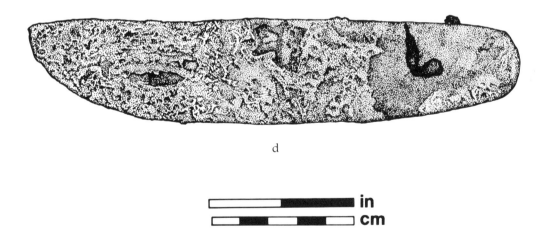

d

in

cm

Figure 8. Protohistoric Copper and Iron Implements. a. a small iron celt or adze, Chase site; b. a copper blade without formal shape, Chase site; c. a copper blade with formalized shape, Pompey Center site; d. a copper blade mimicking the shape of a European knife, Dwyer site (RMSC 10000/ 221).

implements are cutting or scraping tools of one form or another, there is some evidence that copper was adapted for other uses toward the end of the protohistoric period. For example, some experimental efforts were made to use the metal for projectile points and possibly for awls or needles.[34] The occurrence of copper implements on Onondaga sites is summarized in Table 7.

It now seems fairly clear that artifacts of European copper begin to occur on Onondaga sites sometime during the second quarter of the sixteenth century. What remains less clear is when, and to what extent, the Onondaga themselves began to fabricate copper ornaments and implements. While it is possible that the first copper objects to reach Onondaga were made elsewhere and acquired through exchange, it is equally probable that they were made by the Onondaga. The ornamental forms were traditional ones and would have been simple enough to produce. Indeed, the production of ornaments from other exotic materials such as marine shell can be demonstrated on protohistoric Onondaga sites.

Technologically, there is no reason why many of these copper articles could not have been fabricated by the Onondaga. The necessary technology was available, the same set of copper-working techniques used in northeastern North America since the Late Archaic stage (Schroeder and Ruhl 1968). Three techniques were employed. The first was cold hammering to shape the copper without heating it and, at the same time, harden the metal. The second technique was annealing or heating the metal to soften it for additional shaping. Finally, abrasion was also used for shaping as well as finishing a piece of work.

Copper artifacts were probably made by means of the following process. A piece of copper was hammered to the desired thickness and size. If this could not be accomplished before the metal became too hard to work, it was annealed. Once this rough shaping was complete, the piece was trimmed (if necessary), then rolled or otherwise formed into the desired shape. The piece could then be finished, that is, rough edges ground off, polished, and so on. While only a few metallographic studies have analyzed protohistoric copper ornaments, it is clear that they were made using these techniques (Dunbar and Ruhl 1974).

Whenever it started, there is no question that during the last half of the sixteenth century copper-working was actively practiced in Onondaga.[35] There are at least three sources of evidence for this conclusion. The first is the remnants of production—partially completed objects and the discarded trimmings or scrap, which occur at the Chase and Dwyer sites. These remnants also provide additional information on the manufacture of finished objects. Nearly all the scrap from these two sites, nine of eleven pieces, have cut edges. Several (four of eleven pieces) also show evidence of scoring and folding. This was a more cumbersome but still effective means of reducing a piece of sheet metal to the desired size. The presence of scrap copper in the middens at both Chase and Dwyer provides the first hint of that metal's eventual devaluation as a symbolically charged substance.

A second line of evidence also argues for local production. With few exceptions, the forms used for both ornaments and implements were traditional ones. It was the choice of material that changed, not the form or function of the object produced. For example, tubular copper beads parallel bone antecedents quite closely.[36] Disc pendants in copper differ little from those of stone or shell, and are also similar to the traditional bone pendant made from a modified epiphyseal cap. The close similarities between lithic edged tools and those in copper have already been discussed. There are exceptions of course: Both the spiral and hoop-shaped ornaments have no clear precedents in Onondaga material culture, and it is not currently known where these forms originated.

The third category of evidence supporting a theory of local production of copper artifacts, as opposed to their importation, is that the forms utilized vary significantly between tribes. For example, the disc-shaped pendants from Onondaga sites are circular; Susquehannock examples usually have a small, projecting tang where the perforation is located (Kent 1984:204, Figure 51, illustrates an example). Copper was often used for edged tools by the Onondaga; comparable blades are extremely uncommon on Susquehannock sites. These localized differences argue strongly for local production.

Iron artifacts are less common than those of copper and do not appear on Onondaga sites until later in the protohistoric period. The earliest recorded example is an iron celt or adze from the Quirk site.[37] Virtually all the iron artifacts recovered are implements of one form or another. Most appear to have been made, or adapted, from specific European objects, most frequently axes, knives, and large nails or spikes. In the majority of cases the metal has been so reworked that its original form is difficult if not impossible to determine. Only on the later protohistoric sites do fragments, identifiable as pieces of European axes and knives, occur (Table 8).

Protohistoric iron implements occur in three basic forms: formalized blades, unformalized edged tools, and perforators. Formalized iron blades are usually rectangular or trapezoidal in shape and are generally similar to traditional lithic celts/adzes.[38] Dimensions for these blades are summarized in Table 9. One of the examples from the Chase site shows battering on the poll much like that seen on lithic celts (Figure 8a). However, another blade from Chase is centrally perforated, suggesting that it functioned as a hafted knife or scraper.

Table 8

Iron Artifacts from Protohistoric Onondaga Sites

Site	Blades		Perforators	Fragments			Intact European Objects	Total
	Formal	Informal		Axe	Knife	Unidentifiable		
Quirk	1	0	0	0	0	1	0	2
Sheldon	0	0	0	0	0	0	1	1
Chase	2	5	1	1	2	1	0	12
Dwyer	0	0	1	1	1	0	0	3
Total	3	5	2	2	3	2	1	18

0 means trait not present.
Source: See note 2.

The second form of iron blades, like their copper counterparts, does not have a formalized shape. Most of these are irregular pieces of iron with one utilized edge. While it is difficult to be certain, most of these blades seem to have been made from cannibalized axes. In fact, two of the examples from the Chase site appear to be reworked sections of broken axe bits.

The third form of iron implements, perforators, is an extremely simple tool made by abrading either spikes, or possibly kettle bails (handles), to a tapered point.

The technology for reusing iron was probably no different than that which the Onondaga used for working copper. In fact, Hamell has suggested that Northern Iroquoians viewed metal as a generic substance during the protohistoric period, differentiating between ferrous and nonferrous metals primarily on the basis of color, i.e., black metal (iron), red metal (copper), and white metal (silver) (Hamell 1983:16–17). In addition, it appears that most of the iron to reach Onondaga during the sixteenth century was of fairly small proportions and would have been easy to manipulate. The more intensive business of recycling larger iron objects into manageable-sized pieces (Bradley 1980a) does not occur until the early decades of the seventeenth century. Finally, the iron available was wrought iron, a material malleable enough to be worked cold. For all of these reasons, the traditional techniques used to shape and finish copper were probably used on iron as well.

As with copper, the question is not so much "Did the Onondaga make iron implements?" as it is "When did they start and where did they get

Table 9
A Comparison of Protohistoric Iron Celts/Adzes from Onondaga Sites to Other Reported Examples

Site	Location	Maximum Length	Maximum Width	Maximum Thickness	Shape	Comment
Quirk (Beauchamp 1902b:75)	Onondaga Co., N.Y.	52mm	31mm	unavailable	trapezoidal	measurements estimated
Chase (Bradley 1979:164)	Onondaga Co., N.Y.					
#1		88mm	38mm	7mm	rectangular	centrally perforated
#2		42mm	22mm	3mm	trapezoidal	battered poll
#3		65mm	67mm	6mm	square	reworked piece of axe blade [?]
Sopher (Noble 1971)	Simcoe Co., Ontario	105mm	50mm	10mm	trapezoidal	reworked axe blade, weld line visible; measurements estimated
Schultz (Kent 1984:233)	Lancaster Co., Penn.					
#1		145mm	48mm	7mm	trapezoidal	battered poll
#2		86mm	35mm	12mm	trapezoidal	finely finished
King (Smith 1975:65)	Floyd Co., Georgia					
#1		80mm	39mm	10mm	trapezoidal	
#2		98mm	32mm	8mm	rectangular	
#3		102mm	28mm	6mm	rectangular	
#4		85mm	47mm	19mm	triangular	

the idea?" DePratter and Smith have shown that by the 1560s the Spanish were distributing iron "chisels" and "wedges" to interior tribes in what is now the Carolinas, Georgia, Alabama, and Tennessee (1980). Some of these objects are strikingly similar to the examples from Onondaga and elsewhere in the Northeast (Table 9) and may indicate that the initial conception for iron celts, if not some of the implements themselves, could have been European. Suggestive as this may be, it is important to remember that there were ample precedents within Onondaga material culture and that many other indigenous forms besides celts were replicated in copper and iron.

Whenever and however it began, there is no question that during the last half of the sixteenth century the Onondaga were actively reusing iron. One of the Chase celts shows evidence of the scoring-and-breaking technique, the established method of iron reduction during the early seventeenth century. Another example is a large spike or pin recovered from the Dwyer site in association with a grooved piece of limestone. The shaft portion had been partially tapered, apparently with the intention of making some form of perforator. In summary, while the use of iron lagged behind that of copper during the protohistoric period, the same basic technology was used on both metals and many of the same implement forms produced. The European objects that reached Onondaga rarely survived in an un-modified condition. One such example is known from the Sheldon site. This blade, found point down in a post mold, is from a mid-sixteenth century fighting dagger. The style of the blade indicates that it was intended as a *main gauche*, a left-hand weapon designed generally for use with a rapier and specifically for piercing body armor or mail. Blades of this form were commonly used throughout the Mediterranean, from the Levant to Spain, during the sixteenth century.[39] This blade, and a comparable French example dated ca. 1560, are illustrated on Plate 7.

Glass beads, the third category of European material which occurs on sixteenth-century Onondaga sites, are not common. This is again a re-flection, in part, of sampling. During the protohistoric period, glass beads as well as shell and copper ornaments occur primarily in burials, and very little data on Onondaga burials are available.

A total of four glass beads are currently known from three of the protohistoric sites—Quirk (1), Chase (1), and Dwyer (2). Beads have also been reported from the Sheldon site, but were not available for study. Three of the four beads are small and round, and made of an opaque Robin's egg blue glass—Kidd's type IIa40 (Kidd and Kidd 1970). This particular type of bead has been recovered from many other sixteenth- and early seventeenth-century sites. Unfortunately, however, its chrono-logical and geographical distribution is so broad that it is of limited interpretative value.[40] The remaining bead, from the Dwyer site, would be classed in Kidd's IVb category. It is of medium size, oval, and made of opaque Brite blue glass with a white core; there are four stripes, alternating red and white, on the exterior. Meager as this sample is, it does provide one more means for comparing the Onondaga sites with other protohistoric sequences in the Northeast.

Concluding Comments

Before we could look at broader issues such as warfare and trade during the sixteenth century, we first had to build a data base. While the infor-mation on the protohistoric Onondaga is far from complete, it does allow

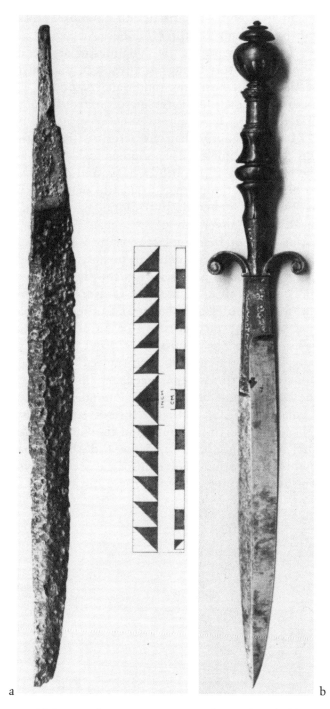

a   b

Plate 7. A Mid-Sixteenth Century Dagger from the Sheldon Site and a
Comparable French Example. a. dagger blade, Sheldon site; b. French dagger
ca. 1560, (photograph courtesy of The Metropolitan Museum of Art,
Gift of Jean Jacques Reubell, 1926, in memory of his mother, Julia C.
Coster, and of his wife, Adelaine E. Post, both of New York City,
26.145.81a–c).

us now to shift the discussion to more process-oriented questions. We will be focusing on three of these.

The first concerns the dynamics of acculturation: Specifically, how did Onondaga culture change as a result of European contact and the increasing availability of European materials? Although we have yet to deal with the historic period, a brief review of sixteenth-century acculturation is appropriate.

It is continuity that characterizes the protohistoric period in terms of the choice of materials, maintenance of the skills for working them, and the forms into which lithics, clay, and bone were shaped. It is against this baseline that the primary dynamic of the period occurs—the integration of European materials into Onondaga culture. With few exceptions this meant the conversion of European products into traditional Onondaga forms. Rather than replacing traditional materials or forms, this assimilation of European material seems to have done just the opposite—it opened up new options within the traditional culture. For example, metal tools appear to have brought greater expression and technical control to the working of wood, bone, and other traditional materials. The point is that while the incorporation of European materials by the Onondaga did cause change, the results were often creative ones.

The other two "process-oriented" questions concern intertribal relations during the sixteenth century. Briefly, these are: To what extent can the relationship between the Onondaga and other Iroquoian peoples be reconstructed? Of particular interest are contacts with the nearby St. Lawrence Iroquois to the north and the Susquehannock to the south. A second and related question is: How did the exchange networks of the late prehistoric period evolve into the trading systems of the protohistoric? The next chapter addresses these questions.

3

Processing the Protohistoric

As interesting as artifacts themselves may be, their real value lies in
their potential for telling us something about the cultural activity
of which they are the material remnant. This is especially the case for the
protohistoric period. We know that significant, even cataclysmic, events
occurred among native groups in northeastern North America during the
sixteenth century. The documentary record, fragmentary as it is, provides
some hint of the transitions and changes, often just enough to allow us
to pose questions about events both big and small. To answer those
questions, however, or even to refine them, we must rely on the archaeological record and our own ingenuity for making the material record
speak.

Thus our emphasis now shifts away from the specific archaeological
data to the broader patterns and processes of the protohistoric period. The
goal is to see the Onondaga more clearly by placing them in the context
of their relations with other native groups. How did these relationships
change during the protohistoric period? To what extent did they stay the
same? How did the gradually intensifying contact with Europeans alter
the dynamics of intertribal relations?

Perhaps the best way to begin answering these questions is to examine
the evidence for warfare and trade—two intertribal dynamics traceable in
some detail from the archaeological record. War and trade are good choices
for another reason: They are among the clearest indicators of a group's
external relationships and priorities. The routes along which war and trade
take place in large part define the vectors of tribal self-interest. As such,
these routes provide a basis for reconstructing how a particular tribe, in
this case the Onondaga, functioned in relation to its neighbors.

A few words about the use of the terms "warfare" and "trade." Both
are loaded with connotations that can be misleading. "Warfare" is used

81

here to describe intertribal hostilities in a way that Iroquoians would have understood. Hostilities could range from "little wars," private feuds or vendettas, to "general wars" which involved entire tribes (Fenton 1978:315–16). The line between these levels of conflict was a fine one and hostilities could, and often did, shift from one level to the other. A second point is that my use of the term reflects less concern with tactics and technology than with the reasons for which wars occurred. As noted previously, the primary purpose of intertribal conflict appears to have been to gain prestige, to seek revenge upon or humiliate an enemy, and to bolster one's own population at the other's expense. In any discussion of Onondaga warfare, this concern for assimilating, not annihilating the remnants, is implicit.

In contemporary westernized societies "trade" means formalized, commercial exchange, usually involving buying and selling and the presence of a market or marketplace. Among native Americans, trade was more a matter of reciprocal exchange through which either perishable or nonperishable commodities could be acquired (Trigger 1976, 1:168–76; Hamell 1983:25). The notion that the pursuit, acquisition, and accumulation of material goods by an individual for his own use could be a positive trait was, as Calvin Martin has pointed out, foreign to a native way of thinking (1978:151–52). For the Onondaga, and probably for most other Iroquoian groups, trade did not have any commercial overtones until late in the protohistoric period. The issue of trade, and routes by which it occurred, is an important one. While it is clear that the Onondaga were receiving European materials during much of the sixteenth century, it is not clear how they got them. An interior tribe, the Onondaga were located more than 300km from the nearest salt water or known point of direct access to Europeans. It is a certainty that finding and maintaining access routes to the source(s) of European goods was a primary goal of the Onondaga during the protohistoric period. How they solved this problem is important not only for reconstructing Onondaga history, but for understanding the broader landscape of intertribal relationships during the century.

In the protohistoric period, Onondaga tribal interests operated along two axes. One ran west/east. This axis was the symbolic longhouse along which the Iroquois confederacy was oriented. The Mohawk guarded the eastern door, the Seneca the western, while the Onondaga tended the council fire at the center. Along this axis, the business of the Confederacy was conducted as well as other intra-Iroquois matters including marriage, maintenance of clan relationships, and probably some trade.

Important as this west/east axis was, it did not define solely Onondaga tribal interests. A second and equally important axis ran north/south connecting the Onondaga both with major fishing sites on Lake Ontario and with their non-Confederacy Iroquoian neighbors, the St. Lawrence

Iroquois to the north, and the Susquehannocks to the south. It was along this north/south axis that two major concerns of the sixteenth-century Onondaga were focused. First was the resolution of hostilities with the St. Lawrence Iroquois and their eventual assimilation. Second was the evolution of trade networks, especially with the Susquehannocks, to facilitate the acquisition of European goods. If the west/east axis was the source of stability and homogeneity for the Onondaga, it was the north/ south axis that provided diversity and change.

Whatever Happened to the St. Lawrence Iroquois?

A great deal has been written about the relationship between the St. Lawrence Iroquois and the Onondaga. Much of it is contradictory. Basically two points of view have been expressed. The first is that a direct relationship existed between the two groups. That is, the St. Lawrence Iroquois and the Onondaga were one and the same, or that the Onondaga were derived from St. Lawrence Iroquois antecedents. This view is closely tied to a migration theory of Iroquois origins and often identifies European contact, and the resulting intertribal hostilities, as the catalyst for migration (Hunt 1940:13–16).[1] Similarities in the material culture of the Onondaga and the St. Lawrence Iroquois of Jefferson County, New York, have been used as archaeological evidence for this direct relationship (MacNeish 1952).

This migration theory of Onondaga origins has been successfully refuted. Through a series of field investigations, Tuck was able to demonstrate that the Onondaga evolved *in situ*, or within the same geographic area which they occupied during the historic period. Tuck concluded that there were no connections between the St. Lawrence Iroquois and the Onondaga, or at least none of significance (1971:206).

It seems as though there ought to be some middle ground between these two diametrically opposed positions. While Tuck's work clearly demonstrates that the Onondaga and the St. Lawrence Iroquois were different groups, it does little to clarify the nature of relations between them. In fact, there is too much evidence *for* a relationship to ignore comfortably. What I propose here is a third point of view, one which posits an indirect but significant relationship between the Onondaga and their St. Lawrence Iroquois neighbors in Jefferson County.

Before reviewing this relationship in more detail, we should clarify a few points about the St. Lawrence Iroquois. Of the major Iroquoian groups in the Northeast, the St. Lawrence Iroquois are probably the least well known. While considerable field work has been done, little comprehensive literature is available.[2] As a result, the term "St. Lawrence Iroquois" is used to describe a large and poorly defined group of Iroquoian peoples. There were at least four major subgroups:

1. A riverine-oriented group on the north side of the St. Lawrence River centered around Quebec City. These are the people to whom Jacques Cartier referred as "Stadaconans" (Trigger and Pendergast 1978:357–58).

2. A more sedentary, agriculturally oriented group on the north side of the St. Lawrence near Montreal. Cartier called these people "Hochelagans." Archaeologically, sites occur from Montreal to Prescott, Ontario, with two significant clusters, one near Cornwall, the other near Prescott.

3. A largely unknown group located around the northern portion of Lake Champlain and along the Richelieu River toward Lac St. Pierre.

4. Another sedentary, agriculturally oriented group located in Jefferson County, New York.

The Jefferson County group can also be divided into several regionally discrete site sequences. The largest and best defined of these is located between Sandy Creek and the Black River, centered near Watertown, New York. At present it appears that over the course of the Late Woodland stage two simultaneous site movements occurred within this sequence. One followed the Black River from the Lake Ontario Lowlands up into the Rutland Hills; the other tracked up into the Rutland Hills along the course of Sandy Creek. Both movements appear to have converged at the Morse site, the terminal site in this sequence. Current estimates place the date of the Morse site somewhere near the mid-fifteenth century.[3]

This branch of the St. Lawrence Iroquois is of considerable interest since they were most directly involved with the Onondaga. Geographically, the two Iroquoian groups were not that far apart. Approximately 100 kilometers separated the sites of the Watertown cluster from the Onondaga sites in the Pompey Hills. Between these two upland core areas lay a large lowland zone bounded roughly by the Oswego/Oneida rivers (and Oneida Lake) on the west and south, and by the Salmon River on the north. This area was characterized by extensive wetlands affording a wide range of floral and faunal resources. Many of the region's most important fishing stations were located along these waterways.

It is fairly certain that both the Onondaga and their Jefferson County neighbors used this area seasonally for gathering, fishing, and hunting. Small Onondaga-related sites can be documented along the southern boundary from at least the Chance phase onwards. There are also indications that seasonal forays, primarily for fishing, may have occasionally taken the Onondaga as far north as the mouth of the Salmon River.[4]

During the Chance and Garoga phases, the pattern of relationship between these two neighboring Iroquoian groups appears to have been one of desultory but gradually increasing hostility. While antagonisms easily could have arisen over access to particular resources, it is likely that they were perpetuated by the traditions of vendetta and assimilation. Indeed, the limited evidence available suggests that this was the case. The continued fortification of village sites, the occurrence of human bone in refuse, and the occasional presence of St. Lawrence Iroquois material traits on Onondaga sites all argue in favor of continuous, low-level warfare.

This situation appears to have changed early in the sixteenth century. There is a dramatic increase in the presence of northern traits on Onondaga sites. While most apparent at the Atwell site, a small village, this change is also evident on the larger sites such as Barnes and Temperance House. These exotic traits occur in several artifact categories, although they can be seen most clearly in ceramics. Most if not all of these northern traits are typical of the Jefferson County St. Lawrence Iroquois.

By the end of the protohistoric period, the pattern of occurrence for these northern traits has again changed. Some disappear entirely. Incised rings on clay pipe stems, for example, or the use of stone discs, seem to be St. Lawrence Iroquois-related microtraditions which did not survive the process of assimilation. Other aspects of St. Lawrence Iroquois material culture not only survive the transition but become part of a redefined Onondaga material culture. This too is most visible in ceramics, both in the way pots were made and decorated. Such changes are clearly evident on late protohistoric sites such as Chase.

What all this suggests, of course, is that sometime during the sixteenth century, a sizable group of Jefferson County St. Lawrence Iroquois was absorbed by the Onondaga. This seems to have occurred during the second quarter of the century. It is at roughly this same time that the people who occupied the sites of the Watertown cluster disappear. Why their dispersion occurred remains unclear. Whatever the cause, and wherever else the remnants were scattered, it now seems certain that a portion of the St. Lawrence Iroquois of Jefferson County were adopted and eventually assimilated by the Onondaga.

The disappearance of the St. Lawrence Iroquois in Jefferson County was not a unique or isolated event. To the contrary, it appears to have been part of a broader pattern, one which affected nearly all St. Lawrence Iroquois tribal groups. For example, at approximately the same time that hostilities were increasing between the Onondaga and the people of the Watertown area sites, a similar process of dispersion and assimilation was taking place north of the St. Lawrence River. Here the protagonists were the Hochelagan group of St. Lawrence Iroquois and their nearest Iroquoian neighbors, the Huron.

Once again, hostile relations between adjacent Iroquoian groups predate European contact. For example, at the Draper site, a fifteenth-century Huron village in the Humber River drainage, about 10 percent of the ceramics are characteristically St. Lawrence Iroquois rather than Huron (Pendergast 1981b). The settlement pattern at Draper indicates that five separate expansions occurred over the life of the village, apparently to accommodate a burgeoning population (Finlayson 1985). From the ceramic evidence it is clear that a good portion of this rapidly growing population was St. Lawrence Iroquois. A similar pattern has been observed on other pre-contact Huron sites (Ramsden 1977a:267–58). On contemporary St. Lawrence Iroquois sites, the situation is much the same. There is a small but significant Huron presence on sites such as Summerstown Station, Roebuck, and Dawson.[5] This suggests that both sides were successful in taking and assimilating captives and that, for a while, a certain reciprocal balance existed between the Huron and their St. Lawrence Iroquois neighbors.

During the protohistoric period, however, this balance shifted in favor of the Huron. Significant quantities of St. Lawrence Iroquois pottery and other material traits continue to occur on Huron sites in both the Trent and Humber drainages (ibid.:257–60; 1977b). At the Trent site, for instance, Burger and Pratt estimate that over 35 percent of the pottery was St. Lawrence Iroquois. They also argue that settlement pattern data support the hypothesis that St. Lawrence Iroquois splinter groups were absorbed by the Huron (Burger and Pratt 1973:14).

On St. Lawrence Iroquois sites the situation is quite different. Although Huron material traits continue to be present on sites such as Glenbrook, it is the extent of ceramic miscegenation that is most notable. Pendergast interprets this as an archaeological reflection of "confused, even chaotic conditions," a portent of the demise of this St. Lawrence Iroquois subgroup (Pendergast 1981a:37). Glenbrook indeed appears to be the terminal site in the Summerstown cluster,[6] and marks the end of a discernable St. Lawrence Iroquois presence in this traditional core area.

While the general process of assimilating St. Lawrence Iroquois remnants appears similar in both the Onondaga and Huron cases, there are differences. One concerns the size and cohesiveness of the refugee population. On Huron sites, the St. Lawrence Iroquois appear to have been more numerous and to have survived successfully as a discernable cultural entity. For example, despite miscegenation, distinctively St. Lawrence Iroquois pottery continued to be made on Huron sites. In contrast, the St. Lawrence Iroquois traits which occur on Onondaga sites seem fragmented, less cohesive, and more hybridized with dominant Onondaga cultural traits. This suggests that the Jefferson County Iroquois absorbed by the Onondaga came in smaller, less organized groups than those assimilated by the Huron.

It is also possible that the mechanism for assimilation was different. For those Huron sites where settlement pattern data are available, such as Draper and Trent, it appears that the St. Lawrence Iroquois were incorporated directly into the major village. In Onondaga, the Jefferson County refugees seem to have been placed initially in an adjacent small village and only gradually absorbed into the main settlement. This suggests that some form of probation may have been required before full tribal membership was granted. At this point, however, the information is simply not strong enough and we can only speculate as to its meaning.

What is most important here is the central role that assimilation played in the ongoing evolution of the Onondaga. In large degree this was the process that created the Onondaga in the first place. The fusion of two smaller, neighboring populations during the Chance phase can, I believe, be viewed as an act of mutal assimilation. It was the merging of group-specific microtraditions, thus creating a new tribal identity, which led Tuck to identify the Chance phase as the beginning of the Onondaga "nation" (1971:215–16). The absorption of St. Lawrence Iroquois refugees during the sixteenth century was simply an extension of this process, albeit on a somewhat larger geographical scale. During the seventeenth century this would be repeated as the Onondaga sought to assimilate remnants of the Huron, Neutral, and numerous other tribal groups. From this perspective, the assimilation of St. Lawrence Iroquois during the protohistoric period becomes one step in a long process of tribal definition. At each step, the Onondaga were themselves redefined as new elements were absorbed and the conception of what was Onondaga changed.

An understanding of this dynamic aspect in Onondaga culture helps to resolve the question posed at the beginning of this section—What was the relationship between the St. Lawrence Iroquois and the Onondaga? In a sense, both Tuck and MacNeish were right. While there is no question that the Onondaga evolved *in situ*, MacNeish was not entirely wrong about the ceramic similarities he observed between Jefferson County sites, such as Durfee and Whitford, and the historic Onondaga. In fact, MacNeish included material from only one Onondaga site in his analysis. That was Pompey Center, an early seventeenth-century site where several St. Lawrence Iroquois traits appear as part of the Onondaga ceramic tradition. The similarities that MacNeish saw may well have been real. In the same way, the tradition of northern origins for the Iroquois as noted by Nicholas Perrot and other eighteenth-century chroniclers may not have been entirely mistaken, especially if they obtained their information from someone who was descended from an adopted St. Lawrence Iroquois.

It should be emphasized at this point that the Jefferson County St. Lawrence Iroquois were not the only native group with whom the Onondaga may have fought during the sixteenth century. We have focused on the Onondaga-St. Lawrence Iroquois relationship in part because of the contradictory nature of the existing literature, and because the available archaeological evidence provides a means for clarifying the issue. Important as this particular resolution was for the Onondaga, many other things were also happening. Given the upheavals and adjustments which occurred throughout the sixteenth century, it is highly probable that antagonisms, if not actual hostilities, characterized Onondaga relationships with many tribal groups.

This raises the broader question of the effect European contact had on intertribal relations, and on warfare in particular. It has often been suggested that the escalating hostilities, endemic throughout the Northeast during the sixteenth and seventeenth centuries, were a direct consequence of European involvement in aboriginal affairs. At its simplest, such a notion implies that, prior to contact, native Americans lived in some sort of Eden where conflict did not take place. This simply is not true. More scholarly explanations argue that the European presence functioned as a transforming agent, altering the established patterns of and reasons for warfare (Hunt 1940:18–22; Jennings 1984:41). This is closer to the mark. It seems clear that an increase in intertribal conflicts did take place during the sixteenth century. European contact seems to have accelerated everything, raised the stakes, changed the scale of warfare. The effect, however, was that of a catalyst rather than an initiator. The changes in intertribal relations, like those in material culture, were characterized by a gradual modification of existing patterns rather than the creation of totally new ones.

One source of difficulty in assessing the changing nature of aboriginal warfare is the implication of an "economic" motive for increased hostilities. It was, the argument runs, the desire for European material goods that accelerated the pace and extent of warfare (Hunt 1940:19; Trigger 1976, 1:221–23; 1978:346). I find this a perilous line of reasoning.

This is not to say that economic factors were of no account, for certainly they were. It also seems indisputable that the desire for European materials was, in large part, the engine which drove intertribal relations during the sixteenth century, undoubtedly heightening old animosities and creating new ones. The pivotal issue here is the term "economic" and what its use implies. If our intent is to see how native Americans fit into an emerging world economic system, then market-oriented terminology and methods of analysis may be appropriate. If, however, we are trying to understand cross-cultural contact and acculturative change from a native perspective, then we must, as Calvin Martin has urged, look at the data from an aboriginal point of view (Martin 1978:150). Perhaps, as Trigger has suggested, a new form of economically motivated warfare did emerge by the end of the protohistoric period (1976, 1:223). Before this can be assessed, however, we need first to examine the economics of the sixteenth century, a century when trade lay as much in symbols as it did in substance.

Networks of Exchange/Patterns of Trade

Just as the effects of European contact can be seen in changing material culture patterns or in the shifting scale of aboriginal warfare, they are also evident in the gradual redefinition of native exchange networks. Over the course of the sixteenth century, the networks through which goods were traded changed as distinctly as did the materials flowing through them.

Pre-contact trade was based on reciprocal exchange rather than a desire for material gain. While the archaeological record is, admittedly, biased as to what was actually exchanged, the emphasis seems to have been on symbolically charged substances—marine shell, native copper, exotic lithics—intended for ritual (including mortuary) use, and which were not locally available. At present, the evidence indicates that a series of overlapping exchange networks operated across northeastern North America during the Late Woodland stage. While the range of these networks was extensive, the quantities of material moving through them was small (Trigger 1976, 1:168–75; Fitzgerald 1982:9, 289–91).

During the protohistoric period this pattern changed dramatically. One significant factor was volume. Whether it was traditional substances, such as shell, or newly available European analogs, more material began to move through the exchange networks than had in the previous several hundred years. Nor did this increased flow diminish as the century went on. One consequence was to emphasize and systematize particular exchange networks as more and more material flowed through them. This was especially the case after 1550 as the presence of Europeans became a less random and more predictable phenomenon. As coastal trading coalesced around particular points, so too the movement of materials inland tended to center on particular corridors. By the end of the century, the character of the exchange system was nearly the opposite of what it had been a century earlier. Instead of small quantities of material circulating widely through an extended series of networks, large quantities now followed increasingly specific routes to a more limited number of destinations.

The final step in the evolution of historic trading systems from the pre-contact exchange networks was the establishment of permanent European settlements early in the seventeenth century. Many of these colonial settlements were, of course, founded specifically to engage in trade. Equally important, however, they also provided a set of fixed points to which the native trading systems could be anchored. It was from this basis that the well known trade routes of the seventeenth century emerged.

We have, therefore, two tasks before us at this point. One is to examine the transformation of indigenous exchange networks into trading systems in more detail. That is, we must take one network as an example and trace its evolution over the course of the protohistoric period. The second, and not unrelated task, is to determine what kind of relationship existed between the Onondaga and the Susquehannocks during the sixteenth century. Archaeological evidence indicates that some form of relationship existed between these two Iroquoian groups and that, whatever it was, it intensified during the last half of the century. What makes this Onondaga-Susquehannock relationship intriguing is that the occurrence of European materials on Onondaga sites parallels the evidence for contact with the Susquehannocks quite closely. This fact suggests that some, perhaps most, of the European goods which reached Onondaga during the sixteenth century came from the mid-Atlantic coast via the Susquehanna rather than from the St. Lawrence as is usually assumed.

The best way to execute both tasks is to choose a class of material exchanged both prior to and after European contact, and one which applies to the Onondaga as well as the Susquehannock. This, on the one hand, allows us to see how that particular network changed over time, and on the other, provides a baseline against which the relationship between two neighboring tribal groups can be assessed. Marine shell is an appropriate material. It is readily indentifiable (to genus if not species) and a considerable amount is known about the sources and availability of commonly utilized species.[7] Shell is appropriate material to track for another reason. Shell was valued in large part because of its potential for life enhancing/ life restorative power when consecrated for ritual purposes. This high cultural value was based on a fusion of ideational and aesthetic concerns focused on light, bright, and white things (Hamell 1983, 1985). The degree to which this material, as opposed to some other, was in demand provides us with an understanding not just of what was highly valued in aboriginal culture, but why an effort was made to acquire it.

Map 7 shows a distribution of Late Woodland stage sites from which marine shell artifacts have been recovered. The sites themselves and information on the genus/species of shell present are summarized in Table 10. These data suggest that prior to European contact, marine shell was widely, albeit thinly, distributed across the Northeast. In general, shell occurs in the form of small finished objects, particularly beads and, to a lesser degree, pendants. The most common forms are small discoidally

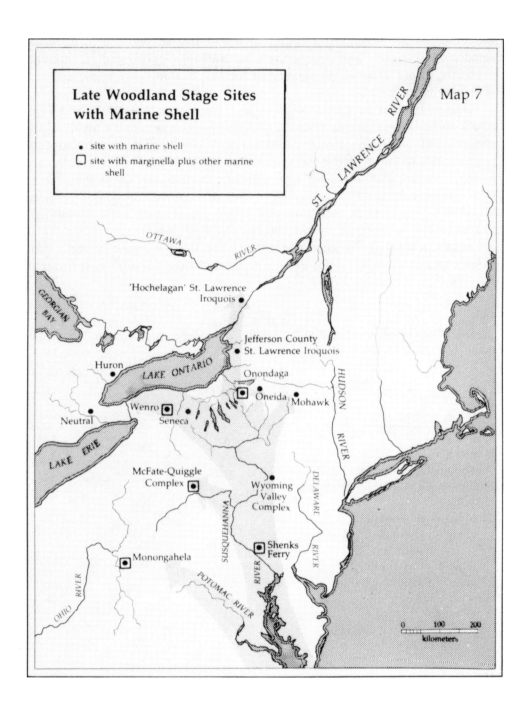

Late Woodland Stage Sites
with Marine Shell

Map 7

- site with marine shell
□ site with marginella plus other marine
  shell

ST. LAWRENCE RIVER

OTTAWA RIVER

GEORGIAN BAY

'Hochelagan' St. Lawrence Iroquois

Jefferson County
St. Lawrence Iroquois

Huron

LAKE ONTARIO

Onondaga

HUDSON RIVER

Wenro
Seneca

Oneida
Mohawk

Neutral

LAKE ERIE

McFate-Quiggle Complex

Wyoming Valley Complex

DELAWARE RIVER

SUSQUEHANNA RIVER

Shenks Ferry

Monongahela

OHIO RIVER

POTOMAC RIVER

0   100   200
kilometers

shaped beads made from either *Busycon* or *Mercenaria* and small tubular
beads made from *Busycon* columella. While these two forms predominate,
a variety of other bead shapes—barrel-shaped, round—also occur. Pendants

were most often made from round to irregularly shaped pieces of shell, usually *Mercenaria,* and were singly or multiply perforated. Columella pendants, either grooved or perforated for suspension, have been reported occasionally as well.

One additional variety of marine shell found on Late Woodland sites is the common marginella *(Prunum apicinum).* These small univalves are encountered frequently along the southern Atlantic coast; North Carolina is the northern limit of their range (Morris 1975:232). Modified either by perforation or by abrading off a portion of the shoulder, these shells were used extensively for ornamentation. They are commonly found on Late Woodland sites of both the Colington (Algonquian) and Cashie (Iroquoian) phases in costal North Carolina (Phelps 1983:39, 44).

Since their source is known, the distribution of marginella shells provides a means for tracing the extent of the exchange network that brought

Table 10

A Distribution of Marine Shell on Late Woodland Sites in the Northeast

Tribal Group (Site)	Unspecified Marine Shell Present	Identifiable Genus/Species		
		Busycon	Mercenaria	Marginella
Shenks Ferry	X	X	X	X
Monongahela	X	X		X
Wyoming Valley complex (Parker)		X		
McFate-Quiggle complex (Kalgran)	X	X		X
Iroquois				
Mohawk (Elwood)	X	?		
Oneida (Nichols Pond)	X		?	
(Olcott)	X		?	
Onondaga (Barnes)		X	X	X
Seneca (California Ranch)	X			
Wenro (Alhart)		?	X	X
St. Lawrence Iroquois				
Jefferson County subgroup	X	X		
"Hochelagan" subgroup (Beckstead)		X		
(Roebuck)	X	X	?	
Huron				
Humber axis (Draper)	X	X		
(Black Creek)	X			
Neutral	X			

Sources: See note 8.

marine shell from the mid-Atlantic coast to sites in the Northeast. At present, it appears that this network extended from Chesapeake Bay up the major river corridors into the interior: for example, along the Potomac River to the sites of the Monongahela culture in the upper Ohio drainage. More pertinent to our case is the network that tracked up the Susquehanna, its branches and tributaries. This network extended along the West Branch bringing shell to the sites of the McFate-Quiggle complex. It reached as far as the Wenro-related sites west of the Genesee River. The North Branch of the Susquehanna and its tributaries, the Chenango and Tioughnioga, brought marginella at least as far north as Onondaga.[8]

It is difficult to know how much farther this pre-contact exchange network extended. Marine shell (*Busycon* and *Mercenaria*) has been found on St. Lawrence Iroquois sites in both Jefferson County and Ontario, as well as on Late Woodland Huron and Neutral sites. To date, however, marginella beads have yet to be reported. My own impression is that most, if not all, the marine shell that occurs on interior Late Woodland sites in the Northeast originated from the mid-Atlantic coast and was transported inland via some variant of the exchange network described above.[9]

The antiquity of this exchange network is unclear. It is possible, however, that this or a similar network was in operation as early as the Frontenac phase of the Late Archaic stage (ca. 2000 B.C.) and continued to function through the subsequent Early and Middle Woodland stages (Ritchie 1944:49; 1969:202–4, 249). In spite of an apparent hiatus during much of the Late Woodland, it is clear that the existence of this exchange network predates any evidence of an Onondaga-Susquehannock relationship. In fact, the origins of the Susquehannock are far from resolved. While serveral antecedent groups, such as the Wyoming Valley complex and the McFate-Quiggle complex, have been identified, it remains unclear how these relate to the emergence of the Susquehannocks (Kent 1984:13–15, 111–32).

By the mid-sixteenth century, a number of changes had occurred in both the exchange network and in what it carried. Nonetheless, the same basic network continued to function. Map 8 shows a distribution of early protohistoric sites from which shell objects have been recovered. The sites and a summary of particular artifact types are presented in Table 11.[10]

One of the more obvious changes is in the nature of the groups still involved in the exchange process. Many of the cultural groups that participated prior to contact had either disappeared or were on the wane by the mid-sixteenth century. For example, on the lower Susquehanna, the people of the Shenks Ferry complex were under pressure from other groups and maintained only a tenuous hold on their traditional core area (ibid.:129–31, 313–14). On each of the major tributary branches of the Susquehanna, previously well defined complexes—the McFate-Quiggle on

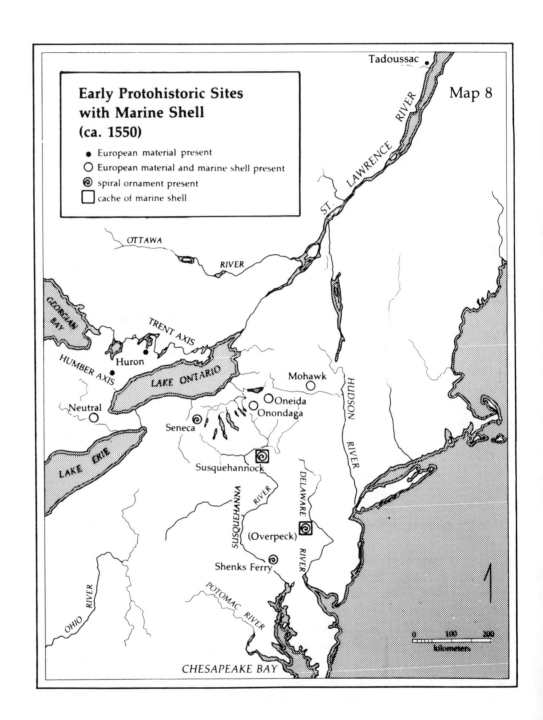

Early Protohistoric Sites
with Marine Shell
(ca. 1550)

Map 8

● European material present
○ European material and marine shell present
◉ spiral ornament present
▢ cache of marine shell

Tadoussac

ST. LAWRENCE RIVER

OTTAWA RIVER

GEORGIAN BAY

TRENT AXIS

HUMBER AXIS

Huron

LAKE ONTARIO

Neutral

LAKE ERIE

Seneca

Mohawk

Oneida
Onondaga

HUDSON RIVER

Susquehannock

SUSQUEHANNA RIVER

DELAWARE RIVER

(Overpeck)

Shenks Ferry

OHIO RIVER

POTOMAC RIVER

0   100   200
kilometers

CHESAPEAKE BAY

Table 11

A Distribution of Marine Shell and European Material on Early Protohistoric Sites in the Northeast

Tribal Group (Site)	Marine Shell			European Material		
	Finished Object	Marginella	Bulk or Semi-processed	Tubular Beads	Spirals or Hoops	Unspecified or Other
Shenks Ferry	X			X	X	
Susquehannock						
(Murray Garden)	X				X	
(Engelbert)	X	X		X	X	X
(Pumpelly Creek)	X			X	X	
(Ellis Creek)			cache	X		
(Overpeck)	X		cache	X	X	
Iroquois						
Mohawk (Garoga)	X			X		X
Oneida (Vaillancourt)	X			X		X
Onondaga (Temperance House/Atwell)	X		X	X		X
Seneca (Richmond Mills)	X			X	X	?
(Culbertson)	X			X	X	X
Huron						
Trent axis (Trent)				X		X
(Benson)				X		X
Humber axis (Parsons)						X
Neutral (Cleveland)	X	X	X	X		X

Sources: See notes 10 and 11.

the West Branch, and the Wyoming Valley on the North Branch—had vanished (ibid.:121–24, 306). At the far end of the network, of course, the St. Lawrence Iroquois were also in eclipse. On the other hand, the Susquehannocks emerged as a clear presence on the North branch. During this Early Schultz phase Susquehannock settlement pattern was characterized by small, dispersed hamlets strung along the river from what is now Towanda, Pennsylvania, north to Owego, New York. The largest concentration occurred around Tioga Point, the confluence of the Chemung and Susquehanna. Current "best guess" estimates suggest that the Susquehannock population may have numbered around 1000 people during this period (ibid.:304–6).

Not only were the participants different, the exchange network itself seems less dispersed, more focused. In part, this change in character was a reflection of what was being transported. The volume of shell moving through the network was greater. While the quantity of shell objects on

Iroquois sites remains modest, it is markedly more than on pre-contact sites. A similar situation appears to have existed on Neutral sites in southern Ontario (Fitzgerald 1982:295–96). Not only was the volume greater, a different form of shell was being exchanged. In contrast to the pre-contact network where finished objects were circulated, unprocessed or partially processed shell now moved through the network as well. Two caches of semi-processed shell have been reported; both were found on Susquehannock-related sites located part way through the exchange network.[11] Complementing this is the increased occurrence of partially completed shell objects on Iroquois sites of the same time period.

Other, more subtle changes also occur. In spite of an increase in quantity, there seems to be less variety in the finished shell objects being exchanged. Discoidal beads remain the most common style and the sizes in which they occur seem more standardized. While tubular beads continue as a minority style, many of the other less common shapes seem to disappear. The occurrence of marginella beads, for example, drops off considerably. What this means is unclear. Perhaps it represents a constriction of the older, more attenuated network or its fragmentation into more discrete, regionally oriented ones. Given the evidence for cultural dislocation and change along the Susquehanna, it is not surprising that the exchange network underwent some alteration as well.

The other major change is, of course, the presence of European materials. All of the sites listed in Table 11 have produced artifacts of European origin, primarily small objects of smelted copper or brass. The point is that the distribution of mid-sixteenth century sites with marine shell is basically the same as that of sites which show evidence of European contact. While this by itself is suggestive, a clearer sense of the relationship between marine shell and European material can be demonstrated by looking at a specific artifact form more carefully. One of the earliest diagnostic forms in which a European material occurs is the spiral "ear ring" (Kent 1984:203). If we look at the distribution of these on mid-sixteenth century sites, we see that they occur primarily along the Susquehanna corridor; that is, on the sole remaining Shenks Ferry site and on three of the four Susquehannock sites. An additional example has been found on a Susquehannock-related site on the mid-Delaware. Only a few of these spirals occur as far inland as Iroquoia.[12] It is quite clear that, despite the changes, marine shell continued to move from the mid-Atlantic coast along the Susquehanna into the interior during the mid-sixteenth century. The distribution of spiral ornaments suggests that European material came inland along the same route.

What about the Onondaga-Susquehannock relationship? It is at just this time that the first tangible indication of contact between the two groups appears. The evidence is largely ceramic and quantitatively not very great. On Onondaga sites, it is the presence of small amounts of Early Schultz Susquehannock pottery, very similar to that found on the sites of the Susquehanna's North Branch. On Susquehannock sites, it is the occurrence of anomalous Onondaga-like face effigies on shell-tempered pots (see chapter 2, note 18). While this evidence is not overwhelming, it does indicate that some form of active contact, perhaps exchange, was occurring between the two neighboring Iroquoian groups.

To summarize, the following series of dynamics characterize the mid-sixteenth century exchange network and the emerging relationship between the Onondaga and the Susquehannock:

—During the Early Schultz phase, the Susquehannocks were functioning as a node in an exchange network beginning to transmit European material and marine shell inland.

—The Susquehannocks were actively seeking access routes south to the mid-Atlantic coast, along the Delaware as well as the Susquehanna, in order to procure the materials in demand.

—A motivating force behind the Onondaga-Susquehannock relationship was the Onondagas' desire for those materials.

During the last half of the sixteenth century, it was the continuation and strengthening of these dynamics rather than the initiation of new ones which characterized the exchange process. The amount of shell moving inland continued to increase, as did the tendency toward more uniformity and less variability in the forms traded. Marginella beads seem to drop out of this portion of the network entirely by the end of the century. While the volume of shell being traded continued to grow gradually, the real increase was in European material. The percentage of European goods on native sites jumps markedly during this period, from just a trace on mid-sixteenth century sites to a significant part of the overall assemblage on sites dating toward the end of the century.[13]

The exchange network itself also seems to become more structured and channelled during this period. The route from the mid-Atlantic coast inland appears to be progressively better defined and more focused on a specific set of destinations. In large part, those destinations were the major Iroquoian villages. By the beginning of the seventeenth century, the concentrations of marine shell and European material which occur on Susquehannock, Five Nations, and Ontario Iroquois sites are unmatched elsewhere in the Northeast.[14] It is important not to oversimplify at this point. Other exchange networks besides the one traced here were certainly operating and were undoubtedly important factors in the proliferation of European goods. On the other hand, whether it ended up on Susquehannock, Onondaga, or Seneca sites, marine shell was still coming north from the mid-Atlantic coast via the traditional route. In all likelihood, so was much of the European material.

The evidence for an Onondaga-Susquehannock relationship is strongest at the end of the sixteenth and beginning of the seventeenth centuries. One line of material evidence for this relationship is the increasing percentage of hybrid Iroquois-Susquehannock pottery on Onondaga sites. Frilled vessels make the most convincing case. On mid-sixteenth century Onondaga sites, the percentage of frilled pottery is small, in the range of 1 to 2 percent. This rises during the rest of the protohistoric period until the early seventeenth century, when frilled vessels are nearly 15 percent of Onondaga pottery. The other hybrid variety, Ithaca Linear, follows a similar pattern, but in smaller percentages. There are other material indicators, for example projectile points made from non-local, but characteristically Susquehannock, materials such as white quartz and smoky grey chalcedony.[15]

While the artifact evidence indicates that a relationship existed, it does little to clarify the nature of that relationship. The settlement pattern data, however, do. As discussed above, a number of changes occurred along the Susquehanna corridor during the sixteenth century as various cultural groups emerged, shifted location, or disappeared. One of the most dramatic examples occurred sometime during the third quarter of the century when the Susquehannocks abandoned their traditional core area on the North Branch of the Susquehanna River and moved well over 300km downriver to the Washington Boro basin. Here they apparently displaced the indigenous Shenks Ferry people, absorbing many in the process. The distance involved is not the only extraordinary aspect of this move. The pattern of settlement that the Susquehannocks chose in their new location was one radically different from what had preceded it. Instead of several small unfortified hamlets spread out along the river, the Susquehannocks now elected to live in a single, large, heavily palisaded village (Kent 1984:16–18, 304–6, 324–25).

Changes so drastic do not occur without good reason. In this case, there were two. One was a desire to get closer to the source of the goods, European as well as shell. This helps explain why they moved so far downriver. But second, and equally important, was the desire to get farther away from the Iroquois. In other words, the Susquehannocks were both pulled and pushed south, pulled by the prospect of greater proximity to and therefore control over the source of tradeable material, and pushed by the threat of their larger and more aggressive Iroquois neighbors.

Some corroboration for this assessment is found in the accounts of John Smith and his companions who met and first described the Susquehannocks and their affairs in 1608. While the Susquehannocks were "a mighty people," Smith also observed that they lived "pallisaded in their Towns to defend them[selves] From the Massawomekes Their mortall enemies" (Barbour 1969, 2:343, 407). Due to difficulties in translation, Smith was able to glean only fragmentary information about these Massawomekes. They were "a great nation and very populous" who lived "beyond the mountaines," perhaps in "some part of Commada [Canada]." The Susquehannocks were "continually tormented by them" and "very importunate they were with Captain Smith and his company to Free Them From these tormentors" (ibid.:360–61, 408–9). Not long after, Smith had the opportunity to see the dreaded Massawomekes himself. Unfortunately, no one capable of interpreting was present, and the English could understand them "but by signs" (ibid.:407).[16]

Smith's account is tantalizing, though simply not detailed enough to identify the Massawomekes. If we factor in the archaeological evidence, however, it seems highly probable that they were Five Nations Iroquois, and that the Onondaga were deeply involved.

All this makes a good case for European material reaching Onondaga during the protohistoric period by coming up the Susquehanna River rather than down from the St. Lawrence. It is a case which, at present, is based primarily on archaeological evidence. It is also one which stands in contrast to most of the current literature.[17]

By now the reader will also have noticed another seeming inconsistency. The preceding section of this chapter examined the relationship between the Onondaga and their St. Lawrence Iroquois neighbors to the north. One of the points made was that during the sixteenth century this relationship had a significant impact on Onondaga material culture. From documentary sources it is clear that by 1535 Europeans had met and exchanged gifts with St. Lawrence Iroquoians as far up river as Montreal. If this is the case, then isn't it reasonable to assume that brass articles at Onondaga sites such as Atwell and Temperance House came from the St. Lawrence? Perhaps, in fact, they did.

As in our earlier discussion of the Onondaga and St. Lawrence Iroquois, we are again confronted with a discontinuity in which the archaeological data suggest one answer and the documentary record another. Here too, however, closer examination reveals that the discrepancies are more apparent than real.

The prevailing interpretation is that virtually all European material found on sixteenth-century Iroquoian sites came from the St. Lawrence. Acquired from explorers or fishermen at first and later exchanged directly for furs, these trade goods gradually found their way into Iroquoia by means of native trade or capture during warfare.

The basis for this view is the work of Henry Perceval Biggar and, in particular, his study on the early fur trade in New France (Biggar 1901).

Working through Hakluyt's *Principal Navigations* as well as manuscript sources, Biggar systematically pulled out all the information pertinent to the North Atlantic coast and the St. Lawrence. What emerged was a cameo sketch of European interest and activity in these areas throughout the sixteenth century.

Biggar divided his material into two sections. One dealt with the early voyages of exploration and attempts to colonize. The second traced the growth of commercial interests, fishing in particular, as antecedent to the fur trade. Here was the evidence of Europeans poking and prowling along the coast as early as 1497—the Cabots, Corte-Reals and various other Spaniards, Portuguese, and English. Most important was Jacques Cartier, whose three voyages to the New World brought him not only along the coast but as far up the St. Lawrence as the Lachine rapids. Exchanging presents with the natives as he went, Cartier's experiences showed that, in embryonic form at least, trade was occurring in the St. Lawrence Valley by 1535.

In the long run, however, Biggar argued that the less spectacular but more substantial coastal fishing had far more impact on the development of trade than Cartier's brief sorties. During the late fifteenth and early sixteenth centuries, the traditional fishing grounds off Iceland were expanded westward toward Newfoundland and the Grand Banks. By the first decades of the sixteenth century, French and Portuguese as well as English vessels were working these waters in ever-increasing numbers. Toward mid-century, the Spanish also became active participants, particularly the Basques whose specialty of whaling brought them as far up the St. Lawrence as Tadoussac. The fishing boom continued, and by the last decades of the century as many as 300 ships a year were engaged in taking cod and mackerel, walrus and whale (ibid.:18–25).

Of particular interest to Biggar was the link between fishing and the beginnings of the fur trade. Although he found that this connection was "not easy to discover," he did speculate on how the transition took place (ibid.:28). As fishermen returned year after year to the same locations occasional trading took place, especially when the Europeans came ashore to dry their fish. This intermittent bartering slowly expanded into a more organized and purposeful trade as the demand for furs increased in Europe. However it began, the trade for furs grew rapidly during the last half of the century. In large part it remained a coastal activity, but after 1580, merchants from St. Malo began actively pursuing furs in the upper St. Lawrence Valley. By the end of the century, competition had become so sharp and the stakes so high that the first of a long series of trade monopolies was granted in hopes of stabilizing the situation (ibid.:28–60).

While subsequent studies have expanded and revised Biggar's work, his arguments still exert considerable influence. In Biggar's view, European-native trade in the sixteenth century was an organic development centered increasingly in the St. Lawrence Valley. This historiographical focus on the St. Lawrence was quite understandable, since New France was Biggar's primary concern. But in presenting his case, Biggar also provided a focus for archaeologists in the United States anxious for interpretative assistance (Ritchie 1954:70–72). As a result, his view of sixteenth-century trade via the St. Lawrence has become a tenet of orthodoxy, almost to the exclusion of other possibilities.

The difficulty with this via-the-St. Lawrence view is that there is virtually no archaeological evidence to support it. There are few if any documented sixteenth-century sites in the St. Lawrence Valley.[18] This is a problem insofar as the area is supposed to have been the focal point for all sixteenth-century native-European trade in the Northeast. Certainly there are sites yet to be discovered and, without a doubt, many others have either been destroyed or obscured by the intervening four centuries of French and English settlement. Even so, the paucity of sixteenth-century sites in the St. Lawrence Valley is striking.

It is not only along the St. Lawrence that European goods are conspicuously absent. There are at present no St. Lawrence Iroquois sites in Jefferson County that can be considered protohistoric, even though the area remained occupied until the mid-sixteenth century.[19] Since the presence of European materials is well documented on Five Nations Iroquois sites of the same period, it is surprising that no evidence of contact has been discovered in northern New York. If the via-the-St. Lawrence view is correct, then the St. Lawrence Iroquois should have had better, more direct access to trade than the Five Nations, who were farther inland.

This does not imply that trade along the St. Lawrence during the sixteenth century was absent. It does, however, demonstrate that trade centered on the St. Lawrence can no longer be asserted as the driving force behind the intertribal dynamics of the sixteenth century.

The discontinuity between archaeological and documentary reconstructions is largely a reflection of twentieth-century scholarship, not sixteenth-century reality. Biggar's interest was to understand the development of trade in Canada, hence his focus on the St. Lawrence. Indeed, much of the modern scholarship on the sixteenth century is concerned primarily with European economic involvement in North America, how it originated and how it became institutionalized. North of Mexico fish and furs were of particular interest. Both drew Europeans toward the St. Lawrence, to its Gulf and the adjacent Grand Banks for fish, and to the river itself as the corridor inland for furs. That the St. Lawrence was of primary importance during the sixteenth century is indisputable—from a European point of view. From a native perspective, however, things were happening in more places and in more important ways than just along the St. Lawrence.[20]

By the mid-sixteenth century, Europeans had touched upon if not penetrated virtually the entire Atlantic coast from Mexico to Labrador. Each point of contact produced its own particular ripple effect, one which touched not only those who actually saw Europeans but also those with whom there were connections due to alliance or exchange. As the trade routes for marine shell in the Northeast have illustrated, the geographical extent of such networks was great. In consequence, it is likely that the effects of each contact spread inland rapidly. Exactly how different native groups responded is largely unknown; however, the results were undoubtedly complex, dynamic, and interactive. Perhaps the best way to sketch this out is to present a brief review of the Onondaga and how they fit into the shifting patterns of the sixteenth century.

Prior to European contact the Onondaga, like most tribal groups, were one node in a series of interconnected exchange networks that stretched across the Northeast. Among those which can be archaeologically documented, that bringing marine shell north from the mid-Atlantic coast stands out most clearly. Other networks which transported materials such as native copper from the Upper Great Lakes or red slate and serpentine marble from the Lake George/upper Hudson River corridor may have been equally important. Networks for even more exotic substances, high-grade chalcedony from Ohio and possibly catlinite from Minnesota, may also have existed.

It was through these indigenous networks that European goods worked their way inland, eventually reaching interior tribes such as the Onondaga. By what route the first European material arrived may be unknowable. While a case could be argued for other routes, I am persuaded that the earliest brass artifacts probably came from the St. Lawrence Valley. The evidence of greatly intensified Onondaga-St. Lawrence Iroquois interactions, and the presence of walrus ivory on one of the first Onondaga sites with evidence of contact, suggest that ties to the St. Lawrence may have existed during the second quarter of the sixteenth century. The documented presence of Europeans well up the St. Lawrence during the same period tends to support the argument that the first European objects to reach Onondaga originated in the north.

Regardless of where the inital European materials came from, Onondaga attention turned to the south during the middle of the sixteenth century. Resolution of hostilities with the St. Lawrence Iroquois and the relative quiescence of European activity after Cartier and Roberval's departure undoubtedly stimulated this change. So did the increasing interest in acquiring marine shell, perhaps for Confederacy-related ritual use. Whatever the reasons, it was to the south, not the north, that Onondaga interests focused during the last half of the century.

By turning south, the Onondaga came into direct contact with the Susquehannocks, who functioned as intermediaries in the exchange network for marine shell. Relations may have been amicable at first; however, the demand for shell and European goods, which were increasingly available through the same network, caused tension and eventually hostility between the two groups. The movement of the Susquehannocks away from Iroquoia was probably a consequence of this deteriorating state of affairs, and belligerency seems to have characterized the Onondaga-Susquehannock relationship for the rest of the sixteenth century. In spite of this, the Onondaga continued to obtain shell and European materials from the mid-Atlantic coast (or roughly from the mouth of the Hudson to Chesapeake Bay). The similarities between Onondaga and Susquehannock assemblages argue strongly for this. That some form of trade continued throughout the remainder of the sixteenth century and into the seventeenth seems certain; whether this relationship was a voluntary or forced one is less clear.

This situation appears unchanged until early in the seventeenth century when the Dutch, increasingly active along the mid-Atlantic coast, began to establish permanent settlements. These included Fort Nassau (1614) and its successor Fort Orange (1624) at Albany, and New Amsterdam (1625) on Manhattan Island. The presence of these settlements radically altered the exchange systems which had evolved over the course of the preceding century. For the Onondaga, it was no longer necessary to deal with the Susquehannocks now that trading could take place in a location both closer and safer. Instead of the old north/south axis, trade could now occur west/east along the axis of the Confederacy. The implications of this realignment were slow to surface.

Inside and Outside the Confederacy

Up to this point, the emphasis has been on the Onondaga and how they functioned as an autonomous tribal entity during the sixteenth century. They could, and often did, act with considerable independence, especially in matters of warfare and trade. But the Onondaga were also the central tribe in the Five Nations Confederacy. What role did the Confederacy play in the shifting, dynamic events of the protohistoric period?

It is difficult to answer this question on the basis of available evidence. While some insights can be gleaned from the archaeological record, they are more suggestive than substantial. No historical accounts exist, and one cannot safely reconstruct what the Confederacy was by "upstreaming" from seventeenth-century descriptions, since this method offers no reliable way to differentiate continuity from change.

Since there is no way to reconstruct what the Confederacy was, let me propose a model for what it might have been. This can then be tested against what data we do have. It has already been argued that the Confederacy was a pre-contact phenomenon, one that was indigenous in both its form and function. The question is, how did these change during the sixteenth century?

The model proposes that the Confederacy operated on two levels during the protohistoric period. These levels are similar to what Wallace has described as the Confederacy's "minimum" and "maximum" purposes (1972:42). The first, or minimal, function of the Confederacy was its original one, to serve as an internal mechanism for peacekeeping. It did this by providing a ritualized means for redressing grievances or injury, thereby preventing vendettas and violence between members. Just as this minimal function was internally oriented, the second, or maximal, function of the Confederacy was directed externally. This aspect of the Confederacy is more controversial, for it implies that there was a conscious effort by members of the Confederacy to "extend the rafters" of the longhouse, that is to include other neighboring tribal groups whether they were interested or not.

Let us start with the internal, peacekeeping function. The model proposes that during the protohistoric period this remained largely unchanged, operating as it did prior to European contact. As a result there was little if any intra-Iroquois hostility. The Confederacy not only alleviated internal tensions, it also served as a vehicle for cooperation and support.

Two lines of archaeological evidence provide indirect support for this interpretation. One is the rather surprising uniformity of the contact horizon among the Five Nations. The introduction of European material seems to occur at approximately the same time on Mohawk, Oneida, Onondaga, and Seneca sites. Little information is currently available for the Cayuga during the protohistoric period. In addition, the general range of contact goods and their frequency of occurrence remain roughly comparable across Iroquoia during the rest of the sixteenth century.[21] This degree of similarity implies some sort of cooperative arrangement. A second indication of the Confederacy's internal functioning is found in the Onondaga's preoccupation with external matters along their north/south axis. It is unlikely that this would have been the case if their west/east axis was not secure. This evidence is not overwhelming, but then neither is the argument radical. Similar interpretations have been proposed by other scholars (Trigger 1976, 1:224).

The degree to which the Confederacy may have functioned externally as a force for expansionism is another story. To even raise this as a possibility risks reviving the specter of Parkman's militant Iroquois full of "homicidal frenzy" and the "insatiable rage for conquest" (1867:436). This was most certainly not the case. Jennings has rightfully dispatched the notion of an Iroquois empire based on might (1984:10–20). Nonetheless, the Confederacy does appear to have had some external function during the sixteenth century. In order to understand what it was, we need to look more carefully at the Confederacy itself, how it came into being and for what purposes.

One fact which has made the Five Nations Confederacy so distinctive to scholars is that descriptions of both its founding and functions have survived through oral tradition. Although there is a degree of variability in the existing versions, these myths have allowed the Confederacy and its origins to be analyzed in comparison with other similar phenomena. The term "revitalization movement" has been used to describe this process of internal culture change, one in which the members of a society deliberately change their culture in an effort to improve it (Wallace 1956). In general, such a process arises because the existing situation is regarded as unsatisfactory; conditions are often chaotic or deteriorating. In response, a moral and spiritual revival takes place, usually led by a charismatic leader(s). The old ("bad") ways are renounced and new ("good") ways are established and then institutionalized, forming a new and "correct" culture.

Wallace argued that the establishment of the Confederacy, as recounted through the origin myth, is an excellent example of a revitalization movement. In the "dark days" before the Confederacy, the Iroquois were beset by blood feuding, cannibalism, and witchcraft. Guided by the Peacemaker and his disciple Hiawatha, the Iroquois renounced their harmful and destructive ways. Through the ritual of the condolence ceremony, the Peacemaker not only ended the violence but established a new structure to maintain intra-Iroquois peace (Wallace 1958).

There is, however, an additional element, latent but present nevertheless. Once the Great Tree of Peace (the Confederacy) was planted, its roots were to extend out in the four cardinal directions. Other nations, when they saw the tree, were to "accept and follow the roots" and become "as props, supports of the longhouse" (Parker 1916:101, 105). These words, admittedly, describe a nineteenth-century conception of the Confederacy but they do illustrate a point. Revitalization, although initially designed to cope with internal problems, can easily be adapted for other purposes. More than one revitalization movement has become fulminant, and after redressing its own internal inequities has gone on to correct those of its neighbors.[22] In the case of the Iroquois, Wallace inadvertently tells us what triggered this fulminant phase. A new "steady state of Iroquoian culture" was not achieved as a result of the Confederacy's formation "if for no other reason than that the arrival of Europeans created new stresses and distortions" (Wallace 1958:124). Indeed they did.

The Confederacy operated only in its internal (minimal) capacity prior to contact. What potential there was for morally charged expansionism remained latent, untapped. European contact, however, sprang it loose. As Hamell has suggested, the most common native perception of arriving Europeans was that of returning culture heroes, supernatural man-beings originating from beyond the world's rim and offering the substances of "power"[23] from the Under(water) World (Hamell 1983:18–20, 26, 28; 1985).

There are good reasons to believe not only that the Iroquois did perceive Europeans in this manner but that their response was a particularly strong one. In the first place, residual aspects of the revitalization process, which as Wallace noted was never quite completed, were operative. When the Peacemaker departed, conditions were still in flux and it was implied that, should the need arise, he would come again (Parker 1916:195; Fenton 1975:143). From this perspective, it would not have been difficult to consider the advent of these strange and powerful man-beings as some form of fulfillment of the Peacemaker's promised return. Put another way, the process which established the Confederacy may also have primed the Iroquois to anticipate (re)contact. When it occurred, the effect was one of confirmation, underscoring the correctness of the revitalized beliefs and any actions which those required.

Another consideration is applicable here. During the late nineteenth century and throughout the first half of the twentieth, a series of localized revitalization movements took place across Melanesia. Known as cargo cults, these millenarian, often militant, movements focused on the acquisition of "cargo", that is, European manufactured goods such as axes, knives, beads, and cloth (Burridge 1960:xv, 29; Worsley 1968) While a detailed comparison between the Iroquois response to Europeans in the sixteenth century and more recent cargo cults is beyond the scope of this study, a few observations are pertinent.

Cargo cults combine elements of two culture-changing processes. These are the desire to reform the culture internally (a revitalization movement), and the response to contact with a new, more technologically sophisticated culture (an acculturation process). As a revitalization movement, cargo cults are characterized by a strong desire for moral/spiritual regeneration and the prophetic vision of a better future. Cargo cults differ from other revitalization movements in that they emphasize the acquisition of European materials, not so much for their intrinsic or material qualities as for their power—power to communicate with ancestors, power to regenerate, power to create a better life. Sometimes the new (European) materials supplement the traditional forms of wealth/power; sometimes they replace them. Problems arise when those who rightfully should have access to these materials are blocked or restricted by distance, by a competing group, or some other factor. In Melanesia, for example, Europeans were occasionally threatened, even attacked, because they were seen as unwilling to share the "secret" of obtaining cargo (Burridge 1960:xvi).

As part of an acculturation process, cargo cults occur in a series of phases.[24] These are summarized in Figure 9. In the initial phase, cross-cultural contact is interpreted as consistent, or congruent, with the indigenous culture's own belief system or creation myth: The newcomers may be perceived as deities or returning ancestors. As a result, the newcomers and their material possessions are eagerly sought and accepted. This phase has rarely been documented. A second phase occurs when inconsistencies

Figure 9
Phases of Cargo Cultism as an Acculturative Process

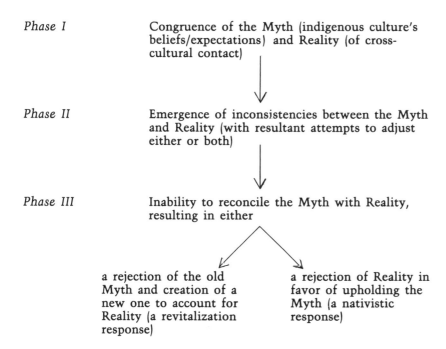

Phase I   Congruence of the Myth (indigenous culture's beliefs/expectations) and Reality (of cross-cultural contact)

Phase II   Emergence of inconsistencies between the Myth and Reality (with resultant attempts to adjust either or both)

Phase III   Inability to reconcile the Myth with Reality, resulting in either

a rejection of the old Myth and creation of a new one to account for Reality (a revitalization response)

a rejection of Reality in favor of upholding the Myth (a nativistic response)

Sources: Hamell 1985 and personal communication; Burridge 1960:28–29; Wallace 1956.

begin to appear between what the indigenous culture's beliefs (the Myth) predict, and what actually happens (the Reality). Perhaps the "gods" don't act the way they should. This phase is characterized by efforts to reconcile or redress the inconsistencies. In the third and final phase, it is no longer possible to reconcile the differences. This requires that a choice be made between rejecting the traditional belief system (the Myth) and accepting the new Reality, or rejecting Reality in favor of upholding the Myth. The latter, or "nativistic," response is often characterized by a strong, even violent rejection of the newcomers and their materials. This has been the most frequently documented aspect of cargo cultism.

Returning to our model of the Confederacy and incorporating the foregoing into it, I propose that the Iroquois response to European contact be characterized as a protracted revitalization movement fueled by the first phase of cargo cultism, and that the Confederacy was the vehicle through which that response was externally expressed. This interpretation helps explain two observable circumstances which are otherwise difficult to understand.

One was the state of generalized belligerency which appears to have surrounded the Five Nations. At the end of the sixteenth and into the seventeenth century, the Iroquois seem to have been at odds with all their neighbors—Algonquian and Huron to the north, Mahican on the east, Susquehannock to the south. While this has been noted by other scholars, it has yet to be explained adequately. One traditional interpretation has linked this situation with the "weak and defeated condition" of the Iroquois after they were reputedly driven out of the St. Lawrence Valley. As discussed above in the section on the Onondaga and St. Lawrence Iroquois, this explanation is not correct. Another frequent interpretation has connected these hostilities with the burgeoning fur trade and the Iroquois desire first for access to European goods, then for maintaining a "middleman" position in the trade. The difficulties with this interpretation have also been discussed.[25] The problem is not that this kind of economic analysis is incorrect, but rather that it easily distorts native behavior and motivations by describing them in Western-oriented economic terms. Eric Wolf's observation that the Confederacy can be seen as "a native American parallel to . . . the European trading companies" is a case in point (1982:167). While the Confederacy may in fact have functioned in this manner, it also functioned in other ways. By focusing just on the economic explanations, one misses the other operative factors. In this case, those additional factors, and Confederacy functions, are of considerable consequence.

The model proposes a different explanation for this generalized (and, from an Iroquois point of view, externally directed) warfare. While eco-

108 EVOLUTION OF THE ONONDAGA IROQUOIS

nomic concerns did play a role, the hostilities were primarily a consequence of the Confederacy in its fulminant phase, a militant Five Nations pushing out against their neighbors in an effort to extend the white roots of peace.

Two lines of evidence support this conclusion. First is the potential for spiritually charged expansionism within the Confederacy itself. As noted above, it was the Peacemaker's wish that the Great Tree of Peace protect not only the Five Nations but grow to embrace all nations. I would argue that this is exactly what was occurring by the end of the protohistoric period—an Iroquois quest for hegemony fired by the vision of a unified and peaceful world. That sense of mission would remain a recurrent and powerful force in Iroquois culture.

It is important not to overplay this expansionism. Iroquois militancy was not a relentless jihad. No monolithic Iroquois armies assaulted adjacent tribes in a concerted program of conquest. Instead, the pattern appears to be one of intensified warfare among traditional adversaries, each of the Five Nations acting largely on its own.

There was another reason for their militancy. Not only were the adjacent tribes outside the structure of the Confederacy, in many cases they also blocked Iroquois access to European materials, materials which the Iroquois felt were rightfully theirs. The overtones of cargo cultism are quite clear here. From an Iroquois point of view, these were materials of "power" perhaps sent by the ancestors in order to aid in reforming themselves and extending the Confederacy. It is no coincidence that most of the hostilities were directed at those neighboring tribes who controlled access to the coast along the major river corridors. These were the Algonquians and their Huron allies on the St. Lawrence and Great Lakes, the Mahicans along the Hudson, and the Susquehannocks astride their own river. From this perspective, the radical relocation of the Susquehannocks downriver as well as John Smith's description of intertribal relations make much more sense.

In addition to belligerent conditions, there is another generalized circumstance which previously defied explanation. This has to do with which tribes had European goods and in what quantities. The Five Nations began to acquire European goods at a very early date, perhaps by the beginning of the second quarter of the sixteenth century. Moreover, during the remainder of the century, they continued to obtain these goods in ever-increasing quantities, amassing more than any other comparable group in the Northeast (the Susquehannocks excepted). This is a significant accomplishment for an inland people with no direct or easy access to the coast. Why were the Iroquois so successful?

In part this question has been answered. The Confederacy was the means for Iroquois success. In its maximal aspect, the Confederacy provided the sense of mission which kept the fires of revitalization burning. As a result, the Iroquois exerted an influence well in excess of their numbers. In its minimal aspect, the Confederacy provided the basis for an internal cooperation and stability which, in turn, allowed all that visionary zeal to be externally directed. This, however, refines the question as much as answers it. While the Confederacy may have provided the Five Nations with the competitive edge necessary for obtaining European goods, it does not explain why those materials were in such high demand. Here we finally reach the essential question about the protohistoric period—What was the motivation for acquiring European goods? Why were they so important?

The answer, to put it most succinctly, is that the initial Iroquois response to Europeans and their materials was not an economic one; it was ideological.[26] The reason one sought European goods was not for material gain, but to obtain their "power." Here again, the parallels with other cargo cults are very strong.

The best evidence for this interpretation lies in how the Iroquois used European materials once they obtained them. As noted in chapter 2, the vast majority of European goods have been recovered from burials. This is significant in two ways. First, mortuary offerings of any sort are extremely uncommon during the Late Woodland stage. This changes dramatically after contact occurs. Suddenly, material offerings are found in many, perhaps a majority of, burials. Not only do such offerings become more common during the rest of the sixteenth century, they also become more lavish, especially for children. Second, the materials most frequently used to accompany the dead are the traditional substances of life-enhancing/life-restorative power—shell, crystal, and copper. The fact that the indigenous forms of these substances and their newly available analogs were used together and interchangeably underscores the ideological value of European material and the uses to which it was put.

There still remains a final question—Why was it necessary to amass so much "power"? Initially this may have been a consequence of the revitalization process that created the Confederacy. As discussed in chapter 1, a radical change takes place in Onondaga culture at the end of the Late Woodland. Not only is there a symbolically charged elaboration of traditional Onondaga forms, such as effigy faces and figures on ceramic vessels, there is also revived contact with long-distance exchange networks. As a result, marine shell, exotic lithics, and native copper are again included in Onondaga site assemblages. It would not be difficult to argue that these were material expressions of the revitalization process, the symbols and substances needed to re-form the old and maintain the new culture.

Whatever the initial motivation for acquiring the substances of power, many more emerged during the sixteenth century: diseases which traditional ritual would not cure, the rapid escalation of old animosities and the outbreak of new ones, change at a pace so swift that traditional solutions could barely keep up. Under such circumstances, acquiring the new as well as the traditional substances of power was more than just a matter of material success; it was the means for survival.

During the sixteenth century, several circumstances combined to maximize the Iroquois' advantageous situation. Although deep in the interior, they were located at the headwaters of four major waterways (the St. Lawrence, the Mohawk/Hudson, the Delaware, and the Susquehanna). As a result, the Iroquois had tremendous flexibility in terms of acquiring European goods. Wherever those materials were available, from the lower St. Lawrence Valley to Chesapeake Bay, the Iroquois were in a position to go and get them. The major sources were to the north (the St. Lawrence) and the south (the mid-Atlantic coast). In each case, it was native groups outside the Confederacy who either blocked access or competed for trade. These external tensions served to reinforce the internal west/east axis of the Confederacy, a bond already strong, having been forged in the fires of revitalization. The result was an internally cohesive and resilient structure, one that could absorb the stresses of change as well as maximize whatever opportunities were presented.

With the establishment of Fort Nassau and the shifting of trade routes west/east to focus on the Hudson Valley, everything changed. What had been the axis of consensus would gradually become one of contention as the Five Nations gradually found they were competing as much among themselves as they were with their non-Confederacy neighbors.

4

The Historic Onondaga
1600-1655

Just a year after Captain John Smith encountered the Susquehannocks and their Massawomeke adversaries, another European explorer had a momentous series of encounters with native Americans. After exploring several sections of the Atlantic coast between Maine and the mouth of Chesapeake Bay, Henry Hudson ventured up the river that now bears his name. One of Hudson's officers, Robert Juet, kept a fairly detailed account of the ship's travels. The countryside, he noted, was full of people and they seemed "very glad of our coming" (Purchas 1906, 13:363). Other Europeans, it seems, had already been there. Not only were the natives anxious to exchange foodstuffs and furs for "beads, knives, and hatchets" as well as other "trifles," they already possessed a considerable quantity of brass and copper.[1]

Hudson's voyage had two significant results. It called to Dutch attention the tremendous economic potential of the New World fur trade and it focused that attention on what the Dutch knew as the North River. The seeds for economic growth could not have fallen on more fertile ground. By the end of the sixteenth century, Amsterdam was the acknowledged center of European commerce and trade. Dutch expertise in shipbuilding and navigation was unsurpassed. Hungry for new markets, Dutch merchants and carriers were expanding their range beyond the Baltic and Mediterranean toward the East Indies, Africa, and the Americas (Scammell 1981:379–86). The success of Hudson's venture brought a flurry of new interest in the North American fur trade. Within a few years, several small companies had been established in order to exploit this new market. By 1614, an outpost known as Fort Nassau had been built close to where Hudson's expedition had met with such success, near present-day Albany, New York. These small companies continued to trade, as well as bicker

112

and squabble among themselves, until they were superceded by the Dutch West India Company in 1621 (Hart 1959).

This rapid expansion in Dutch commercial activity along the upper Hudson River must have had profound effects on native Americans. Previously, contact with Europeans had been desultory at best; now they had come to stay. European materials, always scarce and often capriciously available, could now be acquired in unbelievable quantities through direct exchange. Not only was the supply more reliable but the volume and variety of goods available was exponentially greater. This chapter examines the impact of the dramatic increase in European presence on the Onondaga.

A second aspect of the "historic" period is that Europeans themselves, not just their materials, came to Iroquoia. One result was the gradual compilation of a documentary record, one which describes the Iroquois in increasingly detailed terms. These ethnohistorical accounts serve as a valuable counterpoint to the archaeological evidence and allow a more complete assessment of the Onondaga to emerge.

The first known European to venture into Onondaga territory was Samuel de Champlain. Reluctantly persuaded by his Huron and Algonquian allies, Champlain agreed to assist them in attacking their "Entouhonoron" enemies during the fall of 1615.[2] Traveling by canoe from Huronia, the war party moved southeast along the Trent waterway, crossed the St. Lawrence, and passed into the enemy country on the south side of Lake Ontario. The boats were cached near the mouth of the Salmon River, and the expedition proceeded inland on foot. As they crossed the Oneida River near Brewerton, a small group of Onondaga were captured while fishing; the next day Champlain and his native allies arrived "before the enemy's fort" (Biggar 1922–36, 3:62–66). This site, the subject of considerable debate, was a palisaded fishing village at the head of Onondaga Lake.[3] After six days of skirmishing the attackers withdrew. Champlain departed with two arrow wounds and considerable exasperation about the way in which native people conducted their warfare (ibid., 4:261). The Onondaga, for their part, were not so annoyed with the French as they were with their Huron enemies who showed "very little courage" by bringing Europeans along to help them (ibid.:263). Interestingly enough, Champlain notes in passing that the Iroquois themselves may have received some assistance from the Dutch. The implication is that, by 1615, Dutchmen were also beginning to learn their way around the interior and may have visited as far inland as Onondaga (ibid., 3:54–55; Trelease 1960:33).

It was nearly twenty years before another European visited Iroquoia and kept an account of his travels. Late in 1634, the Dutch, concerned about the slackening of trade at Fort Orange, sent a party of three men to visit "the Maquasen and Sinnekens" and report back on the problem. One of the three, Harmen Meyndertsz van den Bogart, the surgeon at the fort, kept a detailed journal of the trip.[4] Traveling under difficult winter conditions, van den Bogart and his companions passed through several Mohawk villages, finally reaching their destination, a large Oneida town, on December 30, 1634. When they inquired about the trade, the Dutchmen found themselves chastized for their countrymen's stinginess. Van den Bogart also met with a delegation of ten "Onnedagens" who encouraged the Dutchmen to come to their country to trade, as the French did. The French, however, gave better value. If the Dutch would come and trade fairly, they could have all the furs they wanted. Van den Bogart presented the Onondagas with a gift of "knives, some awls and needles," and returned to Fort Orange with their message (Jameson 1909:154).

Slowly, over the first half of the seventeenth century, Europeans began to replace their vague and often fanciful conception of North America's inhabitants with a more accurate understanding. By 1635, the Dutch had learned who the Onondaga were. The French also could now distinguish among the nations of the "Hiroquois" (Thwaites 1896–1901, 8:115). While other Europeans may have reached Onondaga before the middle of the seventeenth century, it was nearly two decades before the next documented visit took place.

In the summer of 1654, Simon LeMoine, a French Jesuit and a proficient native speaker, was sent to assess whether the Onondaga were serious in their protestations of friendship. LeMoine appears to have followed the same basic route as Champlain, by boat to the mouth of the Salmon River, overland to the Oneida River at Brewerton or Caughdenoy, then on to "Onnontage." LeMoine stayed for ten days and had an opportunity to see some of the surrounding countryside as well as study his hosts. He left impressed with both (ibid., 41:91–129).

Based on LeMoine's favorable report, and the Onondagas' earnest request for a mission, two Jesuits were dispatched to "Onontaque" in the fall of 1655. The two were Joseph Chaumont, also a fluent native speaker, and Claude Dablon, a recent immigré. Like van den Bogart, Dablon kept a detailed journal of the trip. The two Jesuits followed the same route LeMoine had used, reaching Otihatanque, an Onondaga fishing village at the mouth of the Salmon River, on October 29, and Onontaque itself a week later. They were warmly received, and, after several days of celebration and deliberation, a small bark chapel was erected to serve as the mission of St. Jean Baptiste (ibid., 42:61–125). Both Jesuits wintered over and Dablon recorded many observations about the Onondaga and their customs in his journal. By spring, it was necessary to report back to Quebec. Dablon left on March 2, while Chaumont remained behind to tend the growing flock of converts.

With Dablon's return, the French found themselves "extremely perplexed" (ibid., 43:127). On the one hand, they were anxious to exploit this successful turn of events and establish not only a mission but a French settlement, "une habitation," in the heart of Iroquoia. On the other hand, they could not easily forget how often their previous efforts had been thwarted by the Five Nations. The decision, however, was to proceed. On May 17, 1656, a large party set out from Quebec for Onontaque in two shallops and several canoes. This time the French took a water route all the way, bypassing the overland path from Otihatanque (or La Famine, as the French called it) and following the Oswego River inland to Gannentaha, Onondaga Lake. The arrival of the French colonists on July 11 occasioned "manifestations of joy on both sides" (ibid.:159). Within a week the French were busily constructing lodgings for themselves and a redoubt for the soldiers who accompanied them. Before the month was out, Ste. Marie de Gannentaha was well underway.[5] For the Onondaga, the once mysterious and distant Europeans now lived next door.

As noted above, the documentary record that accompanied this gradual lessening of distance between the Onondaga and Europeans is extremely valuable. It provides many details about Onondaga culture not discernable from the archaeological record. The documents also provide an independent chronological baseline against which the archaeological data can be plotted and assessed. Finally, the written record also gives us some insight into what people were thinking and what motivated certain decisions, especially among Europeans. Where the documents are less helpful is in understanding what was happening on the native side. In order to see how the Onondaga accommodated to increasing European encroachment during the first half of the seventeenth century, we still must rely on archaeological information.

The remainder of this chapter focuses on that evidence. Two dynamics are of primary concern. First, how did the Onondaga continue to evolve as a cultural entity during a period of tremendous flux? Put another way, how did the definition of what was Onondaga change between 1600 and 1656? Second, how did the Onondaga respond internally to the ever greater availability of European materials? What stayed the same within Onondaga material culture, and what changed?

Settlement and Subsistence Patterns

Ten early historic Onondaga sites are currently known. Five of these are large sites. Listed in the order of their estimated dates of occupation, they include:

Name	Estimated Dates	Estimated Size	Sources[6]
Pompey Center	1600–1620	4 acres	Bradley 1976
Pratt's Falls	1620–1630	3–4 acres	
Shurtleff	1630–1640	3–4 acres	
Carley	1640–1650	4–5 acres	
Lot 18	1650–1655	4–5 acres	

In contrast to the protohistoric period, several changes take place in the patterning of Onondaga settlement during the first half of the seventeenth century. Most obvious is a shift away from the traditional pairing of large and small villages in favor of a single large, consolidated settlement. Exactly when this change occurred is uncertain. The current archaeological evidence suggests that it was early in the century; based on Jesuit descriptions, it is clear that the change took place prior to mid-century.

The new pattern was characterized by a large central town surrounded by a scatter of small outlying hamlets, individual cabins, and fields. Unlike the pattern among the other Five Nations, where the name of a town often changed when it was relocated, the principal Onondaga town kept the same name—Onontaque. All five of these large sites were probably known by that name. Archaeologically, they are poorly documented. No systematic testing or excavation has been done. As a result, it is difficult to discuss either site size or internal characteristics. From what archaeological and ethnohistorical evidence there is, it does appear that all these sites continued to follow the basic Onondaga pattern—a mixture of longhouses and smaller structures surrounded by a palisade.

Other more subtle changes accompanied this shift to a single, large town. The location of these sites is more variable, less patterned than that of the preceding large sites. Some do follow the traditional preference for protected terraces or knolls; others are situated on exposed ridges or in less conventional settings. In addition, the character of site-to-site movement differs from the previous pattern of site relocation. Rather than moving in a more or less systematic manner within one drainage, these large sites move rather randomly in a northwesterly direction, jumping from one drainage to another (Map 9). In spite of these differences, all the large early historic sites, like their predecessors, continue to be situated in the Pompey Hills. The Onondaga, as their name indicates, remained "the people of the great hill" (Beauchamp 1907:147–48).

Two other factors deserve mention. The length of time these early seventeenth-century sites were occupied appears relatively shorter. As discussed in the previous chapters, estimating the length of site occupation is risky at best and, where the archaeological evidence is slim, probably perilous. Nonetheless, it does seem as though the Onondaga towns of the

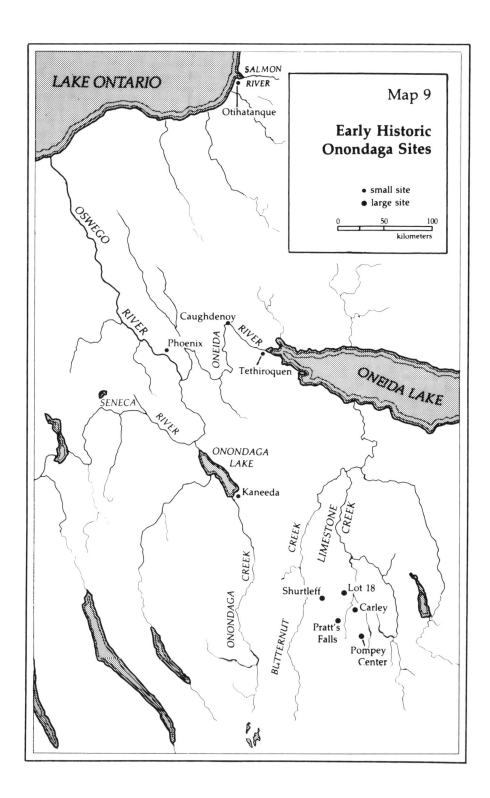

Map 9

Early Historic
Onondaga Sites

• small site
• large site

0   50   100
kilometers

LAKE ONTARIO

SALMON
RIVER

Otihatanque

OSWEGO

RIVER

Caughdenoy

ONEIDA   RIVER

Phoenix

Tethiroquen

ONEIDA LAKE

SENECA

RIVER

ONONDAGA
LAKE

Kaneeda

ONONDAGA   CREEK

BUTTERNUT   CREEK

LIMESTONE   CREEK

Shurtleff

Lot 18

Carley

Pratt's
Falls

Pompey
Center

early seventeenth century moved more frequently than did their sixteenth-century antecedents. Why this was the case remains unclear.

The second factor is the extent to which ever greater exposure to Europeans influenced the form and structure of Onondaga settlement. By 1656 a European community, complete with craftsmen who "worked at all the trades practiced in a city," had been built less than 25km from Onontaque (Thwaites 1896–1901, 43:161, 181). In those early days of good will and cooperation, the French assisted the Onondaga in several ways. One was constructing a new chapel, replacing the earlier bark structure that Chaumont and Dablon had erected (ibid.:181). French carpenters also may have followed through on earlier promises to assist the Onondaga in fortifying their town (ibid., 42:107). Archaeological testing may still be able to document this aspect of cross-cultural contact.

At least five small sites from this period are known either from documentary or archaeological sources.[7] All are located in the lowlands north of the Onondaga Escarpment and appear to have functioned as seasonal fishing and food processing camps. They include:

Name	Location	Estimated Dates of Occupation
Kaneenda[8]	mouth of Onondaga Creek	1600–1625
Tethiroquen	outlet of Oneida Lake	1600–1655+
Otihatanque[9]	mouth of Salmon River	1600–1655+
Unnamed site	Oswego River at Phoenix	mid-seventeenth century
Unnamed site	Oneida River near Caughdenoy	mid-seventeenth century

The apparent increase in the number of small sites, compared with similar protohistoric sites, is primarily a matter of better recording. Several of these fishing camps, for example, were noted by Jesuits as they traveled back and forth between Quebec and Onontaque.

One noticeable change in the distribution of these sites does occur. In contrast to comparable Late Woodland and protohistoric sites, historic period fishing sites spread much farther north onto the Great Lakes Plain (Map 9). This is good evidence for Onondaga expansion into what had previously been a buffer zone used both by them and the St. Lawrence Iroquois. By the mid-seventeenth century, however, with the St. Lawrence Iroquois either gone or assimilated, the land as far north as the mouth of the Salmon River was Onondaga territory (Thwaites 1896–1901, 42:71–73).

Significant changes in settlement pattern usually signal changes in population. While it is difficult to assess the size and composition of Onondaga population during the first half of the seventeenth century, it does appear that two major changes took place. One was population loss, a result of both European-introduced diseases and the escalating scale of intertribal warfare. The extent to which the Onondaga were affected by disease is unclear. Van den Bogart observed that many of the Mohawk villages were seriously afflicted with smallpox (Jameson 1909:141, 156). At about the same time, the Huron were devastated by a series of epidemics (Trigger 1976, 2:501, 526–34). While it is likely that the Onondaga also lost population as a result of the increased exposure to European diseases, there is currently no evidence that any major epidemic took place.

The increased level in intertribal hostilities was also a significant cause of population loss. While documentary accounts are not available for the earlier conflicts, Dablon's account of the Onondaga-Erie war in 1655 makes it clear that the victors suffered nearly as severely as the vanquished (Thwaites 1896–1901, 42:177–83). A year later, another Jesuit observed of the Iroquois: "These victories cause almost as much loss to them as to their enemies and they had depopulated their villages to such an extent, that they now contain more foreigners than natives . . . Onnontaghe counts seven different nations, who have come to settle in it" (ibid., 43:265).

Le Jeune's comment illustrates both the problem and how it was solved. As population was lost, it was replaced through assimilation and adoption. While not new practices, both now occurred on an unprecedented scale. As a result, in spite of massive losses, Onondaga population (and site size) appears to have remained stable during the first half of the seventeenth century, and perhaps even grown. There was a price of course. By 1660, the definition of what, or who, was Onondaga had changed considerably. Within its boundaries were St. Lawrence Iroquois, Algonquians, Susquehannocks, Ontario Iroquois, Erie, and probably others (ibid., 45:207). What is certain is that by the mid-seventeenth century, Onondaga material culture, like its population, had become vastly more heterogeneous.

In contrast to the fluctuations in settlement pattern and population, the basic strategies for subsistence do not appear to have changed significantly during the early historic period. The Onondaga continued to support themselves through a mixed economy in which horticulture, fishing, hunting, and gathering all played a prominent part. In general, little archaeological evidence on subsistence patterns has been collected, and only one faunal sample, from the Pompey Center site, has been studied. White-tailed deer continued to be the preferred game, comprising 84 percent of the sample. Other species included black bear, 5 percent, and smaller percentages of beaver, elk, small mammals, and a variety of upland game birds and waterfowl. Fish remains and freshwater mussel shells were also present.

While the archaeological evidence is slight, the documentary record offers a different and often detailed view of Onondaga subsistence. The journals of van den Bogart, LeMoine, and the other Jesuits contain numerous references not only to what the Onondaga ate but also to how different foods were collected, stored, and prepared. The documents also provide a more balanced assessment of how important particular activities were. The archaeological data, for example, suggest an overwhelming reliance on the hunting of large mammals; the documents, on the other hand, underscore the importance of fishing. Virtually all the accounts mention fishing. While species cannot always be identified with precision, it is clear that a wide range of both freshwater and anadromous fish were exploited and that, through the use of a variety of techniques, fishing took place on nearly a year-round basis (Thwaites 1896–1901, 42:71–73).

There seems to be no question that the Onondaga population could adequately support itself on the diverse resources available. Even the French were impressed with the bounty of the countryside and cited it as one of the reasons for locating their settlement among the Onondaga: "Hunting and fishing render this position an important one; for, besides the fish caught there at different seasons, eels are so abundant in the Summer that a man can harpoon as many as a thousand in one night; and, as for game . . . [it] is always abundant" (ibid.:97).

In spite of this plenitude and the strength of traditional Onondaga subsistence practices, it is likely that European foods and foodways were beginning to affect the Onondaga by the mid-seventeenth century. Liquor and other consumables were increasingly a part of the fur trade. More important, by 1656 the Onondaga could watch the French firsthand as they grew Old World grains, legumes, and herbs, as well as raised pigs and chickens.[10] The immediate impact of such activities on the Onondaga is, of course, hard to gauge. However, it is likely that the exposure to European practices, such as small lot gardening and the keeping of domestic animals, could not but help lay the groundwork for eventual adoption of these activities by the Onondaga.

Material Culture: Native Materials

Two factors were of primary importance in shaping the changes in material aspects of Onondaga culture during the first half of the seventeenth century. One was the increasingly heterogeneous character of the Onondaga population as the remnants and refugees from several other native traditions were assimilated. Just as the St. Lawrence Iroquois from Jefferson County left their mark on Onondaga material culture during the last half of the sixteenth century, so too the Huron, Neutral, Erie, and other people absorbed by the Onondaga during the first six decades of the seventeenth century brought the material characteristics of their cultures with them. The second factor was the radically increased exposure to European materials and technologies. Traditional Onondaga craft skills and material preferences were modified under the influence of European materials which became more familiar and available.

Nowhere is the evidence of change greater than in ceramics. In previous chapters the Onondaga pottery tradition, its changing profile forms and decoration preferences, has dominated the sections on native material culture. During the first half of the seventeenth century, however, that ceramic tradition all but vanishes (Table 12). Sample problems, especially for sites like Carley and Lot 18, undoubtedly make this disappearance seem more abrupt than it really was, since pottery continued to be made and used on Onondaga sites until the last decades of the century. Nonetheless, the virtual dismantling within a few decades of such a longstanding and important tradition is evidence of profound change. In this instance, the change seems to have been a straightforward, functional replacement— a lighter, less fragile form (a copper or brass kettle) taking the place of a heavier, more cumbersome one.

The pottery from early historic Onondaga sites is, in form and decoration, very similar to that from the late protohistoric sites. Despite pottery's rapid demise, the ceramic changes that occur during the first half of the seventeenth century are incremental rather than abrupt or dramatic ones. Both collared and collarless pots were used and appear at about the same ratio as on earlier sites. While overall vessel shape does not change, size does, with the tendency toward smaller pots. The preferred collar

Table 12

Ceramic Attributes from Early Historic Onondaga Sites

Site	Total Rims	Collarless (%)	Chance Round (%)	Chance Straight (%)	Biconcave (%)	Concave (%)	Frilled (%)	High (%)	Medium (%)	Low (%)
			Rim Profile					Collar Height		
Pompey Center	252	21.8	7.1	3.2	15.1	38.1	14.7	33.3	38.1	28.6
Pratt's Falls	—	—	—	—	—	—	—		—	—
Shurtleff	12	8.3	16.6	0	16.6	33.3	25.0	0	16.7	83.3
Carley	2	0	0	0	50.0	50.0	0	0	50.0	50.0
Lot 18	0	0	0	0	0	0	0	0	0	0

0 means trait not present.
— means specific data not available.
Sources: See note 6.

profiles also continue to shift away from the older Chance and Garoga forms toward the newer concave and frilled ones.

There is also a basic continuity in the style of ceramic decoration. Small effigies, both applied and incised, continue to be placed beneath castellations, and incised patterns of opposed triangles or oblique lines remain the most frequently used collar motifs. A wide variety of other motifs and styles are also used, often in exotic ways (see Plate 2f for an example from the Pompey Center site). This is hardly surprising given the extent of miscegenation in the Onondaga population. The overall impression is not so much one of diversity as it is of a ceramic tradition that has become increasingly diluted and eclectic.[11]

It would, however, be incorrect to assume that because pottery disappears the entire Onondaga ceramic tradition died with it. To the contrary, the pattern of occurrence for clay pipes is one of increase rather than decline. While pipes themselves do seem to pass into eclipse during the late protohistoric period, they come back strongly during the first half of the seventeenth century.

Two things are notable about this resurgence. First, all the major, traditional Onondaga pipe forms—trumpet, coronet, bulbous, and effigy—reappear despite a hiatus of several decades. Second, there appears to have been no serious loss of quality in the interim. True, many of the pipes from the Pompey Center site have a crude, somewhat experimental character, but it was not long before pipe making regained its previous competence. By the second quarter of the seventeenth century, Onondaga pipes were again made with as much technical skill and artistic sophistication as were their pre-contact and protohistoric predecessors.

The revival of clay pipe making provides material evidence for two dynamics characterizing the Onondaga during the seventeenth century. Like pottery, pipes can be sensitive indicators of specific cultural traditions. While caution is necessary since many styles were pan-Iroquoian, pipes do help document the increasingly heterogeneous nature of Onondaga culture. The pipes from the Carley site are a case in point. The seven specimens are complete enough for identification. These include one owl effigy, one open mouth effigy, two coiled snake effigies, one coronet, and two pipes described by Tuck as "rimless trumpets" (1971:177). With the exception of the two coiled snake effigies, these pipes are illustrated in Figure 10. Of the seven pipes, three are traditional Onondaga styles: both the owl and the open mouth effigies, and the coronet. On the other hand, the two undecorated snake effigies are unusual for Onondaga and are more typical of the contemporary Ontario Iroquois, particularly Neutral (Mathews 1981b:40–41). The same is true of the two rimless trumpets, both of which fit more easily into an Ontario Iroquois tradition than into the Onondaga one.[12] One additional pipe from the Lot 18 site (Figure 10a) also deserves mention. This unusual style, termed a "pinch-face" effigy, is characteristic of the late Ontario Iroquois and occurs on both Huron and Neutral sites (Mathews 1976:15–16). The occurrence of these Ontario Iroquois styles at the Carley and Lot 18 sites correlates well with mid-seventeenth century documentary references to both Huron and Neutral refugees in Onondaga (Thwaites 1896–1901, 41:95–97, 193, 219; 42:56).

Pipes are also a material expression of another dynamic: a general tendency toward greater elaboration, more embellishment in the material aspects of Onondaga culture. This trend was characterized by an increased concern for detail, much of it symbolically charged, and is evident in most of the surviving crafts which used native materials—clay, lithics, antler/bone, wood, and shell. This tendency can be seen both in the care with which pipes were made and decorated, and in the growing incidence of effigy forms. Effigy pipes, often elaborate, become increasingly common throughout the period. In addition, an ever wider range of zoomorphic and anthropomorphic forms are employed. Considerable discussion has centered on what these effigies represent, and attempts have been made to link particular forms to masks, clan totems or eponyms, and even specific League sachemships (Mathews 1978; Noble 1979).

It is likely, however, that this increased use of effigy pipes is a material reflection of a deep and fundamental aspect of Onondaga culture. However ethnocentric the observations of Dablon and the other Jesuits, it is clear that the Onondaga, like the Huron, were preoccupied with maintaining good and correct relations with the spirit world and all its (super)natural forces (Thwaites 1896–1901, 17:161). This meant avoiding offensive behavior and rigorously heeding whatever demands were made, usually through the medium of dreams. From an Onondaga perspective, compliance with such requests through prescribed ceremonies and rituals was prerequisite to health, abundance, and success in hunting or war (ibid., 42:135, 139, 147–69).

The smoking of tobacco, and pipes themselves, were strongly connected to these beliefs. Not only did pipe smoking promote "good thoughts," but as the smoke rose into the sky it became another medium by which one could communicate with spirit beings (Coyne 1903:25; Hewitt 1928:537, 544; Mathews 1978:158–63). Calvin Martin has argued that during the period following European contact, native Americans lost faith in the traditional avenues and rituals of spiritual redress (1978:148). The increased use of effigy pipes, however, may represent just the opposite—a more intense effort to placate spirit beings, the "keepers of the game," and appease their anger so that disease, disorder, and death might no longer be sent as punishment.

After centuries of continuity, dramatic changes occurred in the Onondagas' use of lithics. The use of both flaked and ground implements dropped

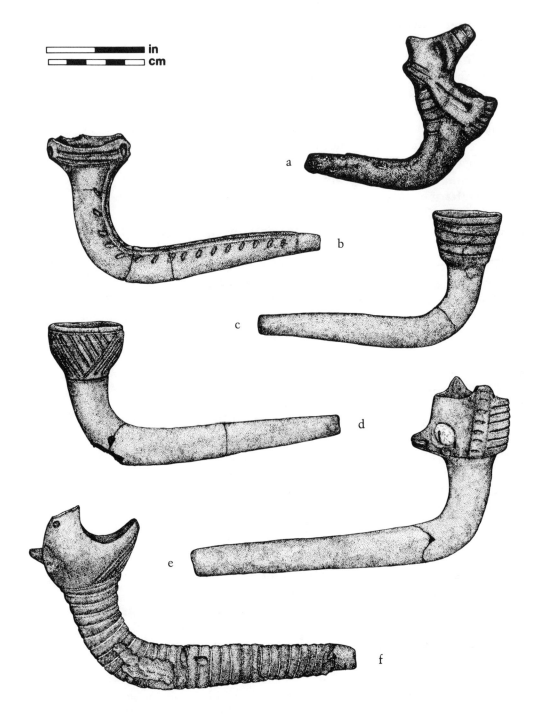

Figure 10. Historic Onondaga Pipes. a. a "pinch-face" effigy pipe, Lot 18 site (RMSC 11119/250); b. a coronet trumpet, Carley site (RMSC 10025/217); c. and d. two rimless trumpet pipes, Carley site (RMSC 10028/217), (RMSC 10027/217); e. an owl effigy with applied copper eyes, Carley site (RMSC 10026/217); f. an open mouth effigy, Carley site (RMSC 10024/217).

off rapidly as the use of metal increased. By mid-century, the occurrence of triangular projectile points and other flaked tools shrinks to vestigial proportions (Table 13). Here, as with pottery, the remaining examples reflect an eclectic diversity in both shape and material. This suggests that the breakdown of the Onondaga lithic tradition may have occurred as much through dilution as it did through replacement. The demise of ground stone tools is especially dramatic; large woodworking tools such as celts and adzes disappear entirely, replaced with metal equivalents. Only abrading stones and food-processing tools such as mullers and mortars appear to be used throughout the period.

There is an important exception to this diminished use of lithics for utilitarian purposes: native-made gunflints (Figure 11c and d). These small, bifacial objects begin to occur on Onondaga sites during the third decade of the seventeenth century and closely parallel the examples described by Kent (1983). While the frequency of lithic projectile points drops sharply during the first half of the seventeenth century, the occurrence of native-made gunflints rises proportionally (Table 13). This illustrates an important point. The decreasing occurrence of lithic points represents more than just a simple process of replacing chert points with metal ones. A conscious shift in what forms would be made also took place. Instead of dying, lithic technology was adapted to meet changing circumstances and new needs. Early in 1635, van den Bogart noted in his journal that the natives had shown him stones with which they made fire. These, he thought,

Table 13

Occurrence of Lithic Implements on Early Historic Onondaga Sites

| Site | Unifacial | Bifacial | | | | | Gunflints | |
	Scrapers	Perforators	Scrapers	Knives Lanceolate and Ovate	Projectile Points Number	Length-to-Width Ratio	Number	Ratio to Projectile Points
Pompey Center	7	1	8	3	100*	1.30:1	0	0:1
Pratt's Falls	—	—	—	present	present	—	—	—
Shurtleff	0	0	2	1	20	1.41:1	2	0.1:1
Carley	0	1	2	0	13	1.59:1	22	1.8:1
Lot 18	1	0	3	1	12	1.83:1	66	5.5:1

* Sample approximately 1200 points seen from site.
0 means trait not present.
— means specific data not available.
Sources: See note 6.

"would do very well for flintlock guns" (Jameson 1909:153). The Onondaga, it seems, had also come to that conclusion.

In contrast to the waning of lithic tools, the making of ornamental/ritual objects from stone slowly accelerated during the first half of the seventeenth century. Here, as with ceramic pipes, the emphasis was on more elaborate and detailed forms. The simple beads and pendants of the protohistoric period give way to more complex and symbolically charged forms such as pipes and effigies (Figure 11). Undoubtedly, the availability of metal tools was a significant factor in the increasingly sophisticated quality of Onondaga stoneworking. Both locally available and exotic materials, especially soapstone and marble, were used. Continuities in form, plus the evidence of partially completed and repaired pieces, argue strongly that most of this sophisticated stonework was done in Onondaga, and not imported.

The patterns for bone and antler artifacts parallel those of lithics quite closely. Utilitarian objects—bone awls and needles, harpoons and other fishing gear—all but vanish by mid-century. While this is dramatic, it represents less change than would appear. As with triangular projectile points, the shift was in material preference, not form or function. The same holds true with many other utensils. Most of the traditional tool kit continued to be made and used; the difference was that the pieces were increasingly fashioned from iron or brass instead of bone or antler. We will discuss this shift further in the section on European materials.

As with lithics, the non-utilitarian use of bone and antler not only continued but steadily grew in sophistication. Simple ornaments, such as the perforated teeth of bear, elk, and wolves, continue to be used throughout the period. Turtle-shell rattles also have been documented both archaeologically and in ethnohistorical accounts (Thwaites 1896–1901, 42:149). Once again the emphasis was on more complex and elaborate forms, particularly effigy figures and combs.[13] Combs illustrate the changing nature of Onondaga craft skills especially well. Not only were the historic period styles vastly more embellished than prehistoric and protohistoric examples, the technical mastery of the medium was significantly greater. Compare the two examples in Figure 12. Much of this changing sophistication in combs seems to occur during the first half of the seventeenth century. Metal tools again help explain the increased technical facility. The motivation for making combs more detailed and elaborate, however, seems to be similar to that which led to the production of effigy pipes.

While the Onondaga undoubtedly made extensive use of wood prior to European contact, little archaeological evidence survives. This changes on sites of the early seventeenth century. Because of fortuitous preservation conditions, usually due to an association with copper, wooden objects are more frequently a part of the archaeological record. In general, the pattern

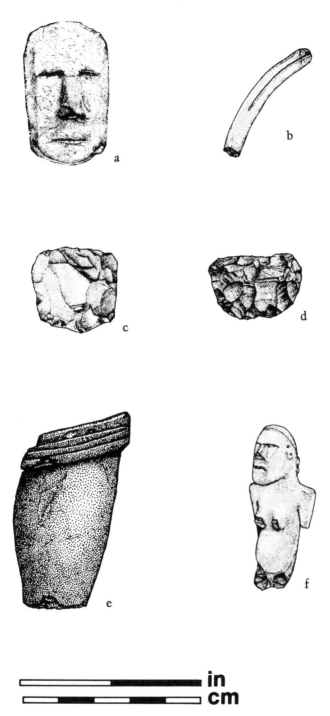

Figure 11. Historic Onondaga Stonework. a. a face effigy pipe bowl, limestone, Pompey Center site (RMSC 10004/218); b. a small snake effigy,
limestone, Pompey Center site; c. and d. two native-made gunflints, Onondaga chert, Carley site; e. a partial coronet trumpet pipe bowl, serpentine marble, Carley site; f. an effigy figure, limestone, Carley site (RMSC
6456/177).

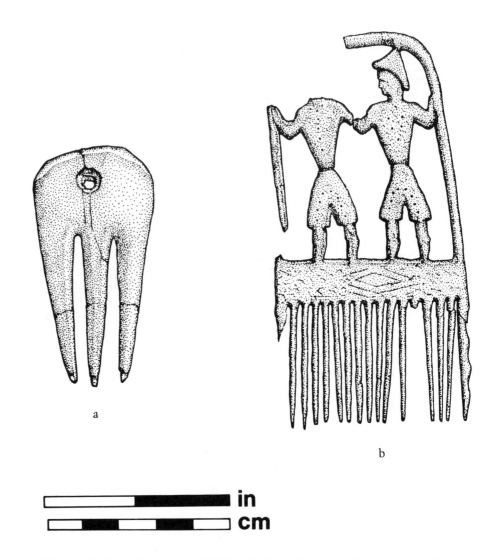

a

b

in
cm

Figure 12. Protohistoric and Historic Onondaga Combs. a. a protohistoric period comb, Atwell site (RMSC AR19289); b. an historic period comb, Jamesville (Pen) site (RMSC 11553/237).

of use is similar to that described for bone and antler. This includes a growing tendency to embellish utilitarian objects such as bowls and ladles, and an increased emphasis on pipes, effigies, and other more complex forms. In nearly all cases, the craftsmanship reflects growing skill and competence. These patterns are discussed in greater detail by Hamell (1978) and Prisch (1982).

While the rising flood of European materials may have diminished the visibility of traditional exotic ones—marine shell and non-local lithics—it did not decrease their value or desirability. Shell in particular remained much in demand. The quantity of shell artifacts, especially beads, rises steadily on early seventeenth-century Onondaga sites. There are, however, distinct changes in form and preference. The small discoidal beads characterizing protohistoric assemblages continue to predominate for a time at the Pompey Center site, then drop off rapidly. In contrast, the occurrence of small tubular shell beads, a minority form on protohistoric sites, increases dramatically on historic period sites like Carley and Lot 18.[14] This increase is accompanied by a change in bead production. Instead of having tapered perforations, as they did during the prehistoric and protohistoric, these beads were now made with a straight hole drilled from either end, apparently with a metal drill. This shift in how beads were made appears to reflect growing Dutch efforts to control and manipulate the production and use of wampum for their own commercial purposes (Ceci 1977:191–283).

A second change is also evident. Not only do shell objects become more common, the range of forms in which shell occurs expands significantly during the second quarter of the seventeenth century. In addition to wampum, shell also occurs as large discoidal beads (10–12mm in diameter), long tubular beads (often up to 80mm), and massive beads, frequently acentric in shape made from *Busycon* columella. *Marginella* beads again appear during this period after an absence of several decades. In addition to a more diverse range of beads, shell crescents, runtees, and effigies also become more common. The effigies are usually zoomorphic in shape and seem to be prototypes for the highly stylized, and probably mass-produced, forms that become common during the last half of the seventeenth century.[15] While many of these shell objects appear to have been brought to Onondaga in finished form, not all of them were produced elsewhere. The occurrence of whole *Busycon* shells, as well as partially worked pieces of whorl and columella, indicate that marine shell continued to be worked by Onondaga craftsmen throughout the period.

The other traditional category of exotic materials is non-local lithics. Here again the shifting preferences and patterns of use illustrate the changing nature of Onondaga interests. For example, at Pompey Center, an early seventeenth-century site, exotics were less than 1 percent of the total lithic assemblage (n = 1200). As argued in chapter 3, the grey chalcedony and white quartz projectile points that occur are but one of the material indicators of an Onondaga-Susquenhannock relationship. At the mid-seventeenth century Lot 18 site, however, the pattern is different in two ways. Exotics now account for more than 15 percent of the lithic assemblage (n = 92), and both the range of material and the uses to which these have been put have broadened considerably. Nearly 10 percent of the native-made gunflints and other flaked implements are made from non-local materials including Pennsylvania jasper, Ohio (Flint Ridge) chalcedony, white quartz, and several other cherts. Two-thirds of the ornamental/ritual objects are made from exotics such as catlinite, serpentine marble, and several varieties of soapstone. Not only are exotic lithics more frequent, they tend to reflect source areas to the north and west of Iroquoia rather than to the south. The occurrence of these exotic lithics provides one more means for tracking the shifting interests of the Onondaga away from the Susquehannocks and toward the Ontario Iroquois and Erie.

Material Culture: European Materials

During the first half of the seventeenth century, the volume of European material reaching Onondaga grew at a phenomenal rate. On early seventeenth-century sites like Pompey Center, these materials comprise in the range of 10 to 15 percent of the total artifact assemblage; on mid-century sites like Lot 18, they comprise 75 percent or more. This section examines two aspects of the increasing flood of copper, brass, iron, glass, and other objects into Onondaga.

The first is the range of forms and materials used by Europeans for trade. What were the most commonly occurring forms? To what extent did these preferred forms change during the period? Where were these materials produced in Europe? How different was the trading merchandise of the rival French and Dutch groups? Definitive answers are not possible for all of these questions. Therefore we will attend primarily to those artifact classes that serve as either chronological or cultural markers.

The second aspect is the Onondaga response to these strange and often unfamiliar objects. Here the emphasis is on two interrelated dynamics: How did the Onondaga use (or re-use) European goods in order to fit their own traditional needs? And at the same time, to what extent did the Onondaga shift their own cultural preferences in order to accommodate European ways? While these acculturative dynamics are discussed further in chapter 6, the material culture patterns that underlie them are examined here.

During the first half of the seventeenth century, objects of copper and various copper alloys continued to be of primary importance in European-native trade. In part this was due to copper's versatility. It was a medium with which native craftsmen were familiar and which could be adapted to a wide range of purposes. Copper's desirability also was a function of

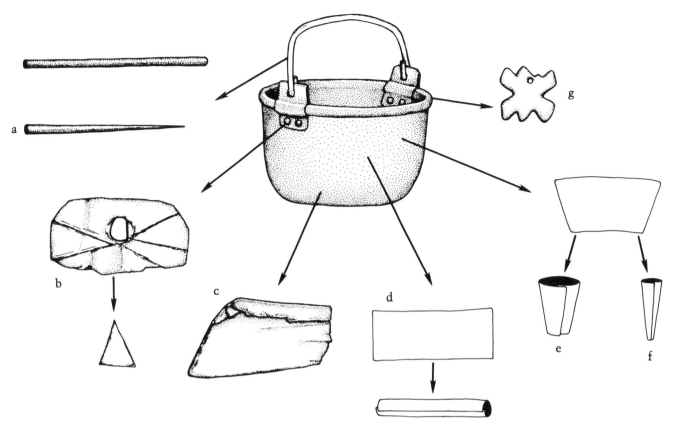

Figure 13. The Recycling of a Copper Kettle. a. iron handle removed and ground into an awl; b. heavier gauge metal from lug scored and cut into triangular projectile points; sheet metal from the body of the kettle converted into: c. a knife blade, d. a tubular bead, e. and f. a conical bangle or pipe bowl liner, g. a pendant.

its symbolic/power overtones. Traditionally endowed with power-related properties, its high cultural value was passed on to the new forms of copper that came from Europeans. While this quality appears to have gradually eroded during the early seventeenth century, copper articles remained in demand in part for this reason.

Of the many forms in which copper was available, kettles were by far the most important. While it remains unclear where they were produced (see Appendix B), they were a mainstay of both Dutch and French trading stocks throughout the period. Regardless of where they came from, kettles became a common occurrence on Onondaga sites during the first decades of the century.

The evidence for kettles on sites like Pompey Center is based, literally, on scraps. Complete kettles are a rare occurrence prior to mid-century. It also appears that the Onondaga were slow to use kettles for the purposes which Europeans intended—cooking. Few if any of the fragments from Pompey Center show signs of burning or charring. Instead, a high percentage show evidence of deliberate dismemberment through scoring and cutting or other means. This indicates that for the first several decades of the seventeenth century, kettles were valued by the Onondaga primarily as a source of usable metal, not as a functional replacement for ceramic vessels (the range of uses to which a kettle could be put are illustrated in Figure 13). This also argues against the rather ethnocentric notion that natives used kettles for cooking until they burned out, and only then salvaged the remnants for other purposes. By the second quarter of the century, however, the direct and immediate recycling of kettles began to wane. The percentage of scrap showing evidence of utilization drops steadily (Table 14), and more of the non-utilized scrap shows signs of having been burned or is encrusted with charred residue. This, plus the concurrent disappearance of native ceramics, suggests that by mid-century, kettles were being widely used for food preparation.

The technology for reworking copper remained fairly simple during the first half of the seventeenth century. Sheet metal was reduced to the desired size by either scoring and folding or by cutting. The increased availability of iron knives and, by the second quarter of the century, scissors, made this a fairly easy process. Once cut out, objects were shaped further by use of the traditional cold working, annealing, and abrasion

Table 14

*Patterns in the Reuse of European Copper and Brass on
Early Historic Onondaga Sites*

Site	Total Copper/Brass Artifacts	Finished Objects		Partially Completed Objects and Utilized Scrap		Nonutilized Scrap	
		No.	%	No.	%	No.	%
Chase	20	12	60.0	7	35.0	1	5.0
Pompey Center	271	58	21.4	198	73.0	15	5.6
Pratt's Falls	—	—	—	—	—	—	—
Shurtleff	176	36	20.4	104	59.1	36	20.5
Carley*	79	34	43.0	30	38.0	15	19.0
Lot 18	125	30	24.0	39	31.2	56	44.8

* Sample includes some material from burial contexts.
— means specific data not available.
Sources: See note 6.

methods described from the protohistoric period. While the Onondaga did not master European techniques such as brazing until much later, there is evidence of native experimentation with joining pieces of copper through the use of rolled "laces" and possibly simple rivets.

It is important not to underestimate the significance of this copper working just because it was technologically simple. In terms of the extent to which it was practiced and the range of objects produced, this craft activity had a major impact on Onondaga culture. It is worth reiterating that nearly 95 percent of all the copper and brass from the Pompey Center site shows some evidence of utilization. Even though this drops off considerably by the middle of the seventeenth century, the rate of use at the Lot 18 site is still well over 50 percent.

Initially, the products of this craft specialty followed protohistoric patterns and emphasized ornamental/ritual forms. These included tubular beads, disc-shaped (and occasionally zoomorphic) pendants, and a few lingering spirals and hoops (Table 15). Other newer forms, such as rings and bracelets, were also made. Another form that became popular, particularly during the last half of the century, was the conical "bangle" or "tinkling cone." These have traditionally been identified as clothing ornaments, designed to enhance the wearer by their sound as well as their appearance (Beauchamp 1903:19). While copper cones were certainly made on early seventeenth-century sites such as Pompey Center, how they were used remains unclear.

Another important category of copper objects was associated with tobacco smoking. These included pipes made completely from metal, usu-

Table 15
Native-made Copper Artifacts (Ornamental and Ritual) from Early Historic Onondaga Sites

Site	Tubular Beads	Pendants	Spirals/ Hoops	Rings	Bracelets	Bangles	Pipe Liners	Total
Pompey Center	13	10	3	2	0	7	0	35
Pratt's Falls	—	—	—	—	—	—	—	0
Shurtleff	3	1	—	1	2	2	0	9
Carley	1	1	1	2	0	0	1	6
Lot 18	6	2	0	1	1	1	1	12
Total	23	14	4	6	3	10	2	62

0 means trait not present.
— means specific data not available.
Sources: See note 6.

ally a piece of sheet rolled and shaped into a trumpet form,[16] as well as conical inserts used to line the bowls of wooden pipes. Some of these copper liners had flanges or other means for attachment. Most, however, were simple cones and are indistinguishable from the large bangles that also occur on early seventeenth-century sites. In addition to pipes and liners, copper also embellished the pipes made from the traditional mediums of wood, clay, and stone. The owl effigy pipe from the Carley site shown in Figure 10e serves as an example. Here, small pieces of copper have been applied to the effigy. While the resulting copper eyes may have made the pipe more attractive, it is likely that the intent was to increase the pipe's efficacy by adding a power-enhancing substance to it. Other examples of copper inlays or elaboration on pipes are discussed by Hamell (1978).

Whatever the preferred forms, the Onondaga continued to use copper for ornamental/ritual purposes throughout the first half of the seventeenth century. By mid-century, the reuse of kettles waned as greater quantities of finished European items—bells, finger rings, and religious ornaments—became available. Even so, the making of ornamental/ritual objects from copper sheet and wire remained a discernable craft activity among the Onondaga until the end of the century.

The sheet metal from copper and brass kettles was converted not only into ornamental/ritual objects but also into a variety of utilitarian forms. On early historic sites such as Pompey Center, the use of copper implements follows the protohistoric pattern emphasizing both unformalized and formalized blades (Table 16). With the increasing availability of iron knives, however, the use of copper for blades drops off quickly on subsequent seventeenth-century sites. The most widespread utilitarian use for sheet copper was as projectile points. Early in the century there seems to have been little uniformity and perhaps some experimentation, with shapes. Stemmed, barbed, and even pentagonal-shaped points were made along with triangular ones. By the second quarter of the seventeenth century, however, copper points were almost exclusively made in an isosceles triangular form and remained that way for the rest of the century. The exceptions were rolled, conical points, a minor style throughout the century. As with the shift from lithic to iron celts, the change from chert to copper projectile points was more one of material preference than of form or function.

Other traditional tool forms were also replicated in copper, although they occur far less frequently than metal projectile points. A flat, centrally perforated needle from the Carley site represents the continuation of an implement used by the Onondaga or their antecedents since at least Owasco times. These native-made copper needles continue to be a part of the Onondaga tool kit well into the eighteenth century (Hinsdale 1927). An-

Table 16

Copper Implements from Early Historic Onondaga Sites

Site	Blades		Projectile Points		Saws	Other	Total
	Unformalized	Formalized	Triangular	Conical			
Pompey Center	3	5	7	7	0	0	22
Pratt's Falls	—	—	—	—	—	—	0
Shurtleff	0	1	19	7	0	0	27
Carley	0	0	23	3	1	1	28
Lot 18	0	1	10	4	1	3	19
Total	3	7	59	21	2	4	96

0 means trait not present.
— means specific data not available.
Sources: See note 6.

other implement form that begins to occur in copper can best be described as a saw. At its simplest, this was a piece of sheet metal with crude teeth cut into one side (a more elaborate example, made from a straightened trigger guard, is illustrated in Plate 9). These small saws become increasingly common during the last half of the seventeenth century, and their occurrence correlates closely with the growing popularity of antler combs. Here again there may be some precedent in native material culture for this implement form. Small, serrated chert blades and unifacial "scrapers" occur on many of the Onondaga sites through the early seventeenth century. While it is unclear how these lithic implements were used, it is plausible that the copper saws from seventeenth-century sites are their functional descendants if not equivalents.[17]

One of the key factors to differentiate historic period sites from protohistoric ones is the prevalence of intact European objects rather than reused fragments. During the second quarter of the seventeenth century, several new categories of copper articles begin to occur along with kettles (Table 17). For the most part, these were small, simple items—bells, thimbles, buttons, mouth harps, religious ornaments—probably used for personal adornment. Many of these objects can also be traced to Dutch sources. For example, the small sheet metal bells found on Onondaga sites are virtually identical to those found on contemporary Dutch colonial sites.[18] Both thimbles and cast brass buttons can also be correlated with Dutch examples.[19] The Onondaga apparently used these items as clothing ornaments. Thimbles were usually perforated through the top and utilized like the native-made bangles or tinkling cones; buttons were either sewn

Table 17

Selected European Copper and Brass Artifacts from
Early Historic Onondaga Sites

| Site | Bells | Thimbles | Buttons | Mouth Harps | Religious Ornaments | | | Total |
					Medals	Crucifixes	Rings	
Pompey Center	1	0	0	0	0	0	0	1
Pratt's Falls	—	—	—	—	—	—	—	—
Shurtleff	3	0	0	0	1	0	0	4
Carley	5	3	0	1	1	0	0	10
Lot 18	9	3	2	2	1	1	12	30
Total	18	6	2	3	3	1	12	45

0 means trait not present.
— means specific data not available.
Sources: See note 6.

onto garments or strung along with beads. Small brass-framed mouth harps are another good marker of Dutch trading activity. Identical examples, stamped *R* on the frame, have been found not only on Onondaga and Dutch colonial sites, but in Amsterdam as well (Figure 14c). Jan Baart, Amsterdam's city archaeologist, feels that these were a specialty product and probably made by one individual.[20]

If many of the small copper and brass objects on Onondaga sites from the second quarter of the seventeenth century appear to have been of Dutch origin, one group clearly was not. These were Catholic religious ornaments—medals, crucifixes, and finger rings. On Onondaga sites these are markers of a French presence. The first occurrence, a well struck medal with Christ on the obverse and a crowned Mary on the reverse (Figure 15a), is from the Shurtleff site. It is likely that the Onondaga who visited van den Bogart in 1634 came from this site. As that delegation pointed out, by the 1630s Frenchmen were coming directly into Onondaga to trade. A similar medal from the Carley site (Figure 15b) suggests a continuation of this pattern. On the Lot 18 site, however, there is a drastic change in both the quantity and kind of religious ornaments. As Jesuit missionaries began to travel into the interior of North America during the 1630s, they quickly learned the value of carrying small objects such as knives, awls, and rings with them in order to barter for necessities or win favors (Thwaites 1896–1901, 12:117–21, 15:157, 18:19). The Jesuits also found that distributing religious ornaments was a successful strategy for raising native interest in Christianity (ibid., 53:251). The dramatic increase in religious ornaments, many of which bear Jesuit-related motifs, suggests

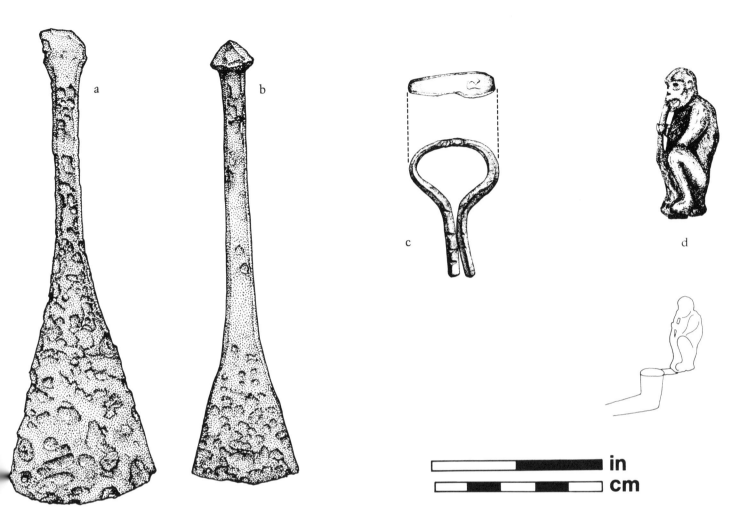

Figure 14. European Items Made for Trade. a. and b. two iron scrapers, Shurtleff site (RMSC 11222/244 and 11223/244); c. two views of a brass mouth harp marked R, Carley site; d. a pewter monkey playing or smoking a pipe, from a pewter pipe, Lot 18 site (RMSC 11159/245).

that the Lot 18 site was the town visted by LeMoine in 1654, and possibly still occupied when Chaumont and Dablon established the mission of St. Jean Baptiste a year later. In addition to twelve religious rings,[21] a small crucifix and a religious medal also have been recovered from the site. The medal, whose chain loop had worn through, bears an image especially appropriate for Frenchmen on the edge of the frontier—St. Christopher, the patron saint of travelers (Figure 15d).

After 1630, a scattering of other copper and brass articles begins to appear on Onondaga sites. Initially this includes a diverse range of objects—

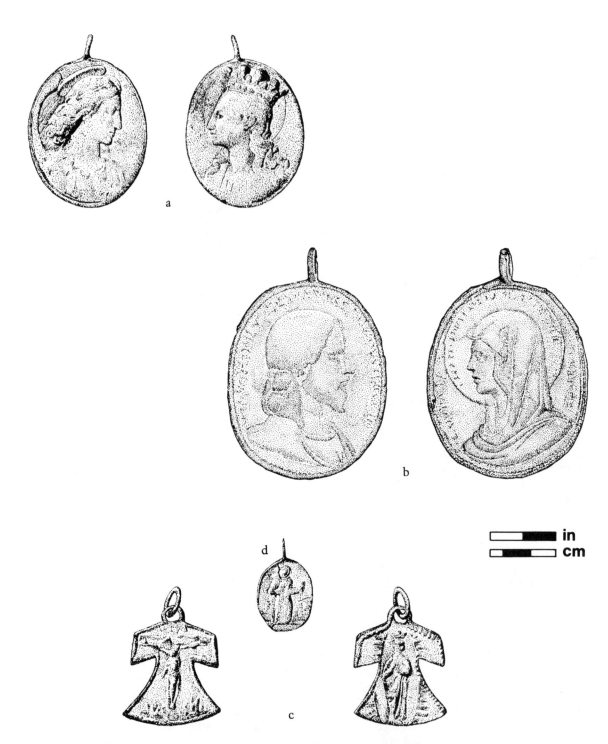

in

cm

Figure 15. Religious Ornaments from Early Historic Onondaga Sites. a. obverse and reverse of a religious medal, Shurtleff site; b. obverse and reverse of a religious medal, Carley site (RMSC 10172/217); c. obverse and reverse of a tau-shaped crucifix, Lot 18 site; d. obverse of a St. Christopher medal, Lot 18 site.

clothing fasteners, fittings from firearms, an occasional tobacco box, a latten spoon. By mid-century, the volume and diversity of copper and brass objects has grown to include everything from book hinges and nested weights to cutlery with fancy cast handles and embroidery scissors. In short, after 1650 almost any small copper or brass item made or used in northern Europe, from precision instrument to bric-a-brac, could and often did occur on Iroquois sites.

Nowhere are the material differences between protohistoric and historic period sites more evident than with iron artifacts. On sixteenth-century sites, iron is present only in small quantities and almost always in reused forms. On sites of the early seventeenth century, not only the quantity but the variety of iron artifacts increases dramatically, and while considerable reworking of iron still occurs, the original forms of these European implements are far more discernable. This tide of iron steadily increased during the century. It was composed not only of the stock trade items—axes, knives, awls, and firearms—but also included a wide range of implements, utensils, and hardware. In 1634, while passing through a Mohawk town on his way to Oneida, van den Bogart remarked on the quantity of ironwork he saw. In addition to doors with iron hinges, he observed that the Mohawk had "chains, bolts, harrow teeth, iron hoops, [and] spikes which they steal when they go forth from here."[22] After the abandonment of Ste. Marie de Gannentaha in March of 1658, it is likely that Onondaga was equally if not more cluttered with iron.

As in the preceding paragraphs on copper and brass, the emphasis here is twofold. First, to track the major classes of iron artifacts on Onondaga sites during the first half of the seventeenth century. Once again, our focus is on the most common forms, particularly on those that are temporally or culturally diagnostic. Second, to examine how the Onondaga responded to these objects. To what degree were these articles adapted to fit into Onondaga culture, and to what degree did the Onondaga themselves adapt in order to exploit the new material?

Iron axes, like copper kettles, were a stock item of trade. Almost invariably native people wanted axes, and virtually all Europeans were happy to provide them. In spite of this, it remains difficult to identify reliably either the sources of axe production in Europe or the characteristics that would differentiate a Dutch axe from a French one. These issues, along with terminology, are discussed in greater detail in Appendix B.

While fragments and reused pieces occur on protohistoric sites, complete axes do not occur in Onondaga until the early seventeenth century. This is not the only change. From the Pompey Center site on, axes and axe parts appear dramatically more often than on earlier sites (Table 18). These early seventeenth-century axes are large, averaging around 20cm in length and weighing about 1.5kg, and of simple construction. With only minor variations in shape and size, this style of axe occurs on Onondaga sites throughout the rest of the century. After 1650, a smaller and lighter version of this standard trade axe form, only 16cm long and 0.75kg, also begins to appear.

That the Onondaga wanted iron axes during the first half of the century is beyond question. What they wanted axes for, however, is another matter. Generally it has been assumed that the desirability of axes was due to their functional superiority over traditional lithic tools. This assertion has been supported by quantitative comparison studies (Saraydar and Shimada 1971; Trigger 1976, 1:412). It may be, however, that iron axes were used in a manner very different from that which Europeans expected. As with copper kettles, axes appear to have been more important as the source of a valuable raw material than as useful tools in and of themselves. This issue is discussed in greater detail below.

Iron knives were another standard trading item. To native people they were equally if not more useful than axes. Since they were lighter and more portable, knives quickly became part of the European's trading kit whether he was French or Dutch, cleric or secular. As with axes, complete examples do not occur on Onondaga sites until the early seventeenth century. From the Pompey Center site on, however, they are quite common. Unlike axes, iron knives came in a wide range of forms, defined and discussed in Appendix B.

Table 18

Distribution of Iron Axes and Axe Pieces on Early Historic Onondaga Sites

Site	Number of Complete Usable Axes	Number of Recyclables—Damaged Axes and Pieces					Ratio of Usable Axes to Recyclables
		Total	Damaged Axes	Blades	Bits	Sockets	
Chase	0	1	0	1	0	0	0:1
Dwyer	0	1	1	0	0	0	0:1
Pompey Center	3	24	2	4	9	9	0.13:1
Pratt's Falls*	3	3	1	1	1	0	1:1
Shurtleff	0	16	3	6	2	5	0:1
Carley	5	4	2	0	2	0	1.25:1
Lot 18	7	3	1	0	2	0	2.30:1

* Sample contains material from burial context.
0 means trait not present.
Sources: See note 6.

The distribution of these knife forms on Onondaga sites varies considerably during the first half of the century. (The data are summarized in Table 19). Variety in form thus is particularly useful since certain styles appear to serve as either cultural or temporal markers. For example, knives with a tapered tang tend to correlate with Dutch trading activities.[23] On the other hand, knives with flat tangs and those with folding blades tend to be associated with the French.[24]

A third stock item of trade was the iron awl. Like knives, awls were an implement fitting readily into native culture. Since they were also light and easy to carry, awls were an ideal choice for barter or gift-giving. Van den Bogart used awls in this manner at least eight times during his journey; only knives were mentioned more often (ten times). In contrast, axes were mentioned only twice. The French, too, recognized the practicality of awls. In his instructions for those about to be sent to the Huron mission, the first item that Father Brebeuf recommended each man take was "half a gross of awls" (Thwaites 1896–1901, 12:119).

As with intact axes and knives, iron awls do not appear on Onondaga sites until the early seventeenth century.[25] After their introduction they become a predictable part of Onondaga material culture. During the first half of the century, awls occur in three distinct forms. These are defined and described in Appendix B, and their distribution on Onondaga sites is

Table 19

Distribution of Iron Knives on Early Historic Onondaga Sites

| | Flat Tang | | | | | Tapered Tang | | | | | | |
| | | No Collar | | Thin Collar | Thick Collar | Conical Collar | | | Cylindrical Collar | Thin Collar | | |
Site	No Heel	Round Heel	Straight Heel			Plain	Slight Groove	Elaborate Groove			Folding Blade	Total*
Pompey Center	1	3	3	2	0	1	4	0	0	0	0	14
Pratt's Falls	—	—	—	—	—	—	—	—	—	—	—	—
Shurtleff	0	0	0	2	0	1	1	3	0	2	1	10
Carley	0	0	0	3	1	0	6	5	0	0	1	16
Lot 18	0	0	0	1	0	0	10	5	1	3	2	22
Total	1	3	3	8	1	2	21	13	1	5	4	62

* Does not include untypable blade fragments.
0 means trait not present.
— means specific data not available.
Sources: See note 6.

summarized in Table 20. While it is difficult to match these forms reliably with either Dutch or French trading activities, some tentative attributions can be made.[26]

Last of the four major categories of iron trade goods is weapons, particularly firearms. No other class of trade merchandise, with the possible exception of liquor, caused more contemporary controversy or has generated more ongoing scholarly debate. I suspect, however, that the whole issue has been somewhat overplayed.[27] As with other highly desired European materials—kettles, glass beads—it is likely that guns were valued initially for their "power" (especially their thunder and lightning) rather than for any practical reason.

Firearms do not occur on Onondaga sites until the second quarter of the seventeenth century. While their frequency increased markedly during this period, the overall numbers are not that great. Table 21 summarizes the occurrence of both gun parts and accessories. Even from this modest sample, several conclusions can be drawn. One is that pistols are represented as often as muskets. That pistols may actually have been preferred would not be surprising given the cumbersome size of most longarms. A second and more important point is that these firearms were not obsolete castoffs dumped on the unsuspecting natives. To the contrary, the parts which have been recovered indicate that, with few exceptions, the firearms which the Onondaga received were first-class quality flintlocks.

This conclusion has also been reached by J. P. Puype after examination of the seventeenth-century locks in the collections of the Rochester Museum and Science Center (1985). Although a scattering of snaphaunce,

Table 20

Distribution of Iron Awls on Early Historic Onondaga Sites

Site	Type I (diamond shaped/curved)	Type II (square/straight)	Type III (diamond shaped/offset)	Total
Pompey Center	5	4	0	9
Pratt's Falls	—	—	—	—
Shurtleff	0	1	2	3
Carley	0	6	0	6
Lot 18	0	10	4	14
Total	5	21	6	32

0 means trait not present.
— means specific data not available.
Sources: See note 6.

Table 21

Distribution of Firearms and Accessories on Early Historic Onondaga Sites

Site	Total Number of Gun Parts	Locks and Lock Parts	Barrel Pieces	Fittings/ Furniture	European Gunflints	Bullet Molds	Bar Lead	Number of Bullets
Shurtleff	5	Lockplate (1) Vertical sear (1)	2	Sheet brass buttplate (1)	1	0	2	4
Carley*	11	Complete lock (1) Snaphaunce cock (1) Pistol cock (1) Trigger (1) Lock plate screw (1)	1	Sheet brass buttplate (2) Cast brass pistol buttcap (1) Iron trigger guard (1) Brass ramrod pipe (1)	1	2	2	31
Lot 18	53	Musket cock (2) Pistol cock (2) Battery (5) Top jaw (4) Pan (6) Spring (6) Trigger (3) Sear (1) Tumbler (1) Lock plate screw (6)	7	Sheet brass buttplate (3) Brass trigger guard (5) Iron trigger guard (1) Brass sight (1)	2	1	8	63

* Sample includes some material from burial context.
0 means trait not present.
Sources: See note 6.

English doglock, and wheel lock parts were present, Puype found that the vast majority of locks were flintlocks and probably of Dutch manufacture. Based on his findings, Puype has proposed a typology that traces flintlock development during the seventeenth century. Several of these types appear to have been made specifically for trade and do not occur on either civilian or military weapons in Europe.[28] An example of one of these locks is illustrated in Plate 8. With its vertically acting sear and a fully developed battery, this lock (Puype's type 5A) from the Carley site was technically up-to-date, even by European standards.

While studies by Mayer (1943) and Puype have clarified what kind of ignition systems Iroquoian firearms had, the weapons themselves remain difficult to characterize. Only a few of the firearms which have been recovered are complete enough to permit description. Hamilton has classified most of these together as Type M or N trade guns (1968:21–27). In general, the muskets appear to have had a round barrel, occasionally with an octagonal breech. These barrels were approximately 1.5m in length and between 0.52 and 0.66 caliber. Stocks had either a nailed on, sheet

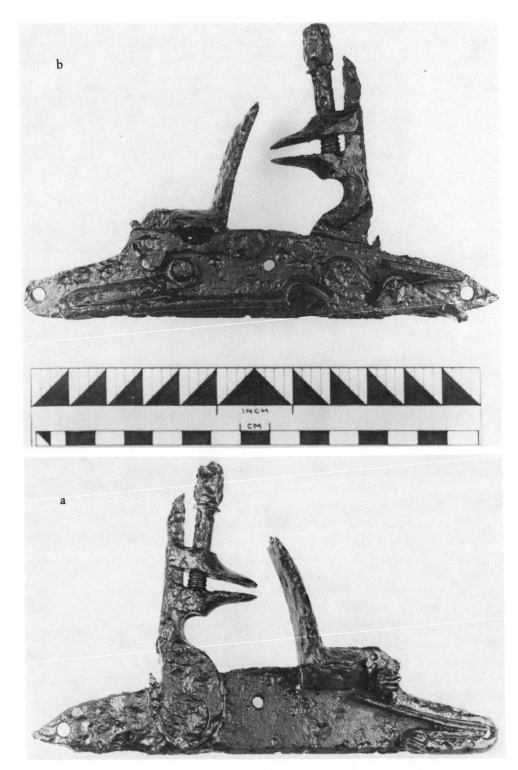

Plate 8. A Dutch Flintlock Mechanism from the Carley Site. a. exterior view; b. interior view, (RMSC 10147/217).

144

brass buttplate or none at all. Simple iron trigger guards were used as were more elaborate cast brass ones with trifoliate finials. Hamilton illustrates an example of this distinctive style of trigger guard in his recent study of colonial guns (1980:24, Figure 3). Not enough information is currently available to describe pistols in any detail.

One additional point about firearms and their use by the Iroquois needs to be made, involving the degree of knowledge needed to repair, as opposed to use, these weapons. On one level, the concepts involved in a flintlock mechanism were not that alien to the Iroquois. Snares and deadfalls also required triggering mechanisms, and the use of flint and steel for creating a spark was doubtless understood. As a result the Iroquois were certainly able to use and even service their firearms by mid-century. Technical repairs, however, especially those that required welding or tempering, were another matter. This was one aspect of European culture that took the Iroquois a longer time to master. Throughout the last half of the seventeenth century, the request for "a smith to mend our arms" was one of the most persistent Onondaga demands (O'Callaghan 1853–1887, 3:776–77).

While axes, knives, awls, and firearms are the most important categories of iron artifacts on early seventeenth-century Onondaga sites, many other iron objects also occur. For example, swords and daggers were often given as gifts or exchanged for furs. Blade fragments and an occasional pommel or cross guard have been recovered from all the early seventeenth-century Onondaga sites. Like axes, however, swords were apparently valued more for their reuse potential than they were for any intrinsic martial purpose, a matter discussed in more detail below.

As with copper and brass objects, it was not until the second quarter of the century that a more diverse range of iron began to flow into Onondaga. Much of this flood was composed of typical European domestic items such as scissors, keys, iron mouth harps, as well as files and other small tools. Nails, spikes, chain, and other kinds of iron hardware also become a common occurrence.

Other items, however, do not have clear European precedents and appear to have been made specifically for trade. The iron scrapers illustrated in Figure 14 are a case in point. Superficially these resemble caulking irons or simple framing chisels; more careful investigation has indicated that they are neither. Given their lightweight construction and terminal finial, it is clear that these implements were designed for hand use, not to be struck with a mallet. While their function is not clear, they would have been efficient tools for scraping skins. In Onondaga, these specialized tools first occur on the Shurtleff site. Given the pattern of their occurrence elsewhere in the Northeast, they appear to have been part of the early seventeenth-century French trading kit.[29]

Despite the increasing availability of finished iron implements, the protohistoric practice of reworking iron continued on Onondaga sites well into the seventeenth century. In fact, given the extensiveness of this practice, it would not be difficult to argue that many iron items such as axes and swords were sought more for their reuse potential than for their intended (European) function.

Axes are a good case in point. While axes are common on all seventeenth-century sites, a distinct shift takes place in the pattern of their occurrence during the first half of the century. On early sites such as Pompey Center, it is pieces that predominate; complete axes are unusual. By mid-century, the reverse is the case (Table 18). Not surprisingly, the evidence for reuse is strongest on the earlier seventeenth-century sites where fragments are more common. This has usually been interpreted as follows: Because axes were scarce, they were used until they wore out or broke; only then were they recycled into other implements (Trigger 1976, 2:411). There is some truth to this argument. Certainly axes were used and, when they broke, reused. However, this assumption implies that axes were so obviously superior to what was traditionally used that once native people acquired them, they used their axes just the way Europeans did. The evidence, on the contrary, suggests a different process was taking place. As with copper kettles, complete axes were often deliberately and systematically dismembered in order to fabricate more "useful" implements.

Axes could be dismantled in a variety of ways. One was to score the blade to remove triangular sections which then could be ground down into celts. Another was to cut the socket open, hammer it flat, then reduce the resulting piece of sheet iron into specific implement forms (Figure 16). Yet another method was to split the axe open along the weld and then unfold it.

The goal of all these reduction processes was to convert large and not particularly useful pieces of iron into traditional implements. As during the protohistoric period, celts/adzes were the most common of these. With the exception of often being larger, the iron celts from the early historic period are very similar to those from protohistoric sites. Two of these celts/adzes from the Carley site are illustrated in Plate 9a and c; metrics for all the available examples are summarized in Table 22. Another lithic form which was replicated in iron was the ovate knife. Often lanceolate or teardrop in shape, these blades were probably hafted pointed end in like their lithic predecessors. A wide range of other implement forms was also produced. At present, these are grouped together as unformalized blades (Table 23). With a larger sample, it is likely that additional categories of formalized blades could be defined.

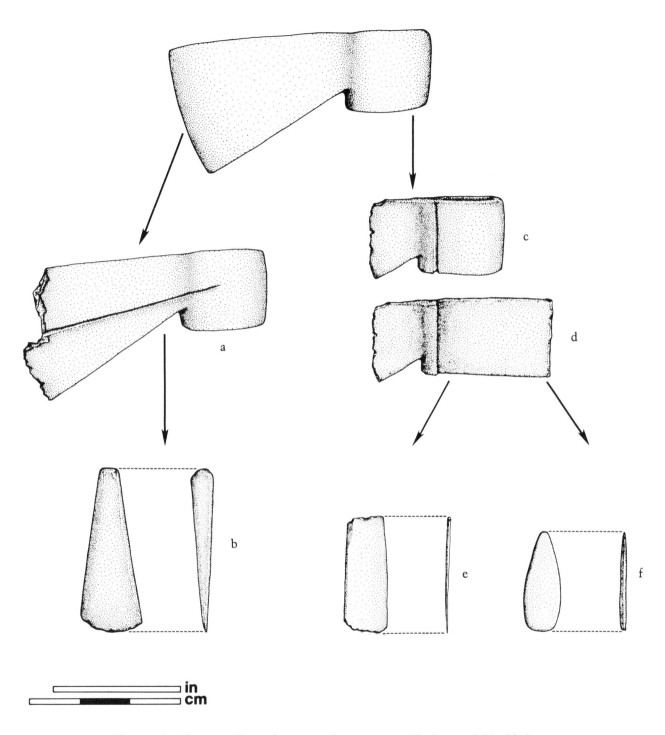

Figure 16. The Recycling of an Iron Axe. a. axe with damaged bit, blade scored in order to remove a celt blank; b. a finished triangular celt/adze; c. axe with broken blade, socket scored to be cut open; d. socket cut open and hammered out flat; two finished implements made from socket: e. a thin rectangular knife or scraper; f. an ovate knife.

147

Table 22
Iron Celts/Adzes from Early Historic Onondaga Sites

Site	Maximum Length	Maximum Width	Maximum Thickness	Shape	Comments
Pompey Center					
#1	61mm	30mm	8mm	Triangular	Finely finished
#2	70	40	15	Triangular	Finely finished
#3	112	26	6	Trapezoidal	Some score marks remain
#4	156	39	9	Trapezoidal	Finely finished
#5	210	38	35	Trapezoidal	Finely finished, nearly square in section
Pratt's Falls					
#1 (Onon. Co. Parks Dept.)	170	39	19	Triangular	Ventral side curved, score marks present
Shurtleff					
#1 RMSC 11005/244	104	49	12	Trapezoidal	Roughly finished
#2 RMSC 11004/244	117	62	19	Trapezoidal	Roughly finished
#3	—	—	—	Trapezoidal	Part of socket attached
	(Measurements not available)				
#4	—	—	—	Rectangular	Finely finished
Carley					
#1	64	44	7	Trapezoidal	
#2	69	26	4	Trapezoidal	Asymmetric
#3 RMSC 10137/217	92	38	11	Trapezoidal	
#4 RMSC 10132/217	118	48	8	Rectangular	
#5 RMSC 10138/217	121	43	17	Triangular	Finely finished
#6 RMSC 10136/217	130	51	8	Trapezoidal	Centrally perforated
Lot 18					
#1	69	37	9	Trapezoidal	
#2 RMSC 11147/245	118	35	21	Trapezoidal	Finely finished

— means specific data not available.

The recycling of axes has been discussed in some detail because it was perhaps the most widespread and systematic means for reusing iron. Many other European forms also were utilized. Swords, for example, were reused in at least two ways. One was to haft the blade for use in spearing game. On his way to Onondaga in 1615, Champlain noted that the Huron also

Table 23

| Site | Formalized Blades | | | Unformalized Blades | Perforators | | Total |
	Celts	Ovate Knives	Sword Blade Scrapers		General	Made From Kettle Bails	
Pompey Center	5	1	0	4	1	1?	12
Pratt's Falls	1	—	—	1	—	—	2
Shurtleff	4	0	1	3	1	8 (of 16)	17
Carley	6	1	2	4	0	6 (of 8)	19
Lot 18	2	1	0	3	0	4 (of 15)	10
Total	18	3	3	15	2	19	60

0 means trait not present.
— means specific data not available.
Sources: See note 6.

used this technique (Biggar 1922–1936, 4:250). An example from the Lot 18 site goes one step further: here one side of the blade has been notched, replicating the shape of a unilaterally barbed harpoon. The tanged end of a sword blade was also reusable. Once the main portion of the blade was detached, a new unifacial edge was ground on the remaining stump. Already hafted, this short but very sturdy adzelike tool could have been used for woodworking or scraping skins. An example from the Carley site is illustrated in Plate 9b. The tang end of a knife blade could also be reworked in the same way. Figure 17 illustrates two such modified knives from the Pompey Center site. The example on the right is particularly notable. With its short, slightly curved blade, this is essentially a prototype of the crooked knife, a tool that occurs on later seventeenth-century sites and is still used by the Onondaga for woodcarving.

Of the many other varieties of iron reuse three deserve brief mention. Unlike the dramatic reworking of axes or swords, these are more modest examples. When a knife blade broke off, it was often still used, probably in the same manner that a lithic edged tool would have been. Many of the knife blade fragments from the Pompey Center site show evidence of regrinding suggesting this kind of continued use. Nails and spikes were also easy to reuse. Little if any adjustment was needed to make these into perforators. Another important source of reusable iron came from copper kettles: The bail or handle, once straightened and abraded to a point, made remarkably serviceable awls. The popularity of this particular method of

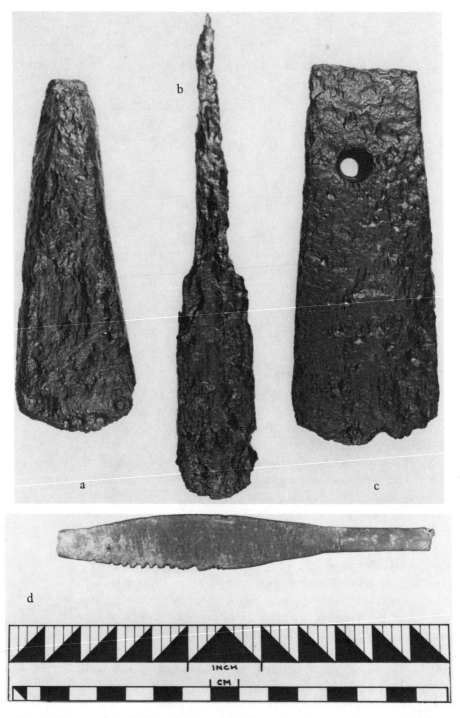

Plate 9. Examples of Onondaga Reuse of Iron and Brass. a. an iron celt, Carley site (RMSC 10138/217); b. a swordblade scraper, Carley site (RMSC 10155/217); c. a perforated iron celt or adze, Carley site (RMSC 10136/217); d. a saw made from a trigger guard, Lot 18 site (Onondaga Historical Association).

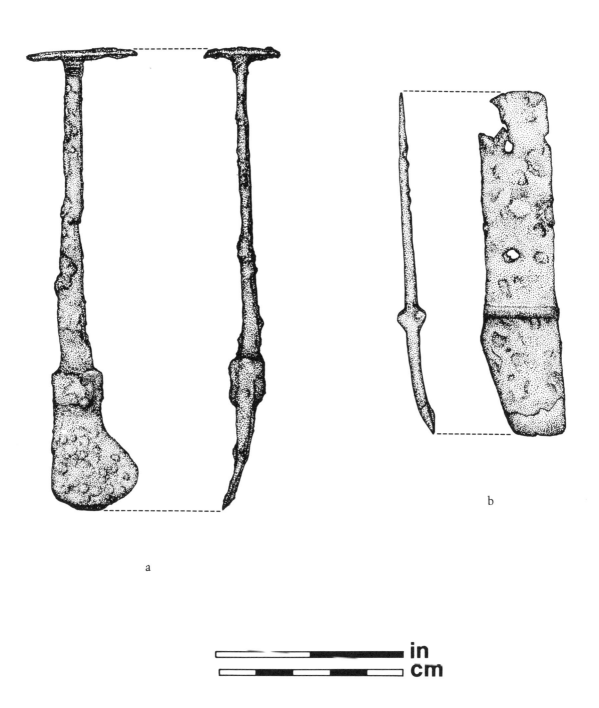

Figure 17. Reused Knife Blades from the Pompey Center Site. a. knife
with tapered tang, iron pommel cap, and a plain conical collar; blade
has been scooped slightly and resharpened; b. knife with a flat tang and
thin collar; blade has been resharpened back to the heel.

151

recycling is underscored by the frequency with which it occurred. At the Shurtleff site, eight of the sixteen identifiable kettle bails have been converted into awls. At the Carley site, six of the eight bails recovered have been reused in this manner (Table 23).

As with copper, the technology of iron reuse was fairly simple. In fact, the basic elements of Onondaga ironworking were adapted directly from their experience with copper. Most pieces were prepared through a combination of cold working and abrasion. There is also some evidence that iron tools were deliberately hardened by cold working the edges (Bradley 1980a:112). Efforts to "anneal" iron may also have resulted in some fledgling attempts to forge it (ibid.).

The technological aspects of Onondaga ironworking during the first half of the seventeenth century are not very impressive. What is remarkable is the degree to which the Onondaga systematically and deliberately converted European items into forms that were traditional to their own culture. Far from being seduced by these new "toil-alleviating tools" (Ritchie 1954:1), native people seem to have been more interested in adapting these implements into useful forms.

Among the new materials introduced to the Onondaga during the first half of the seventeenth century were lead and pewter. Bullets are the most common lead artifact. These, along with casting waste, first occur at Shurtleff and become increasingly common on later sites (Table 21). As noted above, the majority of these balls fall within a 0.50 to 0.65 caliber range and were probably intended for muskets. The actual range in caliber is much greater. For example, at the Lot 18 site, the sixty-three examples recovered range from 0.19 to 0.665. The distribution is remarkably even; there are very few clusters (Bradley 1979:286). This suggests that little effort was made to match the caliber of the ball with that of the weapon. One apparently shot whatever he could get down the barrel.

The presence of both iron bullet molds and bulk lead makes it clear that the Onondaga cast most of the balls they used. Lead was acquired in bar form and then cut into smaller pieces for casting. The most common form of bar lead was trapezoidal in section and approximately 25cm in length. These begin to occur on the Carley site and remain common throughout the rest of the third quarter of the seventeenth century.[30]

A very different kind of lead artifact also begins to appear on Onondaga sites during the second quarter of the century. Lead seals were commonly used on textiles in Europe to identify the town where they were made. Other seals were often added to the cloth as quality control markers. These might indicate the length and type of cloth or the stages of processing which had taken place. As a result, cloth seals are particularly useful in helping to document patterns of production and trade (Baart et al. 1977:110–25; Endrei and Egan 1982). The first cloth seals in Onondaga occur on the Carley site; they remain a common occurrence until the end of the century. Most if not all of these are Dutch and were probably affixed to woolens. Among the towns represented are Leiden, a major textile center in south Holland; Campen, an important trading town of the old Hanseatic League; and Amsterdam, where much of the dyeing and finishing of cloth was done (Bradley 1980b). A fragmentary example from the Lot 18 site—an "Amsterdams anderhalf stael" quality seal dated 1652— is illustrated in Plate 10 along with an identical specimen excavated in Amsterdam. Useful as these seals are to archaeologists, the Onondaga do not seem to have placed any particular value on them. If not cut off and melted for casting, they apparently were discarded.

By mid-century, a scattering of pewter objects was also available to the Onondaga. Some of these were common domestic items integrated into the exchange process. Spoons, and an occasional pewter basin or other vessel, are examples.[31] Other pewter objects, however, appear to have been made specifically for trade. The most notable are pipes. These novel smoking devices occur in two basic forms. One simulates the shape of common European clay smoking pipes. The other, apparently designed to appeal to native tastes, adds a small effigy to the rear of the bowl facing the smoker. While several varieties of effigies have been reported, the two examples from the Lot 18 site portray a seated monkey playing (or smoking) a pipe (Figure 14d). Current evidence suggests that these pipes were part of the Dutch trading stock.[32]

Just as they perfected the means for reusing copper and iron, Onondaga craftsmen also began to experiment with these new metals. The first attempts were simple, primarily cold working lead objects into new shapes. A lead turtle made from a musket ball is an example (Figure 18b). With the introduction of casting technology, the experiments with lead and pewter became more ambitious. The pewter turtle also shown in Figure 18 is an example of the increasing sophistication of this new native skill. Other expressions of this craft included the decoration of stone and wooden pipes with lead/pewter inlays as well as the production of a wide range of effigy figures, brooches, and medals.

While the bulk of the European material reaching the Onondaga during the early seventeenth century was metal, ceramic and glass items were also of considerable importance in the trade. European ceramics, though not common until later in the century, are good markers for documenting the Onondaga's increasing contact with Europeans, particularly the Dutch. The first examples occur at the Pompey Center site. These include Weser slipware, a refined earthenware made in northern Germany and popular in Amsterdam during the late sixteenth century, and Dutch majolica[33] (Plate 11). By the second quarter of the century, a different ceramic assemblage is present. While some majolica continues to occur, there is a

Plate 10. A Fragmentary "Amsterdams anderhalf stael" Cloth Seal, Dated 1652, from the Lot 18 Site and a Comparable Example from Amsterdam. a. fragmentary example, Lot 18 site; b. obverse of a complete seal from Amsterdam; c. reverse of complete example (Collection Amsterdam Historical Museum MH7–59; Photo: DOW/AHM-Afd. Archeologie).

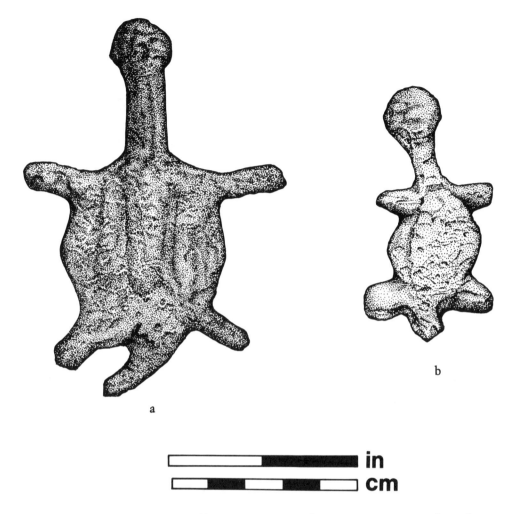

<indent>in
<indent>cm

Figure 18. Two Turtle Effigies, Examples of Onondaga Reuse of Lead and Pewter. a. a cast pewter example, Indian Castle site (RMSC 6001/217); b. an effigy formed from a musket ball and casting sprue, Carley site (Onon. Co. Parks Dept. 76.22.39).

shift toward German stoneware, particularly the gray and cobalt blue vessels from Westerwald (Plate 11). Among other ceramics present are brown, salt-glazed stonewares of Frechen and Dutch lead-glazed redwares. The first evidence of European drinking glasses, German "roemers," also occurs about mid-century (Table 24). This mid-century assemblage of ceramics and glass is similar to objects recovered from Dutch colonial sites such as Fort Orange (Huey 1985:74–75).

As the occurrence of European ceramics changed during the first half of the seventeenth century, so did the Onondaga use of them. Several of

<indent><indent>THE HISTORIC ONONDAGA 1600-1655   155

Plate 11. European Ceramics from the Pompey Center and Lot 18 Sites with Comparable European Examples. a. a piece of polychrome Dutch majolica drug jar reworked into a pendant, Pompey Center site; b. a comparable majolica zalfpot, Amsterdam (Collection Amsterdam Historical Museum Eg3–1; Photo: DOW/AHM-Afd. Archeologie); c. two pieces of Weser slipware pipkin or pot, Pompey Center site; d. a comparable Weserware pot, Amsterdam (Collection Amsterdam Historical Museum Hekl–2; Photo: DOW/AHM-Afd. Archeologie); e. a piece of lead-glazed, Dutch redware pipkin, Lot 18 site; f. a comparable pipkin from the Seneca Dann site (RMSC 372/28); g. a piece of Rhenish stoneware jug, Lot 18 site; h. a comparable jug from the Seneca Dann site (RMSC 2628/ 28). Scale of a, c, e, and g is actual size. Scale of b and d is approximately half of actual size.

156

Table 24
Distribution of European Ceramics and Glassware on Early Historic Onondaga Sites

	Earthenware			Stoneware		Glass
Site	Coarse (Lead Glazed Redware)	Refined (Weserware)	Tin-Glazed (Majolica)	Westerwald	Frechen	Roemer
Pompey Center	0	6	4	0	0	0
Pratt's Falls	—	—	—	—	—	—
Shurtleff	0	0	2	0	0	0
Carley	0	0	0	1	0	0
Lot 18	1	0	0	16	1	1
Total	1	6	6	17	1	1

0 means trait not present.
— means specific data not available.
Sources: See note 6.

the pieces from Pompey Center show evidence of reuse, primarily grinding or attempts at perforation. The majolica pendant shown on Plate 11a exemplifies one style of use. Unperforated ceramic discs may also have been used as dice in the bowl game or other ceremonies of divination.[34] By mid-century, however, European ceramics were being used by the Onondaga in a more European manner, as containers for food and probably liquor.

European clay smoking pipes are another class of artifacts helping trace the extent of Dutch commercial activity. While the Onondaga continued to make and use their own pipes, they also began to smoke the squat white clay pipes made in the Netherlands. Fragments first appear at the Shurtleff site, and by mid-century have become common artifacts on Onondaga sites. Many of these pipes are marked on either the heel or stem, thus enabling identification of their makers.[35] The most commonly occurring mark, *EB*, belonged to an expatriot Englishman, Edward Bird or Burt, who made pipes in Amsterdam from about 1630 until his death in 1665 (McCashion 1975:15; Huey 1985:76–77). The other pipe marks from Onondaga sites also correlate with Amsterdam makers. Further underscoring their origin, these same pipes occur on Dutch colonial sites. For example, all of the pipe marks recorded from the Shurtleff, Carley, and Lot 18 sites have also been recovered from the site of Fort Orange (Paul Huey, personal communication).

Glass beads are one of the most common and, for the archaeologist, useful classes of European artifacts. Infrequent on protohistoric sites, glass beads suddenly become abundant on early historic period sites such as Pompey Center. The value of glass beads to the archaeologist lies to some extent in their numbers. Unlike other kinds of European materials, beads occur in large enough quantities to be studied statistically. The most frequently occurring beads from the early seventeenth-century Onondaga sites are summarized in Table 25.[36] In addition to their numbers, beads are also variable. In color, complexity, and even techniques of manufacture, there was considerable diversity in those exported to North America from Europe. Finally, beads arc a valuable source of data because the styles on Onondaga sites changed rapidly during the century. Many bead types were introduced, became common, then disappeared. By seriating these changes, an historical archaeologist can use glass beads to help establish site sequences and chronologies in much the same way that a prehistorian uses ceramic traits.

Table 26 summarizes the distribution of the most common bead varieties from the early seventeenth-century Onondaga sites. For example, that found at Pompey Center, Kidd IVk3, is a round, multilayered bead with a dark blue exterior. Due to its red, star-shaped medial layer, these have often been referred to as "star" beads. At Pompey Center, they are nearly 15 percent of the total sample. On subsequent sites, however, their percentage drops off sharply. The other three most common varieties follow similar patterns on their respective sites.

Glass beads can function as cultural markers as well as chronological ones. While this is more frequently the case with an assemblage, occasionally a specific variety stands out. Nueva Cádiz beads, for instance, are a hallmark of sixteenth-century Spanish activity (Smith and Good 1982). In the Northeast, black glass buttons are, oddly enough, one of the "bead" varieties used to trace the Dutch. These small, opaque black buttons became fashionable as an embellishment on clothing during the last decades of the sixteenth century, and their popularity continued well into the seventeenth.[37] They also proved to be useful in the New World as gifts or for trade. Henry Hudson, for one, used them along the New England coast in 1609 (Purchas 1906, 13:351). On Onondaga sites, these buttons first occur at Pompey Center. While they continue to be a frequent occurrence until after mid-century, they are most common on the sites with closest ties to Fort Orange (Table 28).[38]

Assemblages of distinctive bead varieties are even more reliable as chronological and cultural markers. This has become especially apparent as more research has occurred in Europe on production sources. Perhaps the most significant work has been done by the Amsterdam Historical Museum, which recently documented several sites that relate to glass beadmaking (Baart n.d.). Of particular interest are those providing evidence

Table 25
Most Frequently Occurring Bead Types on Early Historic Onondaga Sites

Pompey Center (1600–1620) (sample of 1404 beads; 107 varieties)				Shurtleff (1630–1640) (sample of 70 beads; 21 varieties)				Carley (1640–1650) (sample of 991 beads; 66 varieties)				Lot 18 (1650–1655) (sample of 2107 beads; 81 varieties)			
Rank	Kidd No.	No.	%	Rank	Kidd No.	No.	%	Rank	Kidd No.	No.	%	Rank	Kidd No.	No.	%
1	IVk3	192	13.7	1	IIb56	16	22.9	1	IIIa12	357	36.0	1	IIIa1	371	17.6
2	IVa19	191	13.6	2	IIa40	15	21.4	2	IIa27	97	9.8	2	IIIa12	363	17.2
3	IVb31	111	7.9	3	Ia1	5	7.1	3	IIa37	75	7.6	3	Ia1	309	14.7
4	IIa2	81	5.8	4	IVa13	5	7.1	4	Ia1	43	4.3	4	Ia20	216	10.3
5	IVb33	73	5.2	5	IVa5	4	5.7	5	IVb36	38	3.8	5	IIa1	134	6.4
6	IIa48	55	3.9	6	Black Button	4	5.7	6	Black Button	38	3.8	6	Ia16	78	3.7
7	IIa50	53	3.8	7	IIb31	3	4.3	7	IIa40	36	3.6	7	IIa40	66	3.1
8	IIa55	37	2.6	8	Ic1	2	2.9	8	Ia7	30	3.0	8	Black Button	44	2.1
9	IIbb1	37	2.6	9	IIa3	2	2.9	9	IIb*‡	28	2.8	9	IIa55	31	1.5
10	IIa40	31	2.2	10	IIa11	2	2.9	10	IIa1	19	1.9	10	IIIa3	24	1.1
11	IVa3	31	2.2	11	W11*†	2	2.9								
Total		892	63.5			60	85.8			761	76.8			1636	77.7

* Variety not recorded by Kidd and Kidd (1970).
† Large, flat, translucent wire-wound bead, irregular shape, blue green in color.
‡ Small, circular, opaque white bead with three red and three blue stripes.
Sources: Bradley 1976, 1977, 1984; Tanner 1978.

for bead production in the Netherlands, and specifically in Amsterdam, during the late sixteenth and early seventeenth centuries. The largest assemblage was discovered in 1981 while a new sewer was being installed along the Keizersgracht. In all, over 50,000 beads were recovered along with production waste and crucible fragments. This deposit is important because it can be dated with some accuracy. It lay beneath nearly four meters of fill deposited prior to the completion of the adjacent canal in 1610. This dating is also confirmed by the ceramics and drinking glass fragments associated with the beads: All date from the last decade of the sixteenth century (ibid.; Karklins 1985b).

A large sample of the beads from this site (Asd/Kg10) has been analyzed by Karlis Karklins and compared with the bead assemblages from sites in eastern North America. He found that the strongest correlations were with

Table 26

Seriation of the Most Frequently Occurring Bead Types from Early Historic Onondaga Sites

Site	Kidd IVk2–6 Star or Chevron No.	(%)	Kidd IVb56 Round Opaque Robin's Egg Blue with Three White Stripes No.	(%)	Kidd IIIa12 Tubular Dark Blue with White Medial Layer No.	(%)	Kidd IIIa1 Tubular, Red with Opaque Black Core No.	(%)
Pompey Center (n = 1404)	206	14.7	3	0.2	0	0	0	0
Pratt's Falls (n = 0)	—	0	—	0	—	0	—	0
Shurtleff (n = 70)	2	2.9	16	22.9	0	0	0	0
Carley (n = 991)	7	0.7	17	1.7	357	36.0	11	1.1
Lot 18 (n = 2107)	2	0.1	3	0.1	363	17.2	371	17.6

— means specific data not available.
Sources: Bradley 1976, 1977, 1984; Tanner 1978.

the early seventeenth-century sites, particularly those within the Dutch sphere of influence, such as Pompey Center (ibid.:40–41). Table 27 summarizes the fifteen most common varieties from Pompey Center along with their comparable occurrence at the Asd/Kg10 site. While there are some obvious gaps and discrepancies, the overall similarity is notable. In spite of this, it would be premature to say that the beads from the Pompey Center site came from Amsterdam. Identical beads were made in Venice and perhaps elsewhere. Nonetheless, the discovery of these dated and distinctive assemblages in Amsterdam begins to provide a set of reference points against which the data from Onondaga sites can be plotted. When considered along with the other archaeological and documentary evidence, a strong case for the Dutch origin of these beads does emerge.

The glass beads recovered from excavations on Dutch colonial sites are also of value in defining chronological and cultural patterns. The bead assemblage from Fort Orange, for example, can be used as a basis for comparison with the Onondaga sites (Table 28). Not surprisingly, the greatest similarity occurs with Shurtleff and Carley, sites that also show close affinity to Fort Orange in other artifact classes. Other researchers have also demonstrated that the beads from Fort Orange can be used to

Table 27

*Comparison of Glass Beads from the Pompey Center Site
and Asd/Kg10, Amsterdam*

	Pompey Center Site			Asd/Kg10	
Rank	Kidd No.	Number	%	Presence/Absence	Estimated Number*
1	IVk3	192	13.7	present	1
2	IVa19	191	13.6	present	ca. 100
3	IVb31	111	7.9	present	5
4	IIa2	81	5.8	present	ca. 2000
5	IVb33	73	5.2	absent	0
6	IIa48	55	3.9	absent	0
7	IIa50	53	3.8	present	149
8	IIa55	37	2.6	present	29
9	IIbb1	37	2.6	absent	0
10	IIa40	31	2.2	absent	0
11	IVa3	31	2.2	present	ca. 100
12	IVa1	27	1.9	present	ca. 200
13	IVa6	24	1.7	present	ca. 200
14	IIa56	22	1.6	present	145
15	IIa1	22	1.6	present	ca. 2000
Total		987	70.3		

* Based on analysis of the Asd/Kg10 assemblage by Karlis Karklins (1985).
0 means trait not present.

define a sphere of Dutch trading influence (Huey 1983; Kenyon and Fitzgerald 1986).

One final observation on glass beads and their utility to the archaeologist must be made: Beads were a perfect medium for cross-cultural exchange. They made sense, although for very different reasons, to both Europeans and native Americans. For Europeans beads were an ideal trade item. They were trinkets, trifles relatively cheap to make, easy to transport, and with few exceptions dependable as something the native people would want. Native people, on the other hand, appear to have seen glass beads in a different way: as analogs to two familiar substances of value. One was berries, used traditionally in myth and ritual as a symbol of physical and spiritual well-being. The other was crystal, whose ascribed powers were associated with life-enhancing, life-restorative medicine (Hamell 1983, 1985). If our goal as archaeologists is to understand cross-cultural change and continuity, then objects that carried multiple meanings, such as glass beads, are particularly valuable as probes.

Table 28

Comparison of Glass Beads from Fort Orange and
Early Historic Onondaga Sites

		Fort Orange (n = 334; 81 varieties)		Pompey Center (n = 1404; 107 varieties)	Shurtleff (n = 70; 21 varieties)	Carley (n = 991; 66 varieties)	Lot 18 (n = 2107; 81 varieties)
Rank	Kidd No.	No.	%	%	%	%	%
1	IVa11/13	91	27.2	1.1	7.1	1.6	0.2
2	IIIa12	51	15.3	0	0	36.0	17.2
3	IIa31/36/40	32	9.6	2.7	21.4	3.6	3.1
4	IIa6/7	24	7.2	0.4	0	3.0	0.2
5	Ia19	22	6.6	0.3	9	0.2	0
6	Black Button	10	3.0	0.1	5.7	3.8	2.1
7	IIb56/57	8	2.4	0.2	22.9	1.8	0.1
8	IVa19	4	1.2	13.6	0	0.3	0
9	Ib22	3	0.9	0	3.3	0.1	0
10	IIa46	3	0.9	0	0	0	0
11	IIIa1	3	0.9	0	0	1.1	17.6
Total		254	76.0	18.4	60.4	51.5	22.9

0 means trait not present.
Sources: See note 38.

Concluding Comments

One of the goals of this chapter has been to document the kinds of European material that occur on Onondaga sites in ever greater quantities during the first half of the seventeenth century. Where did these materials come from? What chronological and cultural patterns do they represent? Throughout this chapter, an effort has been made to answer these questions in terms of specific artifact classes. In some cases, Dutch cloth seals for instance, it is possible to fit the examples from Onondaga sites into the broader networks of production and trade that created them. For other artifact classes, such as iron axes, answers are not yet forthcoming.

Before leaving this topic, however, I would like to see if it is possible to define assemblages that are chronologically or culturally specific. Three can be identified for the first half of the seventeenth century, at least in a preliminary way. Two of these are Dutch, one early seventeenth-century, the other reflecting the Dutch West India Company and its entrepot, Fort Orange. The third assemblage is French. As noted earlier in this chapter, the documentary record often alludes to what items were given or traded but only in a general way. The goal here is to see how the specifics of the archaeological record can be matched to the objects which Juet, van den Bogart, or LeMoine happened to mention.

Initially, it seems difficult to match Juet's rather offhanded descriptions with the archaeological materials. Knives and "hatchets" are mentioned, and these certainly do begin to occur in quantity at the Pompey Center site. However, no particular styles or varieties stand out as appreciably different from those which occur on later sites. The same holds true for copper and brass kettles. On the other hand, type I awls do not appear after the first quarter of the century and may be considered part of an "Early Dutch" assemblage. Black glass buttons might also be a candidate, even though they also occur on later sites. Glass beads are, by far, the best indicator, particularly the round polychrome varieties which predominate at Pompey Center. In fact, other researchers have termed this "polychrome bead horizon" as the signature for early Dutch trade (Kenyon and Fitzgerald 1986). Weser slipware and early Dutch majolica, though far less common than beads, also seem to be reliable components of an Early Dutch assemblage.

If an Early Dutch assemblage remains somewhat amorphous, the Dutch assemblage from the Fort Orange period is considerably clearer. This is composed of several classes of artifacts which, based on documentary and archaeological research in the Netherlands and the New World, are demonstrably Dutch. Specifically these include lead cloth seals, clay smoking pipes, firearms, small brass items such as mouth harps, buttons and thimbles, and ceramics (particularly later majolica, faience, and lead glazed earthenware). Several other classes of artifacts also appear to belong in this Fort Orange period Dutch assemblage. These include knives with tapered tangs, pewter pipes and spoons, and several varieties of glass beads (particularly IVa11/13 and IIIa12). While not conclusive, current evidence suggests that these are also of Dutch origin.

Defining a French assemblage for the first half of the seventeenth century is more difficult. Although French materials appear to have been present in Onondaga during most of the period, they are more elusive, harder to pin down. Nonetheless, some artifacts do seem to correlate reliably with French activity. Knives with folding blades, or "jambettes," are one example. So are iron scrapers and long tanged arrowheads. Perhaps the most obvious French-related artifacts are Catholic religious ornaments. Other artifacts that appear to belong in a French assemblage include type II and possibly III iron awls, brass kettles embellished with hammered designs on the bottom or sides (and often stamped with a maker's mark), and particular glass bead varieties (especially Kenyon and Fitzgerald's clusters A and B).

This attempt at defining specific assemblages is clearly a preliminary effort, and one that will be refined as both documentary and archaeological research continue. The point is that the massive influx of European material into Onondaga during the first half of the seventeenth century can be broken down into identifiable components. These constituent parts in turn allow the dynamics of change to be traced more clearly.

A second goal of this chapter has been to examine how the steadily increasing rate of contact affected both Europeans and native people. On the European side, many of the initial responses were on a large scale— the formation of new companies, the establishment of colonies—designed primarily to enhance or exploit trade with the natives. In transplanting themselves, however, Europeans frequently found that Old World logic was not always useful for solving problems in the New World and that, in terms of learning what to eat, how to travel, and where to find shelter in this strange and forbidding land, native people could be reliable guides.

As the interactions between natives and newcomers increased, the Europeans also began to learn what Verrazano and others had already found to be true—that native people as consumers had specific and selective tastes. They did not always want what Europeans happened to offer them. For Europeans, the lesson was simple: If a reliable commercial system was to operate, then it must produce the goods native people would accept. As a result, New World market demand began to reshape Old World production during the first half of the seventeenth century.

The growing influence of this market pressure can be seen most clearly in Amsterdam, the great entrepot of seventeenth-century Europe. While collecting, storing, and reselling may have been the key elements in the city's prosperity (Braudel 1984:236–39), these commercial activities were supplemented by the making or assembling of components in order to produce the goods the New World market demanded. This process can be seen in two related ways. One was a division in production where some items were made for domestic consumption while other, different versions were made for trade. Brass and copper kettles, though not made in Amsterdam, are a good example. Axes, knives, textiles, and clay smoking pipes may also follow a similar pattern. Second and closely related was the production of goods solely for export markets. Glass beads are an example.[39] So are firearms which, if not made in Amsterdam, were at least assembled there. Novelty items such as pewter pipes, especially those with effigies, also fall in this category. Although most visible in the Netherlands, this pattern of specialized production for export undoubtedly developed in other countries as well. The trade-oriented ironwork found on French sites certainly suggests as much.

By the late seventeenth century, the manufacture of goods designed specifically for the native American market had become a large and well established practice, one which produced a steady supply of trade guns, trade blankets, trade beads, and other stock merchandise. It was on this foundation, shaped in part by native demand, that new entrepreneurs such as the Hudson Bay Company built their own formulas for success.

What does this, in turn, suggest about the process of acculturation? Recent studies have often used the concept of "donor" and "recipient" cultures to discuss the interactions between native Americans and Europeans, and emphasize the various ways in which one culture borrows and adapts particular traits from another (Foster 1960; Brain 1979:270; Berry 1980). While this may be appropriate for describing some aspects of the acculturative process, it misses the critical element in what happened during the first half of the seventeenth century. The Onondaga data suggest that there was no single donor or recipient culture; native Americans and Europeans taught and learned from one another, modifying both their respective cultures in the process. The interaction was dynamic and reciprocal, not linear and in one direction only.

Regardless of what was happening to the Europeans, it is clear from the data presented in this chapter that the Onondaga were not passive in their response to the Europeans, their ideas, and their materials. Accept them they did, especially the materials. But in the process, the Onondaga frequently altered and redefined these exotic objects to make them more useful within their own cultural tradition. During the first half of the seventeenth century, the Onondaga were a people striving not to resist, but to accommodate change.

5

Accommodating Change

In 1672, after four decades in North America, Nicholas Denys made the following observation about the native people who lived along the North Atlantic coast: "They have abandoned all their own utensils, whether because of the trouble they had as well to make as to use them, or because of the facility of obtaining from us, in exchange for skins which cost them almost nothing, the things which seemed to them invaluable, not so much for their novelty as for the convenience they derived therefrom" (Denys, 1672, 1:440–41). This assessment of how quickly and completely native Americans accepted European objects, and at what cost to their own culture, remains deeply ingrained in our understanding of the contact period. From this perspective, the acculturative process was primarily one of replacement in which traditional native implements and ornaments were displaced by European equivalents almost as quickly as they became available.[1]

A less obvious but more significant component of this interpretation is its underlying assumption. Namely, that by accepting and using European objects in preference to their own, native people made the logical choice, picking a technologically more sophisticated, "superior," European product over a less satisfactory native one. If one accepts this assumption, then all the rest of Denys' analysis—the loss of craft skills, the disintegration and, ultimately, collapse of native culture—follows automatically.

Superficially, it is easy to see why this interpretation has persisted. The evidence for it seems so obvious. After all, iron axes and knives did replace their lithic equivalents. Copper kettles eventually did displace ceramic pottery. Glass and metal ornaments did take the place of the traditional ones of bone and stone. Why then is Denys' assessment so wrong?

To answer this question, we need to return to the acculturative process. We have traced the evolution of the Onondaga and the material aspects of their culture in detail. With this information, we have the basis for examining the acculturative process and how it worked within one native American culture. The evidence indicates that, contrary to Denys' assertion, native Americans were quite capable of coming to terms with Europeans and European materials. For the Onondaga, the first century or more of contact can be summarized in three points: (1) Their response was active and selective, not passive; (2) continuity marked the process as much as change did; (3) many of the changes were creative, innovative ones. From this perspective, the dynamics of acculturative change can be seen as one more stage in the ongoing redefinition of Onondaga culture.

European Material/Native Culture: The Dynamics of Acculturative Change

Before discussing the particulars of the Onondaga response, we must review briefly the salient features of the acculturative process. We begin with the definition. In this study, acculturation is defined as the process of reciprocal interaction that occurs when two autonomous cultures come into contact.

One aspect of the reciprocal, interactive quality of this process deserves particular mention. While each culture does affect the other, the degree of influence is not necessarily equal. To use a simple example, when Jacques Cartier wintered on the St. Lawrence in 1535, the cultural patterns of the French were shaped more strongly by what they learned from their St. Lawrence Iroquois neighbors than were those of the natives by European ways. On the other hand, 120-odd years later, the degree to which the French at Ste. Marie de Gannentaha and the Onondaga influenced each other was significant for both groups. The point is that the acculturative process works differently when the two cultures are equal, at parity, than when they are not.

At the end of the Introduction, three questions were posed as guides to our examination of the acculturative process:

1. To what degree do existing (traditional) cultural patterns and values serve to screen, filter, even define what is accepted and absorbed from another culture?

2. To what extent are there differential rates of change within a culture?

What elements are most susceptible to influence? Which are most resistant?

3. While the acculturative process can have a negative impact, what is its potential for initiating innovation and cross-cultural creativity? What circumstances maximize this potential?

Let us now see what kinds of answers the Onondaga data provide.

The first question is: to what degree do existing cultural beliefs and values influence the perception of materials, ideas, and representatives of another culture. Based on the Onondaga evidence, the answer to this question is: almost totally. Other researchers have come to a similar conclusion. In her study of Virginia's native people, Nancy Lurie observed that "their first adjustments to Europeans [were] made in terms of existing native conditions (1959:36–37, 60). Calvin Martin has stated this even more forcefully. European goods were what native people thought them to be. As a result, they often "assumed a new personality"—a native identity quite different from what the Europeans intended (1975:129). In order to see what he means, let us look at the Onondaga example in more detail.

There is no question that once European materials were available the Onondaga actively and aggressively sought them out. Evidence for the value placed on these materials is seen both internally and externally in Onondaga culture. During the sixteenth century, these materials were used intensively and often in ritual-related ways. Even when the preferred uses shifted toward the utilitarian during the seventeenth century, demand remained high. The degree to which the Onondaga wanted European materials is also evident in their external relationships. Access to those goods appears to have been a primary motive for the Onondaga's intensified interactions with the Susquehannocks during the last half of the sixteenth century. When the source of European goods shifted to the upper Hudson River valley early in the seventeenth century, so did Onondaga interests. The implications of this change for the Five Nations, and especially for relations between the Onondaga and their Mohawk brethren, are discussed in more detail below.

While the Onondaga were unquestionably interested in obtaining European materials, they also were selective about what they wanted. The archaeological evidence bears this out. The range of European materials on protohistoric Onondaga sites is restricted to a few categories—copper sheet, fragments of iron implements, glass beads. Certainly a variety of factors determined this assemblage, among them: availability from Europeans, the distance the materials traveled to reach Onondaga, the degree to which those materials were processed along the way, and, of course, what survives archaeologically. While all these played a role in shaping the protohistoric assemblage, we must also acknowledge that native choice, what the Onondaga chose to accept, was a salient factor as well. Even during the seventeenth century, when the volume and variety of European goods were exponentially greater, the majority of European objects that the Onondaga chose still fell within a few well defined categories.

If the Onondaga were selective in their response to European culture, by what criteria did they make their choices? The evidence indicates two: one ideological (what had symbolic or ritual value), the other utilitarian (what was useful).[2] How these criteria were applied reflects established elements of pre-contact Onondaga culture.

During the sixteenth century, ideological considerations appear to have been the major criteria for selection. The focus of this selection was a set of indigenous though rarely occurring substances (shell, free state metals, and crystalline or white siliceous stone) associated with life-enhancing, life-restorative "power." In the Northeast, the origins of this ideational and aesthetic linkage appear to extend back at least 3500 years. Initially, Europeans may have been perceived as other-worldly man-beings, the traditional keepers of these substances of power. The fact that Europeans frequently offered metal objects, mirrors, and glass "crystals" or beads to the natives they encountered would have reinforced this perception. Archaeologically, it is clear that European analogs were accepted and used as, or in lieu of, the traditional substances of power throughout the protohistoric period.

During the early seventeenth century this ideological basis for selection appears to have waned in preference for a more utilitarian one. Greater availability may have resulted in a dilution of the power that certain European materials were perceived to possess. In spite of this erosion, ideological considerations did remain important. In fact, the definition of the substances of power was expanded early in the seventeenth century to include new classes of European material, particularly glazed ceramics and glassware. By the middle of the century, another factor helped revive the importance of ideological-based selection. With the establishment of the mission St. Jean Baptiste in 1655, an active effort to Christianize the Onondaga began. Under these conditions, the acceptance of rings, medals, beads, or other objects had implications on several levels.

The second criterion for selection was utilitarian. Fenton has observed that Iroquoian culture was remarkable for its ability to utilize whatever came to hand (Fenton 1978:302). This flexible and opportunistic quality characterized not only the Onondaga but their antecedents as well. As discussed in chapter 1, this trait evolved as part of an overall subsistence strategy, one designed to exploit a wide range of seasonally (and often briefly) available resources. Thus European materials may have been considered initially as another, albeit unusual, kind of material to be sought out on a seasonal basis.

By the late sixteenth century, utilitarian considerations appear as significant factors in the selection and use of European materials, particularly metals. Copper was increasingly used for implements as well as ornaments. Iron, which was becoming a more common occurrence, was used exclusively for utilitarian purposes. This pattern continued into, and indeed typified, the first half of the seventeenth century as the Onondaga actively acquired, used, and reused European metals.

Caution is necessary here, for this begins to sound suspiciously similar to Denys' assessment—native people eagerly seeking and accepting European implements because they were so useful. The difference is subtle but significant. What the Onondaga sought out and absorbed were European materials, not European objects. This pattern is quite clear on sites of the late sixteenth and early seventeenth centuries. Copper kettles and iron axes were desirable because they were the most accessible sources of a valuable raw material, not because they were particularly useful in and of themselves. This argument is reinforced when one looks at how these raw materials were used—to make objects that followed traditional Onondaga forms and functions.

This puts the acceptance of European materials in a very different light. Essentially it argues that the initial impact of European materials was conservative, not revolutionary, in that it promoted the maintenance of traditional cultural patterns instead of their change.[3] European materials were accepted not because they were considered different and "superior," but because they made sense from an Onondaga perspective, both in ideological and utilitarian terms. Of course as the level of contact increased, this perception altered. By the seventeenth century, European objects were common enough to be valued for their intended (European) functions as well. Even then, however, the degree to which a European object had utility within native culture remained a primary criterion for determining its value.

The second question about the acculturative process addresses the issue of differential change, or continuity versus change, within a culture. It is accepted that various elements of a culture often alter at different rates, in part because some components are more susceptible to cross-cultural influence than others. Those less susceptible, or more resistant, can be characterized as appropriately by the degree to which they remain constant as by how much they have changed.

At a very general level, the archaeological evidence from sixteenth- and early seventeenth-century Onondaga sites seems to bear this out. During this period, the patterns of settlement and subsistence appear to change much less than those of the artifact record. While European materials became increasingly important to their culture, the Onondaga continued to live in large, semi-permanent, palisaded villages in the Pompey Hills. They followed the same basic seasonal cycle of horticulture, hunting, fishing, and gathering that had characterized their culture for centuries. However, these continuities are somewhat misleading in that they more accurately reflect the biases of the archaeological record than they do the actual data. At present we simply do not know how house size or the composition of faunal assemblages may have changed during this period.

While the information on settlement and subsistence patterns is not strong enough to analyze in detail, the material record is. We know a great deal about the artifact forms, raw material preferences, and patterns of stylistic development characteristic of Onondaga material culture. As a result, this is the appropriate means for assessing relative degrees of continuity and change. There is another reason to focus on the artifact record. It has often been observed that when a non-Western culture comes into contact with a Western one, its technological elements are most readily affected (SSRC 1954:990–91). But here again, change is not monolithic and uniform. Which aspects are most readily altered—how the object is made? What it is made from? Its form? Its function? The Onondaga evidence suggests an answer.

Initially, when comparing the assemblages overall from pre-contact, protohistoric, and historic period sites, the changes seem overwhelming. However, if we track specific components, the process of change takes on a different character. One way to track is via a simple six-cell matrix with "Continuity" and "Change" across the top, and "Material preference," "Form," and "Function" down the left side (Figure 19). With this matrix we can break down the process and see more clearly the dynamics of Onondaga material culture during the sixteenth and early seventeenth centuries.

During the sixteenth century, change was limited and occurred primarily at one level within the culture. That level was material preference; artifact form and function changed little if at all. Examples help to illustrate this. Tubular beads occur on all the sixteenth-century sites. While there is variation in size and shape, the significant change is in material. Sheet copper replaces bone. Pendants follow the same pattern. By the end of the century, the perforated epiphyseal cap or water-worn pebble has become a perforated disc of brass or copper. Again, the material has changed but the basic form and probably the function have not. This pattern also holds true for utilitarian artifacts. While the basic celt/adze form continued to be used throughout the protohistoric period, by the end of the sixteenth century any particular example is as likely to be iron as lithic. In a similar manner, the form and function of utilized flakes and unifacial lithic tools

Figure 19

A Matrix for Summarizing Continuity and Change in Sixteenth- and Early Seventeenth-Century Onondaga Material Culture

Sixteenth Century

	Continuity	Change
Material Preference	X	X
Form	X	
Function (implied)	X	

Seventeenth Century

	Continuity	Change
Material Preference	X	X
Form	X	X
Function (implied)	X	

was perpetuated in the unformalized pickup tools of sheet copper and iron.

While this pattern of change in material preference is quite clear, we should not overstate it. Not all traditional materials were abandoned; many certainly were not. Lithics, bone, and antler continue to be used for both ornaments and implements. The use of marine shell for ornaments actually increased during the protohistoric period.

During the first half of the seventeenth century this pattern shifted slightly. While changes in material preference continued to occur, there was now an increasing tendency to modify form also (Figure 19). Beads exemplify both the continuities and changes. Shell and copper continued to be used for beads (continuity in material), but glass beads soon predominated (change in material). With marine shell beads, however, the significant change was in shape. Most important was the gradual replacement of the discoidal form, predominant during the pre-contact and protohistoric periods, in favor of the short, tubular wampum bead. As wampum rose in popularity, so did other shapes and sizes of shell beads. By the mid-seventeenth century, shell ornaments were made and used in a wide range of bead and effigy forms. Similar levels of continuity and change can be seen in pendants: There is some continuity in material (copper and shell), but new materials such as European ceramics were also employed. More notable was the increasing diversity in form as zoomorphic and other, noncircular geometric shapes superceded the traditional disc.

The same pattern also applies to utilitarian artifacts: continuity in form and change in material, followed by a gradual diversity of artifact form. During the protohistoric period, the basic dynamic was one of limited and specific substitution—copper and iron replacing lithic and bone. The process continued during the seventeenth century, but at a more rapid pace and on a broader scale. This phase of acculturative change can be seen in several artifact classes. Triangular projectile points slowly shifted from chert to sheet copper or brass. Centrally perforated needles were made from copper instead of bone. Celts/adzes continued to be made and used but more frequently in iron than ground stone. Awls and harpoons retained their form but were made from iron (kettle bails and sword blades) instead of bone or antler. Once again, this puts a very different perspective on how much change has occurred. Certainly the materials are different, but in form and function these are the same implements that the Onondaga and their antecedents had used for centuries.

Even here, however, in this very stable portion of Onondaga material culture, some change in implement form also began to occur during the first half of the seventeenth century. In part, new materials promoted experimentation with new forms. For example, while the majority of sheet metal projectile points followed the traditional triangular form, a scattering of stemmed, pentagonal, and other shapes were also made. More important, the increased availability and extensive reuse of European implements often provided an opportunity to improve a traditional form. The reuse of knife and sword blades is a case in point. In adapting these to make edged tools, care was frequently taken to retain and utilize the tanged or handle end. Examples of these implements are illustrated in Figure 17 and Plate 9. By incorporating the existing handle one was spared the effort of rehafting and probably ended up with a stronger haft as well. Here again, however, the degree of change is less than it appears. Certainly there had been a shift in material and, to a degree, some modification in form. But this seems more a matter of reinterpreting a traditional form in order to take advantage of newly available potential rather than replacing an old form with a new one.[4]

To sum up, during the first century of exposure to European materials, continuity characterized the Onondaga response as much as change did. That changes took place and had a profound impact on Onondaga culture and society is undeniable. However, so is the evidence that change was gradual, that it occurred in a phased manner, and that it affected some aspects of Onondaga culture more readily than it did others.

This returns us to the second part of the question: What aspects of a culture are most and least susceptible to cross-cultural influence? Figure 20 summarizes affects on the material aspects of a culture during acculturation. The scale suggests that the first evidence of cross-cultural change

Figure 20
A Scale for Receptiveness to Cross-Cultural Change

Least Resistant/Most Susceptible to Change

— Material preference and related technology for making an object

— Form of an object

— Function of an object

— Cultural values and beliefs that define an object's function

Most Resistant/Least Susceptible to Change

will occur where it is most useful and least threatening to the existing culture. For the Onondaga, this was at the level of material preference. The next level on the scale, and somewhat more resistant to change, is object form. While the choice of material could vary, objects tended to retain a traditional form regardless of whether they were made from traditional materials or novel ones. Gradually, however, the use of new materials appears to have encouraged experimentation in new forms, or at least greater expression of the diversity inherent in traditional ones. The acceptance of novel (European) forms was also a major factor promoting change at the level of object form. Whether these new shapes were incorporated directly, mimicked, or syncretized into the culture, the result was the same—an increase in the number of possible forms which any object might take.

What is clear from the Onondaga evidence is that change could take place at the level of material preference and object form without any significant difference in how the object was used. This is a key point. As Denys' statement indicates, the acceptance of new materials and forms usually presumes things also have changed at a more profound level in a culture. While this may be the case, the Onondaga data caution us against automatically drawing such a conclusion. Two examples help illustrate. By the mid-seventeenth century, copper kettles had effectively replaced native-made pottery. In terms of material and form, this was a substantial change; functionally, however, this substitution appears to have made no significant difference.[5] The same was true for axes. While iron axes almost completely replaced both lithic and iron celts/adzes by the middle of the seventeenth century, it is questionable whether this represented any functional change. Although he was referring to another time and place, Kenelm Burridge's comment on this is appropriate: "Though iron and finished steel tools have replaced the old stone tools, there has been very little substantial change either in the techniques of work or the purposes for which the tools are used" (Burridge 1960:51). Change, while real, can also be superficial.

By the middle of the seventeenth century, the acculturative process had begun to reshape Onondaga culture and society in many ways. But the changes were more a matter of grafting new materials, forms, and perhaps some functions onto an existing set of preferences, not replacing one set of values with another. In fact, at the level of basic cultural beliefs and values, it is questionable how much change had really occurred by the mid-seventeenth century. After 1655, however, matters were different. With resident Jesuits, a French settlement close by, and increasingly imperialistic European neighbors, the pressure for profound and substantial change in Onondaga would increase dramatically.

A final point here. In many ways, the issue of continuity versus change within a culture is largely a matter of perspective; one tends to find what one looks for. For those who want to see evidence of change in Onondaga, it is certainly there. On the other hand, so is the evidence of continuity. Only by assessing both, and each within the context of the other, can we arrive at a balanced understanding of the acculturative process and its impacts.

The final question about the acculturative process focuses on the issues of innovation and creativity. Initially this may seem a strange way to conclude, for acculturation is more often associated with a culture's decline than with its florescence. However, as the Onondaga case illustrates, this is more a reflection of how acculturation has been studied than of how the process itself works. Acculturation is not inherently destructive, nor is it merely a passive transfer or absorption of traits. As a process, it has as much potential for producing new traits as it does for eroding traditional ones. This potential is especially evident when the process is not forced, when the two cultures are at parity, as opposed to a dominant/subservient or conquest situation. Under the right conditions, acculturation is essentially a creative process (SSRC 1954:985).

The creative side of the acculturative process can be seen in Onondaga culture during the sixteenth and early seventeenth centuries. Occasionally the evidence occurs in unlikely guises. Take, for example, the issue of "lost" craft skills. It is generally accepted that as particular European objects like kettles, iron knives, and axes were incorporated into native culture, it was not only the traditional objects, the ceramic pots and lithic implements, that became obsolete, but also the craft skills which produced them. Once again we seem to have returned to Denys' position. However, it is not quite that simple. Certain classes of artifacts did dwindle and vanish by the mid-seventeenth century, but not the crafts themselves. Instead, they shifted focus in order to produce other and sometimes completely new objects. Lithics provide a good example. During the first half of the seventeenth century, lithic projectile points and edged tools were completely replaced by metal analogs. However, the traditional lithic reduction skills were not lost. Instead of making points, the craft was reoriented to produce a new object increasingly in demand—gunflints. A similar phenomenon occurred with ceramics. While native-made pottery had nearly disappeared by mid-century, the making of ceramic smoking pipes became more sophisticated both in technical and aesthetic terms. Rather than fading into obsolescence, traditional craft skills, like traditional materials and forms, were adapted to meet changing circumstances.

What characterized many of the traditional Onondaga crafts during the seventeenth century was not their demise but their amplification and elaboration. This is most evident in the degree to which native-made objects were increasingly embellished. This tendency, discussed in chapter 4, spans several artifact and material classes. Among the notable examples are ceramic pipes, bone and antler hair combs and effigy figures, stone pipes and effigies, and wooden ladles, combs, and pipes. I have argued that a primary motivation for this increased elaboration in Onondaga material culture was spiritual, an effort to maintain good relations with spirit beings (or to placate them if some offense had been committed). Whatever the motivation for embellishment was, the availability of metal tools permitted its fuller expression. Particularly in stone working, and the carving of antler and wood, metal tools promoted a level of technical proficiency and artistic expression not possible previously.

The amplification of craft skills during the seventeenth century was not restricted to the traditional. By the middle of the century, the Onondaga were proficient at several new crafts. Those most notable were related to metal working. While the basic techniques for cold working and annealing were known in the Northeast prior to European contact, there appears to have been little if any tradition of metal working among the Onondaga. Once contact occurred, however, these skills were quickly developed and perfected. By the first decades of the seventeenth century, the Onondaga were proficient at using sheet metal to produce a wide range of implements and ornaments. They had also begun to experiment with several innovative jointing techniques (rivetting, splicing, and lacing). As their skills became more refined, Onondaga craftsmen were able to mimic European forms as well as to create their own. Even with the increased availability of finished European goods, such crafts continued to flourish in Onondaga well into the eighteenth century (Plate 12a and b).

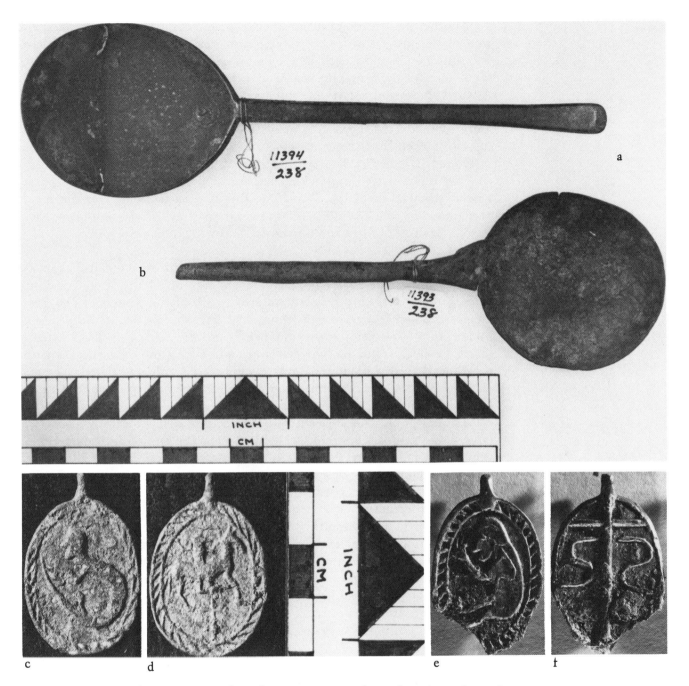

Plate 12. Examples of Late Seventeenth- and Early Eighteenth-Century Onondaga Metalwork. a. a European-made latten spoon, Coye site (RMSC 11394/238); b. a native-made copy from sheet brass, Coye site (RMSC 11393/238); c. and d. a native-cast pewter medal showing both traditional and European motifs, Jamesville site (Onondaga Historical Association); e. and f. another native-cast medal, this one lead, showing a syncretism of traditional and Christian motifs, Jamesville (Pen) site (photograph courtesy of Peter P. Pratt).

177

Another innovation of major consequence was the application of copper working techniques to iron. Although iron was a new metal, the Onondaga were quick to learn its uses. By the first decades of the seventeenth century, the Onondaga were making many of their traditional implements from it. As the volume and variety of iron goods reaching the Onondaga increased during the first half of the century, so did native ability to utilize iron in more sophisticated ways. The manufacture of metal tools was innovative in and of itself, but these implements also promoted creativity elsewhere in Onondaga culture. The role metal tools played in amplifying and enhancing other native craft skills has already been discussed. The point here is that the metal tools enabling this florescence were, for the most part, made by the Onondaga. The metals may have been European, but the conceptions of form and function defining the tools were predominantly native.[6]

By the second quarter of the seventeenth century, Onondaga metalworking skills had begun to move in another novel direction—casting. Initially, this probably was an outgrowth of making bullets. The first effigies produced were simple enough to have been cast in the dirt. By mid-century, however, more elaborate effigies were made as well as intricate inlays for both stone and wooden pipes and even simple medals. As with sheet metal work, Onondaga ability to express not only traditional concepts but new, syncretized ones through this medium became quite sophisticated by the end of the century (Plate 12).

To this point, the creativity of the acculturative process has focused largely on examples internal to Onondaga culture and with limited applicability beyond it. By the middle of the seventeenth century, however, Onondaga contacts with Europeans were sufficiently frequent and substantial to produce cross-culturally significant results. Just as the assimilation of other native people and their traditions produced hybrid forms of pottery or pipes, so too the ever greater exposure to Europeans resulted in more mixing and blending of the traditional Onondaga and novel European materials, techniques, and concepts. While these syncretisms, or cross-cultural hybrids, were a more salient characteristic of Onondaga culture during the last half of the seventeenth century, this aspect of acculturation already produced important results prior to 1650. Perhaps the most important was wampum, the perfect medium for cross-cultural exchange.

The issues concerning wampum, its origins and uses, are too complex to pursue in detail here. But we do need to review briefly how the form and function of this particular shell bead changed over time, and why it was so successful as a medium of exchange. As discussed in chapter 1, the wampum form predates European contact. Although not common, these small tubular beads were one of several marine shell forms that occur in Onondaga at the end of the Late Woodland phase. The beads also occur on Onondaga sites throughout the sixteenth century, and while they become somewhat more common, are never as frequent as discoidal shell beads. By the second quarter of the seventeenth century, however, several changes occur. Wampum beads begin to outnumber discoidal ones. In addition, the beads increasingly appear to have been drilled with metal tools. It is also at this time that the first evidence of beads strung into belts occurs (Wray 1973:16). Clearly, something happened during the first decades of the seventeenth century to change how wampum was made and, perhaps, used.

In order to function successfully as a cross-cultural medium, wampum had to have value both to native people and to Europeans. For the Iroquois, the "value" of wampum was complex. First was the shell itself. When consecrated to ritual use, shell was a substance of life-enhancing, life-restorative power. The conversion of raw shell into beads of a particular shape may have amplified this quality. While shell beads were valued by native people across the Northeast, they were of particular importance to the Five Nations. Wampum was an essential part, in many ways the material expression, of the condolence ritual. This ritual served as the means for consoling the kin of the deceased, and for "raising-up" another to fill the void. Whether at the level of the family, the clan, the tribe, or the Confederacy, the condolence ceremony lay at the heart of all Iroquois social relationships.[7] According to Iroquois oral tradition, the relationship between wampum and the condolence rite can be traced back to the origins of the Confederacy itself. This linkage was especially significant for the Onondaga since they were the wampum keepers, the record holders of the Confederacy. Wampum also had special meaning for the Onondaga because, by tradition, it was first discovered in Central New York.[8]

The value of wampum to Europeans can be expressed more simply: It facilitated trade, especially for furs, and it was a medium they could control. There is a strong correlation between the changing form and function of wampum early in the seventeenth century, and the rise of Dutch commercial activity in the Northeast. Ceci has argued that this was not coincidental, and that the Dutch actively sought out and used wampum as a component in constructing their successful fur trade system.[9] Yet, where did the idea originate? Why did Dutch commercial acumen focus on shell beads? The answer appears to lie a hemisphere away in West Africa, where Dutch entrepreneurs had encountered another native culture that placed a high value on specific forms of shell.

It remains unclear whether the use of cowrie shells (*Cypraea moneta* and *Cypraea annulus*) in West Africa predated the arrival of the Portuguese early in the sixteenth century. After 1515, however, Portuguese merchants began to transport large quantities of cowries (usually as ballast) from the islands off the east coast of Africa to the Niger Delta. Here they were readily accepted and used as currency (Johnson 1970). By the end of the century, Dutch traders, especially from Holland and Zeeland, had established regular trade with Benin, virtually excluding the Portuguese (Ryder 1965:195). While the Dutch did not continue to import cowries as the Portuguese had, they certainly learned that specific forms of shell possessed substantial commercial value.

The step from West Africa to northeastern North America was not as great as the distance may suggest. By the end of the sixteenth century, Dutch maritime interests had outgrown the Baltic and Mediterranean carrying trade and were contesting Iberian claims on both sides of the Atlantic. Numerous companies sprang up to capitalize on the economic potential of places as diverse as the Cape Verde Islands and the Caribbean (Scammell 1981:384–85). It is worth remembering that when the Dutch West India Company was established in 1621, it was chartered both for the slave trade in Africa and the fur trade in North America.

While it remains unclear exactly how and when wampum was redefined as a result of cross-cultural contacts, the available data suggest that changes took place on two levels. One was form. Based on archaeological evidence, it seems likely that prior to contact and into the early seventeenth century, wampum may actually have been strings of discoidal shell beads. Perhaps this is what Robert Juet saw in 1609 when he described the "stropes of Beades" that native people brought aboard the *Half Moon* to help restore a "dead" (drunk) chief (Purchas 1906, 13:368–69). By the second quarter of the century, however, wampum clearly refers to small tubular beads as well as to the belts into which they were strung. This change in form was accompanied by a change in function as wampum began to take on a new, Dutch-inspired commercial value in addition to its traditional ritual ones. The point here is that by the middle of the century, wampum was an acculturative product, a blending of traditional native and novel European conceptions. It was precisely for this reason that it worked so successfully.

The re-definition of wampum during the first half of the seventeenth century is important. It was among the first of the cross-cultural hybrids to emerge from the acculturative process. It was also one of the most influential, serving not only as currency but as the emblem of Iroquois diplomacy during the later seventeenth and eighteenth centuries. It was also a harbinger of things to come. The same forces that reshaped Onondaga material culture and re-defined wampum would soon start to re-form the Confederacy itself.

Re-Forming the Confederacy: The View from Onondaga

With the establishment of Dutch settlements in the upper Hudson River valley early in the seventeenth century, much began to change in Onondaga. Not only were European goods more plentiful, the preferred source was now closer and lay east along the axis of the Confederacy rather than south among the troublesome Susquehannocks. At first, the change must have seemed a great improvement; however, events would not bear out this optimism.

Like other elements of Iroquois culture, the Confederacy had changed during the sixteenth century. Nonetheless, its primary function remained unaltered—to serve as the means to redress grievances and keep peace among its members. The presence of the Confederacy, however, did not preclude conflicting interests, competition, or even violent disagreement among members. This section briefly examines how relationships within the Confederacy, specifically between the Onondaga and the Mohawk, were strained to the point of rupture during the first six decades of the seventeenth century. Although often expressed in terms of trade advantage and access to Europeans, the issue at base was one of tribal prerogative and prestige. By 1658 the problem was so serious that it threatened the very structure of the Confederacy. Pressured by harsh new economic and political realities, the tensions ultimately forced re-definition of the Confederacy, expanding what it stood for and how it would operate.

Initially, access to trade precipitated the tensions. From an Onondaga viewpoint, the Mohawk had all the advantages. A west/east axis of trade placed the Mohawk closest to the Dutch. Not only did location give the Mohawk the most direct access to European commodities, it also placed them in a position to regulate the flow of trade between the Dutch and the other Iroquois nations. It was neither malice nor greed that prompted the Mohawk to profiteer in this manner. Their geographic location entitled them to certain privileges, of which this was one. The Arendaronous, easternmost nation of the Huron confederacy, exercised a similar prerogative in the trade between the French and the other Huron nations (Thwaites 1896–1901, 20:19).

Jealous protection of this privileged position quickly became the hallmark of Mohawk intertribal relations. In 1620, when the Dutch tried to expand their markets to include the northern Algonquian tribes, Mohawk intervention subverted the attempt.[10] During the same period, the Mohawk also fought with their Mahican neighbors over access to the Dutch. By 1628, the Mahicans had been eliminated and Mohawk control of the trade was consolidated further.

It is hard to assess the extent to which Mohawk policy restricted trade; however, it certainly had some effect. In 1633, Killian van Rensselaer charged the Mohawk with interfering in the Dutch trade with other tribes and lamented that the Dutch were too weak to do anything about it (Van Laer 1908:248). By the following year, the "trade was doing very badly," and a small expedition was sent to visit the Iroquois to find out why. What Harmen van den Bogart and his companions discovered was that the Onondaga were trading with the French.

Regardless of which party initiated this trading relationship, once the contact was made both sides found it advantageous. For the French, it provided an entree into the Confederacy: a chance to deal with the other Iroquois nations and bypass the troublesome Mohawk. It is perhaps not coincidence that the first European recognition of individual Iroquois tribal identities occurs during this period. For the Onondaga, the French were an alternate source for the European goods they now required. More important, the Onondaga could deal directly with the French, avoiding Mohawk interference in their economic affairs. This mutual self-interest was the bedrock upon which a century of Onondaga-French relations would be built.

Attractive as this French alternative was, it was not immediately a practical option for the Onondaga. The French capability for trade developed much more slowly than that of the Dutch. While New Netherland had a small population and was burdened with cumbersome regulations and inefficiency, New France suffered even more from underpopulation and bad management. With the arrival in 1638 of a new governor, William Kieft, and the establishment of a free trade policy the following year, Dutch commercial capacity grew rapidly while the French continued to flounder (Trelease 1960:60–61; Trudel 1973:181–82, 210–11). Only after 1645, when control of trade was granted to inhabitants of New France, did the French commercial capacity begin to develop. In the meantime, while dealing with the French might have been preferable, the Onondaga had no choice but to continue to trade with the Dutch.

While the Onondaga and French courted each other, the relationship between the Mohawk and the Dutch also grew stronger. This was due in large part to the efforts of Arent van Curler, who negotiated treaties of friendship between the two parties in 1642 and again in 1645 (Trelease 1971:115–17). The Onondaga found themselves in a dilemma. They were obliged to trade with the Dutch, but this meant dealing with the Mohawk as well. This arrangement was increasingly difficult since what was in the self-interest of one tribe was considered by the other a threat to its economic prerogatives and prestige.

By the early 1640s, hints of this conflict began to show. In 1642 the Mohawk, who declared themselves the "enemy of the French," captured two Frenchmen. Members of the "upper nations" of the League, "not wishing to irritate the French," interceded and asked that the men be released (Thwaites 1896–1901, 21:21, 23, 29, 45). As a result, a large contingent of Iroquois met with the French that spring to work out an exchange. The discussions covered a variety of issues, including an invitation to the French "to make a settlement" in Iroquois territory where "all the Hiroquois nations could come for their trade" (ibid.:39). Who proposed this offer is not specified, but it was clearly a proposition reflecting Onondaga rather than Mohawk interests.

The whole episode ended in failure and recrimination, however. The discussions were abruptly terminated when a group of warriors attacked several canoes of unfortunate Algonquians happening to pass by.[11] Despite Iroquois efforts to renew the negotiations, the talks collapsed. To the French and most subsequent commentators, this incident was viewed as one more example of Iroquois perfidy and duplicity (ibid.:49; Trigger 1976, 2:635–37). It is better considered the prelude to an intra-Iroquois feud, the first round of a Mohawk-Onondaga conflict that would escalate in the following years.

In 1645, a treaty brought about temporary peace between the Mohawk and French. It did little to resolve the growing tensions between the Mohawk and Onondaga. Clear evidence of the rivalry surfaced when the Jesuit Isaac Jogues traveled to Mohawk country in May, 1646, to reaffirm the agreement of the previous year. While addressing the Mohawk, Jogues mentioned that the French also wanted to visit the Onondaga and planned to go by way of the shorter Lake Ontario route. The Mohawk elders were quick to respond. It was much too dangerous to reach Onondaga by that route, they said coolly. The only safe route was the one that went through the Mohawk territory first (Thwaites 1896-1901, 29:57). Jogues, however, considered it inexpedient to depend on Mohawk advice and proceeded to deal directly with the Onondaga. When he returned to the Mohawk again that fall, both he and his French companion were unceremoniously killed, victims in part of an intra-Iroquois quarrel (ibid., 31:117–19).

This thread of Mohawk-Onondaga enmity runs through many of the complex events between 1645 and 1650, a period marked by spreading intertribal warfare. Consider, for example, the dissolution of the Huron. The Huron presented a problem for the Onondaga. They were old and traditional enemies, yet they were also firm allies of the French. If the Onondaga hoped to keep their options open with the French, then they had to be cautious in dealing with the Huron.

Early in 1646, under growing pressure from the Seneca, the Huron approached the Onondaga hoping to negotiate a separate peace agreement. To their surprise, the Onondaga expressed considerable interest in the proposal. One of the reasons given for this unexpected rapprochement was that the Mohawk had become "unbearable even to their allies" (ibid., 33:123). The Onondaga were both jealous and angry over what they considered Mohawk intrusions in Onondaga affairs. Peace with the Huron would not only give them the opportunity to expand their trade with the French, it would teach the Mohawk a lesson in humility (Trigger 1976, 2:733). Emissaries were exchanged to make the arrangements, and the prospects for an Onondaga-Huron settlement seemed good.

The Mohawk, of course, were outraged. In January, 1648, when a new delegation of Huron ambassadors departed for Onondaga to conclude the negotiations, they were intercepted by a large Mohawk war party. All were killed except for the Onondaga who was guiding the party and two Huron who managed to escape. When news of the attack reached Huronia, the main Onondaga negotiator, who had remained as a self-appointed hostage, killed himself out of shame and despair (Thwaites 1896–1901, 33:125, 127).

Once again the Mohawk had successfully thwarted the Onondaga attempt to outflank them. When the final destruction of Huronia occurred later that summer, it was the Seneca and Mohawk who were primarily responsible (Trigger 1976, 2:762).

The lines of the Onondaga-Mohawk feud sharpened further when the Onondaga again approached the French in 1653. On June 26, a delegation of sixty Onondaga arrived at Montreal "on behalf of their whole nation" wishing to know "whether the hearts of the French would be inclined to peace" (Thwaites 1896–1901, 40:89, 163). To demonstrate their good faith, they warned the French of an impending Mohawk raid on Three Rivers.

The French response was guarded, Governor Lauson pointing out that past examples of treachery had made them suspicious. To this the Onondaga spokesmen patiently explained that "a careful distinction must be made" between the actions of the different Iroquois nations; Onondaga behavior was not the same as that of the Mohawk (ibid.:165).

The discussions continued all summer. The Onondaga spokesmen traveled to Quebec to plead their case and demonstrate their good intentions. Finally persistence paid off, and a peace treaty was concluded in September of 1653 (ibid.:191) With this agreement the way was now open for the Onondaga to achieve their real goal—renewal of direct trade with the French. To this end they once again invited the French to come and build a settlement in their territory (ibid.:219, 221; 41:45). This time the French were ready to consider the offer, and later that fall Simon LeMoine was sent to visit Onondaga and make the preliminary arrangements.

The Mohawk, still hostile toward the French, joined the peace agreement reluctantly (ibid., 41:93, 95, 163). News of LeMoine's mission to Onondaga brought a predictable response. "We, the five Iroquois Nations, compose but one cabin," a Mohawk spokesman explained. "It is with us

Mohawks, that you should begin; whereas you, by beginning with the Onondaga, try to enter by the roof and through the chimney." To proceed in this matter was quite dangerous, he concluded, with thinly disguised hostility. The French might find themselves blinded by the smoke and thus "Fall from the top to the bottom, having nothing solid on which to plant . . . [their] feet" (ibid.:87, 89).

This time, however, the Mohawk threats came too late. LeMoine's trip to Onondaga was highly successful and he returned to Quebec impressed by the sincerity and enthusiasm with which he had been received. Sites for the proposed settlement had been discussed, and the Onondaga were anxious to receive missionaries as well as trade (ibid.:131–35). Additional negotiations were to be conducted at Onondaga (ibid.:117).

The Onondaga's long courtship of the French came to fruition in July, 1656, when the promised expedition arrived and began to build a settlement on the east shore of Gannentaha (Onondaga Lake). It was an impressive array. Many of New France's best personnel came. They brought artillery, a wide range of craftsmen, and Jesuits to proselytize among the other Iroquois nations. It all suited the Onondaga perfectly. They had reasserted their claim as the diplomatic center of the Confederacy. Once again, it was to Onondaga that all parties came for council.

The seeds of failure were inherent in the Onondaga success. Ste. Marie de Gannentaha was abandoned by the French less than two years after its founding. Amidst the denouncements of Iroquois treachery, one astute observer reflected on some of the reasons the mission had been predestined to fail. The Onondaga had been "sincere in asking for the French to settle among them." They had had several reasons for doing so. One of them was that "The Mohawks sometimes treated them rather roughly when they passed through their villages to go and trade with the Dutch, [and] they wished to free themselves from this dependence by opening commerce with the French" (ibid., 44:151). The problem was that success for one side had come to mean humiliation for the other. The Onondaga's successful wooing of the French brought the Mohawk to "a jealousy almost verging on fury" (ibid., 43:129). This time the situation had gone too far. The Mohawk were as "bent on thwarting this design" as the Onondaga were on promoting it (ibid., 44:149). The result was intra-Iroquois war. "The two sides fought with each other until the ground was stained with blood and murder. Some believe that all this was a mere feint to mask the game better; . . . I greatly doubt whether Iroquois policy can go so far" (ibid.:149–51).

It was indeed no game, but rather the climax of a long-standing intra-Iroquois feud, one which threatened to destroy the very foundation of the Confederacy. A way had to be found to defuse the problem of conflicting tribal self-interests. Only slowly did a solution evolve.

The Onondaga-Mohawk dispute was a symptom, but not the cause, of the problem. By the middle of the seventeenth century the accelerating pace of acculturation had redefined the material aspects, not only of Onondaga culture, but of all the Five Nations. The Confederacy, however, was slower to change. While there is no clear evidence of how the Confederacy operated during this period, it is likely that it was little different from what has been proposed for the sixteenth century. The Confederacy's primary function remained an internal one, keeping the peace among its members. While the Confederacy's external functions were nebulous, a definite if rather disparate desire to "extend the rafters" and bring neighboring tribes under the Tree of Peace remained present. In spite of this, matters of trade and war continued to be tribal prerogatives and not issues over which the Confederacy had authority. The difficulty was that, by the middle of the seventeenth century, this system no longer worked. As the Onondaga-Mohawk feud demonstrated, it was not possible to keep peace internally unless external issues were also kept under control.

In the decade that followed the abandonment of Ste. Marie de Gannentaha, the need to resolve the problem of conflicting tribal interests became acute. Indeed, the Five Nations could ill afford to scrap among themselves. Decades of warfare and disease had nearly bled them out. While population could be augmented through assimilation and adoption, these very processes threatened to dilute the Iroquois still further. By 1664, the fabric of Iroquois society and culture was wearing dangerously thin. Even to outside observers the once mighty Five Nations appeared to be "within two finger-Breadths of total destruction" (ibid., 49:147–49).

Such vulnerability could not have come at a more inopportune time, for events far from Iroquoia soon brought even heavier pressures to bear on the beleagured Five Nations. In 1663, France's new twenty-four-year-old king, Louis XIV, exercised royal prerogative and took control of New France. No longer would decisions be made by a nearly moribund Company; instead, New France would be a royal province governed directly by the Crown. This was not the only change. Three years earlier, Charles II had been restored to the English throne. Also a man with ambitions, Charles wasted little time, first claiming Dutch territories in North America, then seizing them in 1664. For the Iroquois, these changes were both sudden and significant. Instead of compliant Europeans, men whose politics were as laissez-faire as their economics, the Five Nations now found themselves situated between two aggressive and imperialistic powers. The old days when commercial exchange or hostilities could be pursued with little thought as to the political consequences, were gone. From now on, trade and warfare would be increasingly intertwined with the policies of the Confederacy.

For the Iroquois, the problem required solution on two levels: how to strengthen the Confederacy internally by defusing the potential for conflicting tribal interests, and how to strengthen it externally in order to confront their ever more assertive European neighbors. In part, the solution was one of continuity, reaffirming what already worked. The Confederacy would continue to function internally as it had previously. At this level, the Onondaga role was key. As Father LeMercier observed in his *Relation* of 1667–68, "Onnontae [was] a large village and the center of all the Iroquois nations,—where every year the States-General, so to speak, is held to settle the differences that may have arisen among them" (ibid., 51:327). This policy, he noted, was "very wise . . . since their preservation depends on their union" (ibid.). Indeed it did. To preserve that union in the face of trying and divisive conditions was the critical need. To accomplish this something else had to happen.

Here too, the solution was typically Iroquoian, one based on the tacit understanding that the interests of all the members outweighed those of anyone in particular, just as survival of the clan or lineage always took precedence over that of the individual. The solution to the problem of intertribal conflicts was to augment the Confederacy's traditional authority and let it speak for the members on matters of trade and war. Rather than risk the inevitable disputes which would arise if each tribe negotiated on its own, the Confederacy would now broker the interests of all the Five Nations.

Expanding the Confederacy's authority so that it could control what previously had been tribal prerogatives was a significant change, one as great as any that had occurred in the material culture of the Five Nations. The implications of that change, in turn, redefined how the Confederacy would function. In effect, the traditions of social reciprocity had evolved into the politics of balance. Toward the end of the decade, a new Confederacy strategy, one based on balancing conflicting interests and demands, began to emerge. At this level too the Onondaga held a pivotal position.

Webb has argued that this new policy was largely the work of an Onondaga sachem, Daniel Garacontié, and that it first became evident in June, 1667, when Garacontié successfully negotiated an advantageous as well as peaceful settlement for the Five Nations with the French governor, Courcelles (Webb 1984:269).[12] Three years later, Garacontié again parleyed with the French "in the name of all the Iroquois," not just the Onondaga (Thwaites 1896–1901, 53:47). When Courcelles was recalled to France, Garacontié continued to treat with his successor, Louis de Buade, Comte de Frontenac, speaking "in the name of the Five Nations, as they had only one mind and one thought" (O'Callaghan 1853–1887, 9:103). The fulfillment of this new policy of balance occurred four years later when Garacontié concluded negotiations with the English and, in concert with New

York's Governor-General, Edmund Andros, proclaimed the establishment of the Covenant Chain (Webb 1984:297–301).

By 1677 the Confederacy was a different entity from what it had been two decades earlier. From this point on, it was the Confederacy that "declared war and made peace, sent and received embassies, entered into treaties of alliance, . . . [and] in a word, took all needful measures to promote their prosperity, and enlarge their dominion" (Morgan 1851:66–67). The kind of League which Lewis Henry Morgan would memorialize more than a century later had finally come into being.

There was another significant implication of this enhancement of the Confederacy's authority. It is no coincidence that the Covenant Chain became a meaningful, not merely metaphorical, term at the same time the Confederacy assumed its new powers. As discussed above, the Confederacy had always had an external aspect, whether it was actively expressed or not. During the sixteenth century and well into the seventeenth, the Confederacy expressed that desire to "extend the rafters" primarily through militancy. With the expansion of the Confederacy's power, another, more controlled means for bringing others under the Tree of Peace was available.

While Jennings has correctly observed that the League and the Chain were different and should not be confused, he still puzzles over the origin of the Covenant Chain (Jennings 1984:368–69). The Chain itself was a series of treaties and alliances designed to stabilize, to balance the competing interests of the English colonies, the Five Nations, and other tribal groups. Strip away the European legalisms, however, and a very Iroquoian concept remains. At base, the Chain was a set of reciprocal social, and now political, obligations which bound the participants together so that internal differences could be minimized. In a sense, the League and the Chain were the same principle, only manifested in different directions, the League internally among the Five Nations, the Chain externally to all those who cared to join. It was not military prowess which saved the Five Nations from oblivion during the last half of the seventeenth century, it was diplomatic finesse, "their exceptional ability in treaty negotiation" (ibid.:xviii). The Covenant Chain was the medium through which the League could "extend the rafters" to include not only other native people but their ambitious colonial neighbors as well.

By 1677 the Confederacy, like the wampum belts which conveyed its treaties and keyed its records, was a product of acculturative change. In spite of the cross-cultural influences, however, it was the Iroquois themselves who were the architects of their own success. Just as they had learned to use metals and reorient traditional crafts in order to meet new needs, so too they re-formed the Confederacy. The Onondaga played a central role in this process. For a century and a half they struggled to accommodate changing conditions and new circumstances. But change had also accommodated them. From an independent and autonomous tribe they had become the balance point of the League.

Appendix A

Native Materials: Descriptions and Definitions

Pottery

In general, the Onondaga made two types of vessels: collarless pots and collared pots. Since these differ in both profile and decoration, they are analyzed as separate categories. A collarless pot is a vessel with only an expanded or flared lip, usually above a constricted neck (Figure 21a). A collared pot is a vessel with a collar, or vertically expanded section, above a constricted neck. The collar consists of a lip, collar face, and collar base (Figure 21b). These structural components are defined below.

lip	The uppermost edge of the vessel.
collar face	The exterior of the collar, extending from the exterior lip edge to the collar base; this is where most of the decorative motifs occur.
collar base	The lowest point on the collar, where the vessel "breaks," or begins to curve into the neck.
neck	The constricted area between the lip and shoulder of a collarless pot, or the collar base and shoulder of a collared vessel.
shoulder	The upper excurvate surface of the body.
body	The globular part of the vessel below the neck.

Of the many attributes that can be analyzed, perhaps the most useful is the rim profile, or the cross section of the vessel above the neck. This study uses three collarless and five collared profiles.

On collarless pots, the three profile groups include plain lip, everted lip, and thickened lip:

191

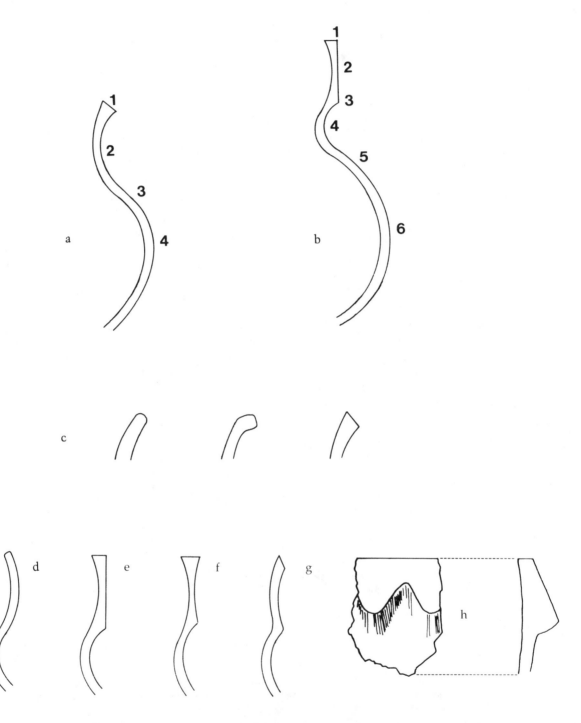

Figure 21. Onondaga Pottery Profiles and Terminology. Pottery Terms a. a collarless pot: 1. lip, 2. neck, 3. shoulder, 4. body. b. a collared pot: 1. lip, 2. collar face, 3. collar base, 4. neck, 5. shoulder, 6. body. Collarless rim profiles: a. plain, b. everted, c. thickened. Collared rim profiles: d. Chance round, e. Chance straight, f. biconcave, g. concave, h. frilled.

plain lip	On these vessels there is little or no thickening or eversion of the lip; in profile, the vessel walls are usually of uniform thickness (Figure 21).
thickened lip	On these vessels the lip is markedly thickened; the top lip surface remains flat while the exterior lip edge protrudes over the vessel's exterior surface (Figure 21).
everted lip	On these vessels the top of the lip is markedly everted in relation to the interior and exterior surfaces; generally, the top lip surface has a slope of at least 30° (Figure 21).

On collared pots, the five profile groups include Chance round, Chance straight, biconcave, concave, and frilled.

Chance round	On these vessels the exterior surface, or collar face, is convex while the interior is concave. There is usually no thickening of the collar base (Figure 21).
Chance straight	On these vessels the collar face is straight while the interior is concave. The collar base is usually thickened, resulting in a sharper "break" between the collar and the neck (Figure 21).
biconcave	On these vessels the lip is flat and somewhat thickened. The collar base is always thickened. This results in a profile where both the interior surface and the collar face are concave (Figure 21). This profile developed from the earlier Chance straight style.
concave	On these vessels the lip is everted rather than thickened. The collar base usually is thickened. The collar face is concave while the interior is convex and concave. The resulting profile has somewhat of an S shape (Figure 21). This profile was a further evolution of the biconcave form.
frilled	On these vessels the prominent feature is an exaggerated basal notching in which the remnants of the collar base have been pinched up into relief. This distinctive technique usually occurs on collars of low to medium height and may be expressed in one of three forms. The "frills" may be lobed (mammiform), pointed, or truncated (see Figure 21 for front and profile views of a lobed frill).

Smoking Pipes

For this study a series of general categories are used that encompass the majority of available pipes. These are based primarily on bowl shapes, and each general category can be subdivided into more specific varieties. These general categories are: trumpet, square trumpet, bulbous, barrel-shaped, human effigy, and animal effigy. This schema is not presented as the means for a thorough and complete analysis of Onondaga pipes. However, it presents enough detailed information to enable others to use it comparatively.

The trumpet bowl category can be divided further into four varieties: proto, plain, rimmed, and ringed.

proto trumpet | Bowls of this style are basically conical in shape. The lip has little flare and is usually rounded at the edge. This style of bowl is usually not decorated (Figure 22).

plain trumpet | This style has a pronounced rim that flares out horizontally from the bowl. The lip is generally tapered at the edge. This style may or may not be decorated (Figure 22).

rimmed trumpet | This style is similar to the plain trumpet except for a distinct vertical edge on the rim. This vertical edge is frequently the only part of the bowl to be decorated (Figure 22).

ringed trumpet | This variety is also similar to the plain trumpet, although the flare of the lip is not necessarily as great. The distinguishing feature is a series of deeply incised lines running horizontally around the bowl. Sometimes these bands are accompanied by rows of punctates (Figure 22).

Trumpet pipes with squared bowls occur in four varieties: square, coronet, collared square, and collared coronet.

square trumpet | This bowl probably began as a variant of the plain trumpet. Instead of being round, the bowl has been molded into a square. Like the rimmed trumpet, there is a distinct vertical lip edge that is often decorated (Figure 22).

coronet trumpet | On this distinctive variety, the top of the bowl at each corner has been pinched or molded up and resembles a small castellation. Again, the vertical lip edge is often decorated (Figure 22).

collared square trumpet | Here the rim of the bowl has been vertically expanded, perhaps to resemble the collar of a pot. If this enlargement is 10mm or more in height, this would be termed a collared bowl. This vertical lip edge is usually highly decorated (Figure 22).

collared coronet trumpet | These bowls have the same vertical expansion as collared square bowls, with the addition of pinched-up corners (Figure 22).

Although pipes with bulbous bowls do not occur in a great variety of forms, they have been given a variety of names.

bulbous bowls | These bowls are round or oval in vertical section with walls that are usually quite thick at the midpoint. Although occasionally plain, bowls in this category are usually decorated, often with encircling horizontal rings or cross-hatched, diagonal lines (Figure 22).

The barrel-shaped bowl probably derived from the bulbous bowl and occurs in two varieties: short and elongated.

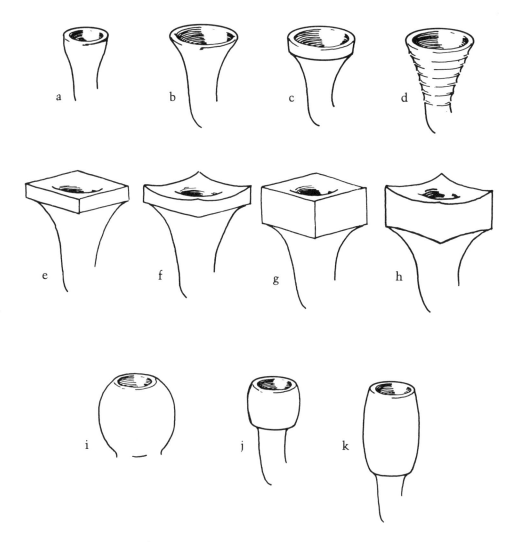

Figure 22. Onondaga Pipe Shapes and Terminology. a. proto trumpet, b. plain trumpet, c. rimmed trumpet, d. ringed trumpet, e. square trumpet, f. coronet trumpet, g. collared square trumpet, h. collared coronet trumpet, i. bulbous, j. short barrel, k. elongated barrel.

short barrel   These bowls have the same general shape as a barrel—broadest at the center and tapering somewhat at either end. Also included in this category are bowls cylindrical in shape. Short barrel bowls are 20mm or less in height (Figure 22).

elongated barrel   Height is what distinguishes these bowls from the short variety. Elongated barrel bowls are greater than 20mm high. These bowls are usually, though not always, decorated (Figure 22).

Appendix B

European Materials: Descriptions and Definitions

Kettles

Given its importance in the trade between Europeans and native Americans, surprisingly little is known about the typical copper "trade" kettle. From the late sixteenth century through at least the third quarter of the seventeenth, these kettles were used across the Northeast and appear to have been standardized in form. The overall shape was characterized by straight sides, a relatively flat bottom, and a mouth that was wider than the base. Although size could vary considerably, these kettles were always of one-piece construction. The body was initially formed by the battery method and then finished on a lathe. In general, these kettles were made from a thin-gauge sheet, usually less than 1mm thick. The lip was formed by rolling the edge of the kettle over an iron reinforcing wire. These kettles were rarely marked (Figure 23a).

The bail, or handle, also of iron wire, was attached by means of two lugs. Three lug types occur on Onondaga sites. Most common is the "square with folded corners" type. This lug was formed by taking a rectangular piece of heavier-gauge sheet copper, folding it in half over the kettle rim, and rivetting it in place. A single large perforation was made for the bail, and the upper corners were folded over again for reinforcement (Figure 23c). A variant was made by cutting the corners off rather than folding them over (Figure 23d). A second type has been termed an "omega" lug because of its shape. This was formed from a long, thin rectangular piece of copper sheet rolled into a tube. The ends were then hammered flat and the piece folded in half so that the flattened ends were side by side. The two flattened ends were then rivetted to the kettle (Figure 23e). The third and simplest type of lug was made from one piece of sheet copper (Figure 23f). Both "omega" and one-piece lugs are an uncommon occurrence on Onondaga sites prior to 1655.

At present it is not known where these trade kettles were produced, although the evidence points to German manufacturing centers along the Rhine or in the vicinity of Antwerp. Wherever they were made, this form of kettle differs in substantial ways from two other seventeenth-century forms. One is the style of copper kettle used on Dutch domestic sites from the thirteenth century through the seventeenth. These vessels were constructed from three or more separate pieces

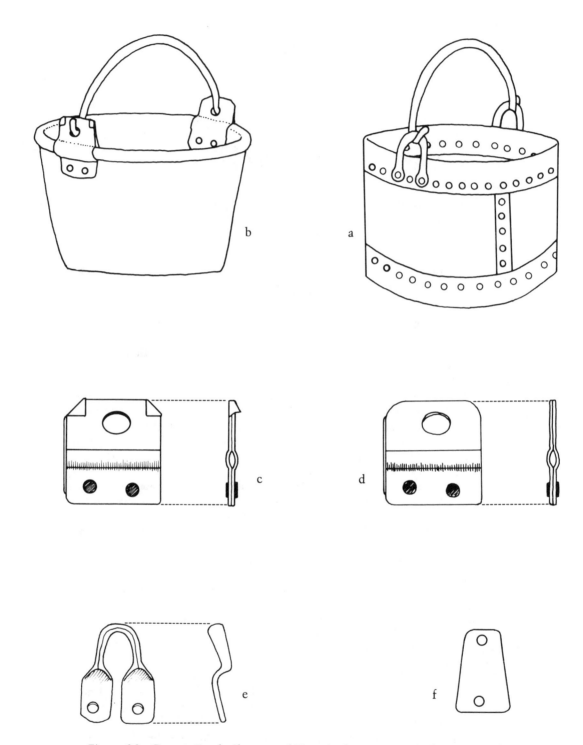

Figure 23. Copper Kettle Shapes and Terminology. a. a typical seventeenth-century trade kettle, b. a typical seventeenth-century Dutch domestic kettle, c. a square kettle lug with folded corners, d. a square kettle lug with cut corners, e. an "omega"-shaped kettle lug, f. a one-piece kettle lug.

of sheet copper fastened together by rivets. The sides are vertical, and the entire vessel is of heavier-gauge metal (at least 1mm thick). While iron wire is also used for the bail, the lugs are cast rather than made from sheet (Figure 23b). For one of the few examples of this form reported from the Northeast, see Brawer 1983:54.

The second form occurs most commonly on French-related sites and is subtly different from the typical trade kettle. While both are of a similar one-piece construction, the two forms differ in several minor ways. Unlike the typical trade kettle, the French-related variety often has lugs with cut corners rather than folded ones. These kettles are also characterized by: a more frequent occurrence of maker's marks, embellishment by patterned battery work, and more varied vessel shape. For examples of these traits from the Grimsby site, a pre-1650 Neutral cemetery, see Kenyon 1982:66 (N-141), 222 (N-604). Comparison of these examples to those described by Brain (1979:164–79) from the Tunica site supports the assertion that these traits are French-related.

Axes

Unlike kettles, axes have been a subject of scholarly inquiry since early in this century. Major studies include Beauchamp (1902:59–68), the first to catalogue archaeological examples and compare them with historical accounts, and Russell (1967:248–53), who attempted to differentiate between French, Dutch, and English style trade axes. Current evidence suggests that most of the axes which occur on sixteenth- and early seventeenth-century sites in the Northeast were made in the Basque Provinces, regardless of the nationality of who traded them. By the second quarter of the seventeenth century, however, the Dutch had apparently begun to make their own axes for trade.

Another approach to studying axes has been to use systematic measurement in an effort to define significant statistical clusters and relationships. This was first attempted by Kidd (1955). The system of description and measurement used in this study is adapted from one devised by Gordon DeAngelo and used by Pratt (1976:234–38). Figure 24 illustrates the terminology used to describe a typical trade axe.

Axes from Onondaga sites generally fall into two size categories. Large axes have the following average dimensions: overall length, 200mm; bit width, 95mm; poll height, 55mm; eye length, 60mm; and weight, 1.5kg. Smaller axes, which begin to occur about mid-seventeenth century, have the following average dimensions: overall length, 165mm; bit width, 75mm; poll height, 45mm; eye length, 44mm; and weight, 0.75kg. Measurements for all available Onondaga axes are listed in Bradley (1979:415–16).

Marks were often struck on the axe blade near the socket. While these have often been termed "armorer's marks," it is not clear what they signify. The marks that have been recorded from Onondaga examples are illustrated in Figure 25.

Knives

At least two attempts have been made to classify the variety of iron knives on seventeenth-century sites in the Northeast (Hagerty 1963; Garrad 1969). The system used here is based on these precedents and on the observed characteristics of the knives recovered from Onondaga sites.

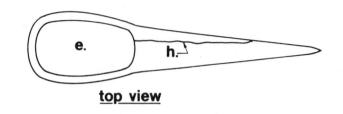

top view

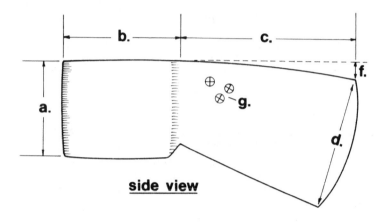

side view

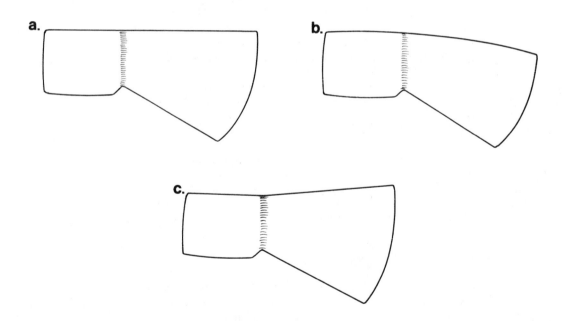

Figure 24. Iron Axe Terminology and Blade Shapes. Terminology: a. poll, b. socket, c. blade, d. bit, e. eye, f. "drop" of the blade, g. maker's mark, h. weld line. Blade shapes: a. straight, b. steep drop, c. raised.

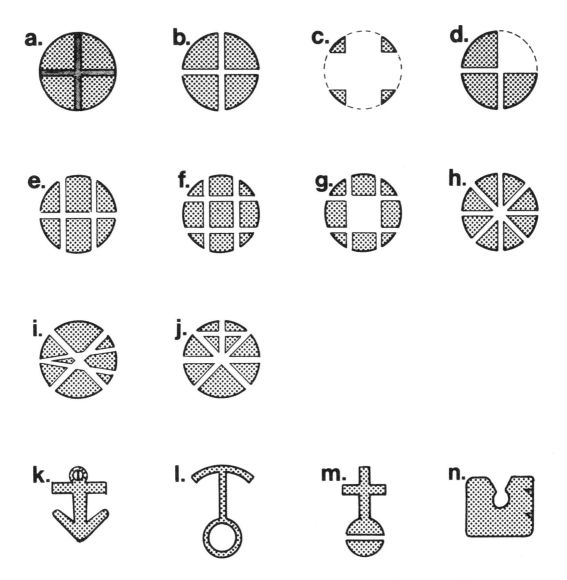

Figure 25. Iron Axe Marks from Protohistoric and Early Historic Onondaga Sites (not to scale). a. simple cross in circle, style 1; b. simple cross in circle, style 2; c. simple cross in circle, style 3; d. simple cross in circle, style 4; e. compound cross in circle, style 1; f. compound cross in circle, style 2; g. compound cross in circle, style 3; h. compound cross in circle, style 4; i. compound cross in circle, style 5; j. compound cross in circle, style 6; k. anchor; l. modified anchor; m. orb; n. rectangular.

Knives can be divided into three basic categories: those with a flat tang, those with a tapered tang, and those with a blade that folds into the handle. The tang is the portion of the knife to which the handle is attached. The shape of the blade has not been used as a criterion for two reasons. Blades are rarely intact enough to measure shape accurately. In addition, the original shape of the blade has often been changed by resharpening. Since the tang and collar sections were seldom modified and are usually better preserved than the blade, they are more reliable as attributes for classification.

The three basic categories can be further subdivided as follows:
I. Knives with a flat tang
    A. without a collar (the collar is a thickened section that separates the blade from the tang)
        1. no heel (Figure 26a)
        2. rounded heel
        3. straight oblique heel (Figure 26b): the heel is the unsharpened edge of the blade nearest the collar
    B. with a collar
        1. thin collar—2mm or less (Figure 26c)
        2. thick collar—greater than 2mm
II. Knives with a tapered tang
    A. conical collar
        1. plain
        2. slightly grooved (Figure 26d)
        3. elaborately grooved (Figure 26e)
    B. cylindrical
    C. thin—2mm or less (Figure 26f)
III. Knives with a blade that folds into the handle (Figure 26g)

Awls

Although they were an extremely important item in native-European trade, iron awls have received little attention from archaeologists. One exception is Stone's detailed description of examples from Fort Michilimackinac (1974:155–59).

The awls from Onondaga sites can be divided into three types (Figure 27). Type I awls are double-pointed, slightly curved, and up to 80mm in length. These awls are diamond-shaped in section with maximum dimensions of 5mm wide and 4mm high. Type II awls are double-pointed, straight, and up to 100mm in length. The average length appears to be about 80mm. These awls are square in section and have a maximum thickness of 3–4mm. Type III awls are double-pointed, straight but offset or stepped in the middle, and up to 120mm in length. Like Type I examples, these awls are also diamond-shaped in section and appear to have the same maximum height and width dimensions.

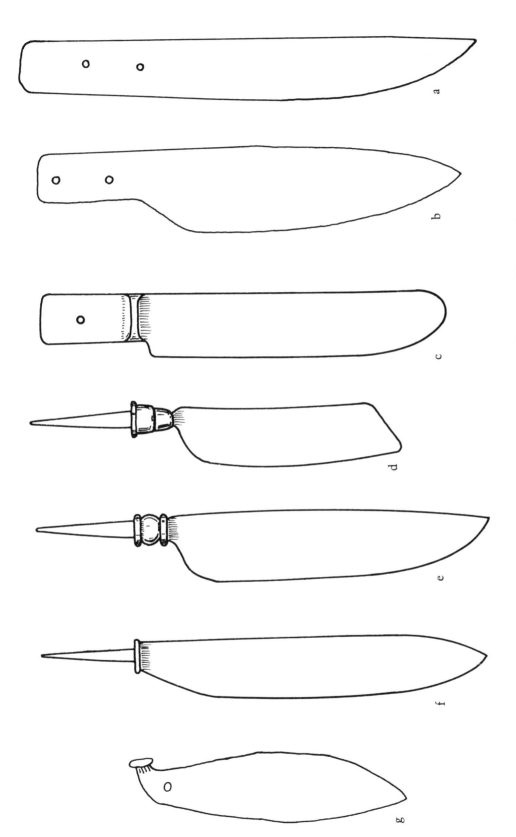

Figure 26. Iron Knife Shapes and Terminology. a. flat tang with no collar or heel; b. flat tang with no collar and an oblique heel; c. flat tang with a thin collar; d. tapered tang with a simply grooved collar; e. tapered tang with an elaborately grooved collar; f. tapered tang with a thin collar; g. blade from a folding knife.

203

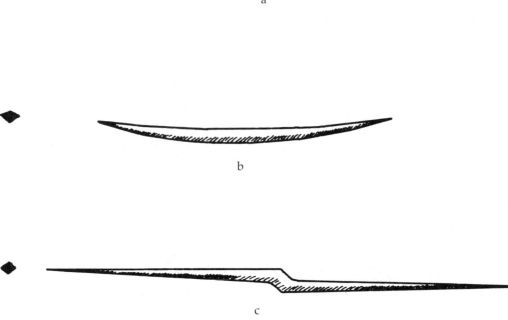

Figure 27. Iron Awl Shapes. a. a type I awl; b. a type II awl; c. a type III awl.

Appendix C

Historic Onondaga Sites from 1655 to 1779

A brief discussion of the later seventeenth- and eighteenth-century Onondaga sites is presented here in order to complete the site sequence as well as to continue documentation of the changes in Onondaga material culture. The sites are listed in chronological order and are summarized in terms of major historical events and artifact characteristics.

Site	Estimated Occupation
Indian Castle	1655–1663
Indian Hill	1663–1682
Bloody Hill II (small)	1675–1685
Jamesville	1682–1700
Sevier	1700–1720
Coye (small)	1730–1750
Onondaga Castle	1720–1779

Indian Castle (ca. 1655–1663)

This appears to be the site occupied by the Onondaga while the French were at Ste. Marie de Gannentaha (1656–1658). It may also have been the location where the mission of St. Jean Baptiste was established by Fathers Dablon and Chaumont in 1656.

Native Material: Shell is at the height of its popularity, appearing in runtee, crescent, and effigy forms, as well as in many bead shapes. Marginella beads are again present. Native pottery is represented by only a few vestigial sherds; however, pipes are common with animal (bear, turtle, bird) and human effigies prevalent. Combs occur more frequently. Native-made gunflints are still a common occurrence.

European Material: Religious artifacts, particularly rings with the IHS or L and heart motif, are common. Glass bottle fragments (globe and shaft) appear for the first time. Glass beads are common and predominantly tubular with heat-rounded ends. Red is the most frequently occurring color. Many Dutch-related items occur, such as Campen cloth seals and an undated medal of William, Prince of Orange (probably William II, who reigned 1647–1651). There is considerable evidence of native metal working, especially the making of coiled bracelets and ear ornaments from copper wire.

Indian Hill (1663–1682)

This appears to be the town where the mission of St. Jean Baptiste was reestablished by Father Garnier in 1667. According to a Jesuit resident, the Onondaga lived here for nineteen years. This site, and the smaller Bloody Hill II (or Weston) site, are probably the towns described by the Englishman Wentworth Greenhalgh. Although he stated that the town was "not fenced" in 1677, recent archaeological work has documented the presence of a substantial palisade (A. Gregory Sohrweide, personal communication).

Native Material: While shell is still popular, catlinite and red slate are increasingly used for ornaments. Ceramic pipes continue to be common; effigy and ring bowl styles predominate. Combs are frequent and portray animal effigies or geometric patterns. There is evidence of extensive and sophisticated wood carving, especially ladles, bowls, pipes, and combs.

European Material: Religious ornaments remain prevalent, although there is a greater diversity in motifs. European ceramics (tin glazed wares and Rhenish stoneware) and bottle fragments are more common. Glass beads are plentiful and predominantly round instead of tubular, with red and black most frequent (Kidd IIa1, IIa6). While Dutch cloth seals and clay smoking pipes remain present, French-related objects are also common, including marked knife blades, an undated Louis XIV medal, and many coins (lairds and double tournois). There is still considerable evidence of sheet copper working plus more evidence of lead/pewter casting.

Jamesville (1682–ca. 1700)

Jean de Lamberville described the move to this site in 1682. Later accounts describe the town as having a triple palisade built with the assistance of the English. Archaeological testing has verified a triple palisade (Pratt n.d.). The town was burned during Frontenac's invasion of 1696 but was apparently reoccupied for a short period afterwards.

Native Material: Catlinite is now the preferred medium for ornamentation and occurs in a variety of bead, pendant, and effigy styles. Shell remains popular, particularly long tubular beads and runtees as well as effigy forms such as fish and turtles. Native pipes are beginning to decline, although some well made styles such as ring bowls with face effigies continue to be made. Combs remain varied and sophisticated.

European Material: Items of English manufacture, especially smoking pipes and cloth seals, begin to replace those of Dutch origin. However, Jesuit-related religious ornaments still remain common. European ceramics and bottle glass are now a frequent occurrence. Glass beads are common and include a mixture of older tubular and round types as well as new polychrome and wire-wound varieties (Kidd WIb, WIIc). Native metal working continues to thrive, especially the casting of small lead and pewter medals.

Sevier (ca. 1700–1720)

The Onondaga appear to have resided here briefly prior to relocating in the Onondaga Creek valley. During this period the French attempted to build a blockhouse and chapel in Onondaga (1711).

Native Material: Red slate is the most popular medium for ornamentation, although catlinite and shell continue to be used. Small face effigies are a commonly occurring form. There is a noticeable decline in both the quantity and quality of native-made pipes and combs; forms are simpler and less embellished with detail. The carving of ladles and other wooden vessels remains a strong tradition.

European Material: English ceramics, bottle glass, and smoking pipes are common. An increased number of buttons and buckles indicates a greater usage of European clothing. Religious ornaments continue to occur as do other indications of French presence, including jack knives with French makers' names on the blade and brass crescents inscribed with "Dieu et Roi de France." While glass beads are less common than on previous sites, wire-wound varieties occur more frequently.

Onondaga Castle (ca. 1720–1779)

Onondaga Castle is a general name for a series of towns occupied by the Onondaga during the eighteenth century. Among the more important were: Ka-na-ta-go-wah, located on the east side of Onondaga Creek and occupied between 1730 and 1750; a large but scattered town on the west side of the creek near the fort that Sir William Johnson built for the Onondaga in 1756; and a small site (Coye) in the uplands east of the Onondaga Valley, possibly the village of "Tue-tah-das-o." These towns were described in 1743 by John Bartram and, over the next decade, by a series of Moravian missionaries. All the Onondaga settlements in the Onondaga Valley were destroyed by an American raiding party in 1779.

Native Material: Although less common than on previous sites, catlinite and red slate remain popular mediums for ornamentation. A few shell beads and gorgets continue to occur. Simple pipes and combs still persist; the majority of the pipes are of a stemless (Micmac) style. Some wooden and antler utensils continue to be made.

European Material: During this period the adoption of European materials becomes so widespread that native refuse begins to look very much like that from colonial frontier settlements—a scatter of broken ceramics, bottle glass, clay pipes, and scraped hardware. There is ample evidence of British imperial concern, including "Brown Bess" musket parts and a variety of medals (George I, George II, and Duke of Cumberland). Glass beads, predominantly wire-wound, are present but not very common. While some trade silver occurs, there is evidence of native metal working in both copper and silver.

Although many Onondaga left their homeland after Van Schaick's raid, others chose to remain in Onondaga Valley. The treaty signed at Fort Schuyler in 1788 recognized Onondaga land claims and established a one hundred-square-mile tract, of which the current reservation is the remnant.

Notes

Introduction

1. The terms "League" and "Confederacy" are often used interchangeably in describing the social and political structure for which the Five Nations Iroquois are so well known. In this study, these terms have different meanings. Confederacy refers to an indigenous, peace-keeping mechanism which operated among five culturally and linguistically related Iroquoian tribes and was based on the ritual redress of injury or grievance. Under the Confederacy, external matters such as warfare and trade remained tribal prerogatives. League refers to a more formalized structure which came into being during the third quarter of the seventeenth century. Under the League, the traditional mechanism of redress was expanded so that internal disputes could be mediated, thus allowing the Five Nations to speak as one on external political and economic matters.

2. There is considerable literature on the topic of acculturation. My definition draws most heavily on the exploratory formulation developed by the Social Science Research Council Summer Seminar on Acculturation (1954). Other sources include Linton 1940, Spicer 1962, Berry 1980, and Smith 1984.

3. The direct historical approach to archaeology was first proposed by Julian Stewart (1942). For a discussion of this method as well as its more recent variants, see Smith 1984:13–14.

1. The Indigenous Onondaga

1. In contrast to proto-Iroquoian groups, Algonquian antecedents are not well understood. What evidence is available suggests that proto-Algonquian groups remained more dispersed and less affected by the nucleation forces which seem to characterize the proto-Iroquoians (Kraft 1975:59–60).

2. Salient sources on the Owasco include Ritchie 1944:29–101; 1969:272–300; and Ritchie and Funk 1973:165–252. Wright (1966:22–53) is still the primary source on the Glen Meyer and Pickering branches of the Early Ontario Iroquois stage. The best review of the St. Lawrence Iroquois and their antecedents is Pendergast 1975. While the origins and forebears of the Susquehannocks are yet to be clarified, by far the best effort is Kent 1984.

3. The major pollen studies available for Central New York are Sheldon 1952 and Cox 1959. Other relevant sources include Yeager's (1969) pollen study in Western New York and

Funk and Rippeteau's effort to synthesize pollen and other paleoenvironmental data with their cultural sequence for the upper Susquehanna Valley (1977:49, 55).

4. The O'Neil site, dated A.D. 1150 ± 80 and A.D. 1160 ± 80, is discussed in Ritchie and Funk (1973:70–85). The undated Cabin site is described by Tuck (1971:34–45). The other three small Owasco sites are Jack's Reef #2 and Smith's Island (Ritchie 1944:83–86) and Wickham #3 (Ritchie 1946).

5. Beauchamp (1900:112–20) gives some indication of the density of sites along these waterways, although his descriptions seldom permit cultural or temporal identification. Beauchamp's manuscript, "Antiquities of Onondaga," contains much more detailed information on most of these sites. A cursory review suggests that several have Owasco components.

6. Such locations were also favored for the construction of fish weirs. Beauchamp (1900:113, #6) describes an example in the Seneca River near Baldwinsville: "It is a stone eelweir with three bays of unequal length reaching up the river as it tended to the north shore. It was built of fieldstone and was about 1,200 feet long . . . Part of another is below the Jack's Reef bridge, and others are found elsewhere." Although these weirs are undated (and perhaps undatable), they suggest that fishing activities occurred in these locations over a considerable span of time.

7. Fish remains from the Chamberlin site were not identifiable. On the nearby Maxon-Derby site, an earlier (Carpenter Brook phase) Owasco site dated A.D. 1100, over 85% of the faunal remains were fish, predominantly common bullhead (*Ictalurus* species) (Ritchie and Funk 1973:166, 210). The identifiable fish remains from the Cabin site were sucker (*Moxostoma* species) (Tuck 1971:44). A larger range of fish was probably taken, especially during the spring and fall spawning seasons. See Cleland (1982) for a summary of freshwater species and their availability. It is likely that anadromous fish (particularly shad and salmon) and eels were also taken. Although this has yet to be documented archaeologically, in Central New York, both eel (*Anguilla bostoniensis*) and shad (*Alosa sapidissima*) were recovered from the Bates site in Chenango County (Ritchie and Funk 1973:235).

8. Celts and adzes differ both in shape and in the way they were hafted. Celts, or ungrooved axes, are generally symmetrical in plan and in section. Based on several examples recovered with wooden handles still attached, it is clear that celts were hafted with the cutting blade parallel to the handle. While adzes are generally symmetrical in plan, they are asymmetric in section and were designed to be hafted with the cutting edge perpendicular to the handle (Beauchamp 1897:12, Figure 1a and b; Willoughby 1935:141–44).

9. Replicating studies have demonstrated that these chipped discs were not used as hoes (Lindner 1983). They occur most frequently on sites where there is strong evidence of fishing. The early Owasco Maxon-Derby site, for instance, produced eight examples; over 85% of recovered faunal remains were fish (Ritchie and Funk 1973:210–11, Plate 101, #4–6). The suggestion that these discs were bottom weights for seines was made early in the twentieth century based on evidence from the Susquehanna Valley (Wren 1914:84, Plate 27). Kraft offers a similar interpretation for the chipped discs (and rectilinear forms) from Delaware Valley sites (Kraft 1975:113–18). For a discussion of seine technology, see Cleland 1982:774–75.

10. The importance of fishing activities on some of these sites is underscored by the quantities of fishing-related implements recovered. At Jack's Reef, for example, Ritchie notes that "literally hundreds of harpoons whole and fragmentary and nearly 100 fishhooks" were recovered (1944:84).

11. Marine shell beads (of both *Mercenaria* and *Busycon* species), as well as small tubular beads of copper, were excavated by Ritchie at the Sackett, or Canandaigua, site (Ritchie 1936:50–51). Marine shell and small, native copper beads also occur, albeit rarely, on Glen Meyer and Pickering sites in Ontario (Wright 1966:39, 96; Kenyon 1968:31).

12. For a more detailed discussion, see Lenig 1965; Ritchie 1969:302–12; Tuck 1971:47–92.

13. Ritchie and Funk estimate the population at the Kelso site (eastern village) at about 330, based on longhouse size and number (1973:275).

14. Tuck 1971:78–79. Tuck gives a detailed account of house shape and size at Furnace Brook and Howlett Hill. Ritchie and Funk also present a concise review of Oak Hill structures (1973:167–68).

15. Identifiable species include: sheepshead, sucker, catfish, pike or pickerel, largemouth bass, and sunfish (Tuck 1971:70).

16. For additional details of Oak Hill ceramics, see Lenig 1965 and Tuck 1971.

17. These small effigies are quite unusual and do not seem to occur on either earlier or later sites in Central New York. Examples from Furnace Brook are described and illustrated by Tuck 1971:66 and Plate 14, #11; examples from Kelso are in Ritchie and Funk 1973:273 and Plate 151, #17–19.

18. In typing the triangular projectile points from the Kelso site, Ritchie and Funk recorded twenty as Levanna and three as Madison (1973:275).

19. While the paleoenvironmental data are sketchy, there does appear to have been a climatic shift toward cooler conditions some time after ca. A.D. 1200 (Funk and Rippeteau 1977:55; Yeager 1969:37–38).

20. There are additional Chance phase sites in the Pompey Hills, although they are poorly documented. These include the Sperry site (a large village?) and the Fietta site (a small hamlet?) (F. LaFrance 1977:2–4; A. D. LaFrance, personal communication).

21. The initial C^{14} date from Burke was 360 ± 80 B.P. (Yale-2375) or ca. A.D. 1590. Using the Stuiver and Suess correction factor, Tuck revised this date to A.D. 1480 ± 80 (1971:136), which still seems too late. By comparison, the Getman site, a late Chance phase village in the Mohawk Valley, is similar to Burke in several ways. Yet Ritchie and Funk's C^{14} date for the Getman site is ca. A.D. 1390 (1973:307). While the C^{14} dates reported by Tuck seriate well, I believe they are fifty to one hundred years too late.

22. The Burke site, like Kelso, was apparently a double village. Tuck's excavations revealed two sets of overlapping palisade lines (1971:126). There is no material culture difference or other discontinuity to suggest two separate occupations. Since all excavations to date have focused on the northern end of the site, its full extent is not known. In the mid-1970s, however, A. D. LaFrance surface-collected a considerable quantity of material in an area he designated Burke II, approximately 200–250m south of Tuck's excavation. The material from this locus appears to be virtually identical to that from the Burke site proper. Until additional settlement pattern work is done, it will remain unclear whether one phase of the Burke site extended far enough south to include the Burke II locus, or whether this was a small, satellite hamlet outside of the main village.

23. For evidence of a palisade at Keough, see Tuck 1969:237. An assessment of this site is complicated by the presence of an overlapping historic period Onondaga site, the Jamesville, or Pen, site which was occupied from ca. 1682–1700. For evidence of a palisade at Carley II, see LaFrance and LaFrance 1976:1.

24. This work was done largely by junior high school students under the direction of the American Heritage Center, Fayetteville-Manlius Junior High School, and West Genesee Junior High School.

25. One exceptional and unusual feature was excavated at the Burke site during the American Heritage Center project. This was a small, rock-filled pit located within the second (burned) longhouse. The pit at first appeared to be a large post mold, approximately 6 inches in diameter and 18 inches deep. Since the entire feature was densely packed with rocks, it had clearly been used for some other purpose than supporting a post. At the very base of the pit, beneath the rocks, a single artifact was recovered—a face effigy carved from a human patella (Plate 1). The nature and location of this feature as well as the object found in it strongly suggest witchcraft-related activity.

26. This western group does not actually disappear, but rather lapses back into obscurity. As Tuck notes, Iroquoian sites from the Baldwinsville area are known (1971:136–38). In addition to these, there are numerous other sites in the western portion of Onondaga County between Baldwinsville and Elbridge. Beauchamp lists at least a half-dozen stockaded, pottery-

producing sites in this area (1900:113–19). Few if any of these sites have been systematically tested, recorded, or reported. Niemczycki has argued that these sites as well as Maxon-Derby, Chamberlin, and even Kelso may be ancestral to the Cayuga rather than the Onondaga (1984:94).

27. Tuck also argues that this population shift and fusion result in the establishment of a two-village settlement pattern which continued until the late seventeenth century (1971:139). This has yet to be demonstrated convincingly for either Chance phase or Garoga phase sites.

28. In addition to the sites already mentioned in the Pompey Hills (note 20) and the Baldwinsville-Elbridge area (note 26), another cluster of Chance phase sites may have been located in the drumlins just north of the Onondaga Escarpment in the eastern part of Syracuse and the adjacent town of Dewitt. One site in this group is Mount View, briefly described by Tuck (1971:137–38). A better example is the Lyndon site. Material from this apparently palisaded site, collected by Stanley Gifford in the 1950s, resembles most closely that from the Christopher site.

29. Examples of these effigies from the Burke site include a bear (Burke II locus) and a finely made human face reported by Tuck (1971:133). A similar human effigy from the Christopher site (Plate 1) is illustrated courtesy of Peter P. Pratt. Several other comparable effigies from Pompey are included in the collection of Otis M. Bigelow, New York State Museum; unfortunately, none have specific site provenience. A particularly unusual pipe from the Burke site was recovered by Peter P. Pratt during his preliminary investigations in 1959. This style, often referred to as a "moon" pipe, is more closely associated with the St. Lawrence Iroquois or Ontario Iroquois (Weber 1970:210–11). Beauchamp illustrates a comparable example from Jefferson County (1898:134 and Figure 220).

30. Beauchamp (1902a) illustrates a large number of bone implements and ornaments, reputedly from the Christopher site. Nearly all of these are from the collection of Otis M. Bigelow, a prominent purchaser of artifacts from the Central New York area. Bigelow's collection was, in turn, purchased by the New York State Museum in 1914. Unfortunately, little of this material has reliable provenience information (Clarke 1915:63–65, 68). In addition, much of the bone work in Bigelow's collection also appears, upon examination, to be forgery.

31. Observations on material culture patterns are based on the examination of several small surface-collected assemblages. The site has also become a subject of controversy due to the reputed presence of a trenched-wall longhouse (McDowell-Loudan 1984).

32. The Conway site had Garoga as well as Chance phase traits and may have been used over a fairly long period (Weinman and Weinman 1982:8). There are other suggestive references, such as the "prehistoric Iroquois pits and burials" located along the Oneida River west of Brewerton, which may well relate to the Garoga phase (Ritchie 1944:84).

33. Insect infestation of fields also may have been an important factor (Starna, Hamell and Butts 1984). In addition to these ecological variables, a variety of cultural factors undoubtedly influenced duration of occupation.

34. Ten fragments of cranial bone have been recovered from Barnes. Most are small pieces of parietal, two are partially fused sections of parietal and temporal bone. One piece of parietal is heavily charred. Gibson also reports recovering a section of mandible with several intact teeth (Gibson 1968:10). Since the large faunal sample from the site has not been professionally evaluated, it is possible that fragmentary post-cranial bones may also be present.

35. The most thoughtful and thorough analysis of this delicate issue is Jaenen 1976:143–47; also see Abler 1980 and Fenton 1978:315–16.

36. This standardization of ceramic motifs is one of the few exceptions to the Garoga phase tendency for artifacts to be more detailed or embellished than comparable Chance phase materials. Tuck argues that this trend toward greater ceramic homogeneity may be material evidence of the increased security, mobility, and exchange which resulted from establishment of the Confederacy (Tuck 1971:219–22). Current evidence suggests that ceramic

homogeneity increased throughout the Garoga phase and that the founding of the Confederacy may have served to accelerate this ongoing, centripetal process.

37. MacNeish termed the opposed triangle under horizontal lines motif Onondaga Triangular. Opposed triangles without the overhead lines was considered a separate motif, Syracuse Incised. Parallel oblique lines beneath horizontal ones were termed Otstungo Incised (MacNeish 1952:59–60, 76–77).

38. There is some evidence that other Iroquoian people also used this technique, in particular the St. Lawrence Iroquois in northern New York (Skinner 1921:149; Parker 1922:337).

39. Two triangular points made from exotic material have been found at the Barnes site. One is glossy opaque white chert, probably of Ohio origin; the other is a translucent, smoky grey chalcedony of unknown origin. Both points are well within the morphological range of other points from the site. Exotic material apparently was also used for ground stone tools. Celts of *verte antique*, a metamorphosed serpentine marble from the New York/Vermont border, have been found at the Nursery and Barnes sites. A muller and hammer of fine-grained, extremely dense diorite, possibly from a Pennsylvania source, also come from Barnes.

40. Most of these discs are made from either a red or grey shale; schist and phyllite examples occur as well. Although some of these materials could have been found in local glacial deposits, others appear to have been imported, possibly from eastern New York. The red slate, for example, is likely to have come from a source on Lake George. Sizes range considerably, between 17mm and 40mm in diameter, with an average of roughly 25mm. Thickness is more consistent, averaging about 3mm. Similar stone discs are commonly found on St. Lawrence Iroquois sites both in Canada and Northern New York (Wintemberg 1936:62, 66; Parker 1922:337–38).

41. Modified deer or elk phalanges are the only ornamental/recreational form which occurs with any regularity on earlier Onondaga sites. Examples are known from: Cabin (2), Furnace Brook (2), Burke (1), and Barnes (7) (Tuck 1971:43, 69, 135; Bradley 1979:67). There has been much speculation about how these objects were used. The most likely explanation is that they were part of a cup-and-pin game (Guilday 1963). Native use of this game has been described by contemporary observers: "The little Hiroquois have the . . . pastime [of] throwing a bone with a hole in it, which they interlace in the air with another bone" (Thwaites 1896–1901, 7:97).

42. Elaborate combs are well documented from Middle Woodland contexts in Central New York. Ritchie illustrates several examples from a cremation burial at Jack's Reef (1944:148–50, Plate 69). Ritchie also notes a three-toothed comb from Canandaigua (1936:48). This aside, there are no reported occurrences of combs on any Late Woodland period site in Central New York, Owasco or Iroquois, until McNab.

43. Turtle-shell examples are an unusual occurrence in the archaeological record during the Late Woodland stage. The only Central New York example from a Late Woodland context prior to the Barnes site is a perforated fragment of carapace at Maxon-Derby (Ritchie and Funk 1973:212).

44. Seven of these beads are discoidal in shape and range in size from 5–6mm in diameter and 2–3mm in thickness. All are white and were probably made from either quahog (*Mercenaria mercenaria*) or the whorl of a species of whelk (*Busycon*). One additional bead made from *Mercenaria* is more massive and barrel-shaped. Approximately 10mm in length and 6mm in diameter, this bead was taper-drilled from each end. Three tubular shell beads have been reported from Barnes, but only two have been available for study. Both were taper-drilled and made from the *Busycon* columella. The final bead is a modified marine snail shell of the family *Marginella (Prunum apicinum)* (Morris 1975:232). The final shell artifact from Barnes is a partially completed pendant of *Mercenaria*. Roughly circular in shape and 20mm in diameter, this shell disc was partially perforated on one side.

45. The blade-shaped piece, excluding soil contaminants, contained two to three parts per million silver with the balance copper. The perforated disc contained approximately 50ppm silver with the balance copper. The trace of silver indicates that the probable origin

of this copper was the Lake Superior region (Griffin 1961:147). This and subsequent spectrographic tests cited were arranged with the help of Henry Wemple, Vernon Center, New York. The tests were performed by Edward Hall, Analytical Chemistry Lab, General Electric Company, Electronics Park, Syracuse, New York. Unless otherwise noted, testing was performed with a Jarrell-Ash 70–000 series emission spectrograph utilizing a 3.4-meter Ebert mount.

46. Ritchie illustrates several assemblages of marine shell and native copper ornaments from Middle Woodland period mortuary sites in Central New York. These include: René Menard Bridge Component Nos. 1 and 2 (Town of Aurelius, Cayuga County), Pickins Component [Brewerton], and Jack's Reef (Ritchie 1944:146–51, Plates 66–70). The last reported occurrence of copper in Central New York prior to Barnes is a small awl from the White site, Hunter's Home phase, Middle Woodland, which is C^{14}-dated A.D. 905 ± 250 (Ritchie 1969:258–61, Plate 87, Figure 21).

47. These concepts are discussed in detail by Hamell 1983 and 1985.

2. The Protohistoric Onondaga

1. The first to state this interpretation of Onondaga origins was Beauchamp (1905a:133–34, 147), and it was reiterated by Parker (1922:155–56). Additional archaeological evidence supporting a connection between sites in Jefferson County and Onondaga sites in Pompey was advanced by Harrington (Parker 1922:339) and MacNeish (1952:56–65, 84).

2. The most important manuscript source is Beauchamp's encyclopedic "Antiquities of Onondaga." The "Antiquities" is important because it documents not only Beauchamp's own collection but also those of several of his contemporaries, notably William Hinsdale and Otis Bigelow, who were less careful about recording provenience information. Among more recent avocational excavators whose collections and records contain important unpublished data on protohistoric Onondaga sites are Stanford Gibson, Robert Ricklis, Herman Weiskotten, and Theodore Whitney. Currently, the members of the William Beauchamp Chapter, New York State Archaeological Association (NYSAA), continue the tradition of responsible avocational excavation. Chapter members Albert D. LaFrance, Ferdinand LaFrance, Dr. A. Gregory Sohrweide, and Tyree Tanner permitted me to examine material in their collections. The data summarized in Tables 4, 7, and 8 are compiled from all the available sources and collections, including material in the author's possession.

3. The sources cited are limited to published reports. A more complete description of the collections from, and sources pertaining to, all the protohistoric Onondaga sites is presented in Bradley 1979.

4. Mortuary practice is another area for which information is lacking, especially, as Tuck has noted, on pre-European contact burial patterns (1971:101). Gibson (1968:9) has reported briefly on two small burial plots at the Barnes site which were characterized by single, flexed interments without material accompaniments. This appears to typify the Onondaga pattern prior to European contact. While there is only meager information about protohistoric burials, it is clear that substantial changes took place. Most notable was a dramatic increase in mortuary offerings of both native and European material. Lamentably, nearly all the protohistoric Onondaga cemeteries have been destroyed. An account in the *Post Standard* (Syracuse, New York) of September 12, 1899, summarizes what was an all too common occurrence: "Relic hunters have been busy the past week excavating on the old Indian Fort three miles north of here. . . . One man dug into a grave Saturday and found an almost entire skeleton of an Indian with his personal property buried with him. A man that was standing by offered him $10.00 for his find, which was accepted."

5. Little is known about this site. In 1946, William Ritchie salvaged a late protohistoric burial on the site (Ritchie 1954:45). The materials and records are located at the Rochester Museum and Science Center, Rochester, New York.

6. Adjacent sections of this palisade were traced by Ted Whitney, Stan Gibson, and Robert Ricklis. A composite map drawn from their field records is presented in Bradley 1979:99. During their excavation, Whitney and Gibson recovered a section of one of the smaller, pointed posts. Analysis of the wood has identified the species as *Tsuga canadensis*, or Eastern hemlock.

7. The same phenomenon has occurred in other Iroquois site sequences. For example, the Garoga site, the type site for the terminal Late Woodland Garoga phase, has since been demonstrated to be a protohistoric Mohawk site (Ritchie and Funk 1973:313–32; Lenig 1977:77–78).

8. The Dwyer faunal sample was recovered by Albert D. LaFrance and the author during reexcavation of a portion of the palisade line in 1976. The human remains were scattered throughout a shallow, mixed refuse midden which also contained other faunal remains as well as native and European materials. The human remains include six fragments of parietal, two teeth (a heavily worn, upper central left incisor and moderately worn second molar), two phalanges (distal and proximal) of the foot, and a medial fragment of a sternum.

9. Lenig 1977:73–74. It should be noted that most of Lenig's data are from Onondaga sites.

10. For discussion of the Huron ceramic tradition(s) see Wright 1966 and Ramsden 1977a. For discussion of the St. Lawrence Iroquois ceramic tradition see Wintemberg 1936 and Pendergast 1966. In spite of the differences, there is some overlap between these two ceramic traditions. This is discussed in Pendergast and Trigger 1972; Pendergast 1981a; 1981b. Overlap is particularly evident on the lowland St. Lawrence Iroquois sites in Jefferson County, New York. Observations concerning this Huron influence on St. Lawrence Iroquois sites in Jefferson County, New York, are based on discussions with Earl Sidler and James Pendergast. Also see Pendergast 1982.

11. Carinated shoulders—that is, ridged as opposed to rounded in profile—are a frequent feature on both Huron and St. Lawrence Iroquois pots. At Glenbrook, for example, 53.1% of the shoulder shapes were carinated (Pendergast 1981a:55). Although not common, handles do occur in both ceramic traditions. See Wintemberg 1936:145, #10 and 151, #21, for examples from the Roebuck site similar to those from Onondaga sites. Among the unusual castellation styles are broad, turret, and overhanging varieties.

12. Motifs involving criss-crossed lines would most often be typed as Lanorie Crossed (MacNeish 1952:64, 153) for collared vessels, and as Lanorie Crossed Lip (Pendergast 1966:11–12) for collarless vessels. An occasional example of Warminster Crossed (MacNeish 1952:32) also occurs. Depending on collar height and profile, horizontal motifs can be typed as Ontario Horizontal (MacNeish 1952:16), Fonda Incised (ibid.:76), Salem Horizontal (Pendergast 1966:7–8), Low Collar Horizontal (ibid.:20), or Copeland Incised (Wright 1966:73). The use of blank triangles and rectangles (often outlined with dashes), rows of punctates, and ladder plaiting are all traditional St. Lawrence Iroquois ceramic motifs (Pendergast 1966; 1981b).

13. The tradition of finishing and/or decorating pottery with either cord impressions or check stamping appears to have lasted longer among the St. Lawrence Iroquois than the Onondaga. At Glenbrook, for instance, 7.5% of the body sherds were corded and nearly 5% check stamped (Pendergast 1981a:55). On St. Lawrence Iroquois sites in Jefferson County, New York, both dentate stamped and cord impressed motifs continue to be used on collared vessels throughout the Late Woodland period (Earl Sidler, personal communication).

14. Engelbrecht's primary finding was that ceramic similarity increased among the Five Nations Iroquois tribal groups from roughly A.D. 1500 to 1640 (Engelbrecht 1972:10).

15. Not all the northern traits that occasionally occur on late Garoga phase and early protohistoric Onondaga sites survived to become a part of the Onondaga ceramic tradition. Among those which did are: the greater prevalence of low collar vessels; use of more diverse castellation styles, especially turret and broad forms; more common use of horizontal and criss-crossed collar motifs, as well as the incorporation of right triangles and rectangles in collar motifs. Among those traits not incorporated are: the use of overhanging castellations

and handles; the underlining of collar motifs (Durfee Underlined); the use of large punctate circles either in rows or to form face effigies; corn-ear type pottery (Pendergast 1966:9–11); and neck or shoulder decoration.

16. Kent 1984:15–17, 304–5. Most of these small Susquehannock sites are burial rather than habitation sites. The Engelbert site in Nichols, New York, is a good example (Stewart 1973). Several of these small sites are located in the Binghamton area and would have been about 100km south-southwest of contemporary Onondaga sites.

17. This distribution of Ithaca Linear pottery on protohistoric Onondaga sites is approximately the same as that of Schultz Incised examples. The Atwell site has produced fourteen pieces of Schultz Incised and five of Ithaca Linear type ceramics. On the Chase site, ten pieces of Schultz Incised and two of Ithaca Linear were found. See Bradley 1979:103–4, 153–54 for additional descriptions.

18. MacNeish 1952:50. As the names imply, both Genoa Frilled and Ithaca Linear were initially defined as Cayuga pottery types. Since the protohistoric sequence among the Cayuga is poorly understood at present, it is not clear how these ceramic forms are related either to the Susquehannock forms or to those which occur on other protohistoric Iroquois sites. For a current assessment of how these ceramics fit into both Cayuga and Seneca development, see Niemczycki 1984:35–41.

19. One of the few instances of ceramic miscegenation is the occasional occurrence of Onondaga style effigies on Susquehannock vessels. Examples include the Athens Faces— several large, carefully executed effigies recovered from burials at Tioga Point in Athens, Pennsylvania (Wren 1914:Plate 6, #1–5, 7). These faces were found on pots recovered from two different burials at the Murray Garden site. Other artifacts recovered from these burials included a marine shell gorget and beads as well as a brass spiral ornament (Parker 1938:47–49). Although the vessels themselves are Susquehannock, the face effigies are very similar to those on late Garoga sites such as Barnes. Compare with the example illustrated by Tuck 1971:152, #6. A second example of an Onondaga style effigy on a shell-tempered Susquehannock pot is also illustrated by Wren 1914:Plate 19, #9. This small, stylized face from Northumberland, Pennsylvania, is very similar to examples on protohistoric Onondaga sites. See Beauchamp 1898:96–97, Figures 51 and 54 for comparable pieces.

20. These include a fragmentary example from the Atwell site (New York State Museum #BX31866), a nearly complete but unprovenienced example from Pompey (New York State Museum #BX31914), and a complete example from the south side of the Oneida River near Oak Orchard (Beauchamp, "Antiquities" 10:#618). Oak Orchard was another traditional Onondaga fishing location (Sohrweide 1963).

21. This pipe, found in 1863, has previously been illustrated by Beauchamp (1898:123 and Figure 181). Compare with the example from the Morse site illustrated by Mathews (1981a:9, Figure 5). Sassi also illustrates a double bird effigy pipe from the Morse site, possibly the same specimen (Sassi n.d.:81, Figure xxix). While Mathews (1981) has argued that multiple effigy pipes do not correlate with any particular Iroquoian group, large complex effigy pipes of this style are more typical of the Jefferson County St. Lawrence Iroquois pipe tradition than that of the Onondaga.

22. Conical antler points have been recovered from the Pickering and Chase sites. Similar points are a frequent occurrence on St. Lawrence Iroquois sites in Jefferson County, New York (Earl Sidler, personal communication; Harrington, in Parker 1922:335) and in Ontario (Wintemberg 1936:26–27 and Plate I, #17; Pendergast 1966:58; 1978:138). Two examples of notching, or incised tally marks, are known from Onondaga. One is a harpoon from the Temperance House site, the other a walrus ivory dagger from Atwell (see note 29 below for additional information on the latter piece). Once again, this is a common trait on St. Lawrence Iroquois sites in northern New York (Earl Sidler, personal communication; Skinner 1921:130–31 and Plate XXV) and, to a lesser degree, in Canada (Wintemberg 1936:57 and Plate XIV, #27–31; Pendergast 1981a:23 and Plate 8, #16).

23. While several examples are reputed to have been found at Atwell, Beauchamp illustrates only one (1902a:Figure 303). Harrington observed that these cranial bone gorgets

were sufficiently common on certain St. Lawrence Iroquois sites in Jefferson County, that "nearly every local collection has one specimen" (Parker 1922:388). They also occur frequently on late St. Lawrence Iroquois sites in Canada (Wintemberg 1936:73–74 and Plate XV, #32–33; Pendergast and Trigger, 1972:135, 261 and Plate XVI, #11; Pendergast 1981a:36 and Plate 8, #22). While these cranial bone gorgets, or rattles (two tied together), are occasionally found on the protohistoric sites of the other Five Nations Iroquois, notably Oneida and Seneca, they do not appear on protohistoric Susquehannock sites (Barry Kent, personal communication). Clearly, this form of trophy was part of a northern Iroquoian tradition.

24. The use of both anthropomorphic and zoomorphic effigies is a salient characteristic of protohistoric Onondaga material culture. Effigies are most common on ceramic pots and smoking pipes, but they also occur on bone, antler, stone, and shell artifacts. While the occurrence of effigies is easy to document, the reasons for their use remain more elusive. Among the many possibilities are: social factors such as the increased visibility and importance of the clan system; cultural factors such as the influence of other tribal traditions as a result of either assimilation or more frequent exchange; spiritual/religious factors, for example a revivalistic response to European presence; or technological factors—the greater facility which metal tools allowed in working traditional mediums such as stone or antler. The point is that these effigies are a material manifestation of very complex and dynamic times. Any interpretation of them has to take that complexity into account.

25. It is possible that the situation would be different if more burial data were available. Given their value as symbolically charged substances, it is not surprising that the great concentrations of European material on protohistoric Iroquoian sites occur in burials.

26. The majority of the white shell is quahog (Mercenaria mercenaria), although some of the discoidal beads appear to be fashioned from the outer whorls of whelk (Busycon species). It is likely that the black discoidal beads were also made in this manner.

27. See Slotkin and Schmitt 1949 on the issue of pre-contact wampum. The majority of these beads were drilled in the pre-contact manner—a tapering perforation from either end; a few of the beads from the Dwyer site, however, have straight and uniform perforations, possibly done with a metal drill. Both quahog and whelk columella were used to produce these beads. Of the two bead forms, discoidals occur more frequently, outnumbering tubulars three to one.

28. A fragmentary pipe from the Chase site is made of this material. Though not common, the dark grey soapstone also occurs on protohistoric Susquehannock sites (Smith and Graybill 1977:54).

29. This piece, recovered from the Atwell site, is approximately 175mm in length and appears to have been made from the distal portion of a split walrus tusk. It is decorated with incised lines as well as tally marks. The ivory from which this dagger was made appears to have been fresh, not the mineralized variety occasionally found in Pleistocene deposits around Lake Champlain (Harington 1981:44). It is unusual for walrus ivory to occur on a site so far inland. Cartier, however, noted the presence of "sea oxen" not only in the Gulf of St. Lawrence, but as far up river as Grosse Island (Biggar 1924:34, 103, 199). Ivory artifacts, though rare, have been reported on St. Lawrence Iroquois sites in both eastern Ontario and Jefferson County, New York (Wintemberg 1936:21–22; Parker 1922:76, 356 and Plate 16). Beauchamp also reports "an implement made of a walrus tusk" from Brewerton (1902a:325 and Plate 40, #342).

30. The composition of these metals is somewhat variable even within the subgroups They break down as follows (percentages are by weight):

Material	Range	Average
Smelted copper (six samples)		
lead	1.02–1.95%	1.5%
tin	unavailable	trace (up to 100ppm)

continued next page

Material	Range	Average
zinc	0–trace	0
antimony	unavailable	up to 0.005%
nickel	unavailable	up to 100ppm
Brass *(four samples)*		
lead	1.5–2.5%	2.0%
tin	0.4–4.5%	2.5%
zinc	10–20%	15.0%
antimony	unavailable	up to 0.005%
nickel	unavailable	up to 100ppm
Bronze *(one sample)*		
lead	2.5%	
tin	10.0%	
zinc	5.0%	
antimony	up to 0.005%	
nickel	up to 100ppm	

31. Other examples from Iroquoia occur on the Oneida Diable site (Pratt 1976:213, Plate 22, #8) and Seneca Adams, Tram, and Cameron sites (Wray and Schoff 1953:55 and examination of collections in the Rochester Museum and Science Center). Susquehannock-related examples have been reported from the Engelbert site (Dunbar and Ruhl 1974:4–5) as well as other sites in Bradford County (Kent 1984:302–5). Several examples are also known from southern New England (Bradley 1983:31).

32. While these spirals have been referred to as "Basque earrings" (Kent 1984:203 and Figure 51), there is no evidence to suggest that they are of Basque origin. They occur on several of the protohistoric Susquehannock sites. It is important to note, however, that at least one example has been found in a Shenk's Ferry burial appearing to predate Susquehannock occupation of the Washington Boro basin (Cadzow 1936:51–52). Hoop-shaped ornaments have occasionally been referred to as bracelets; however, excavated examples indicate that they were probably neck or breast ornaments (Ritchie 1954:45 and Plate 12, #25; Dunbar and Ruhl 1974:4, #5).

33. This type is best documented on protohistoric Seneca sites. Two complete hafted examples, one with a lithic blade (RMSC258/94) and one with a copper blade (RMSC236/94), have been recovered from the Adams site. In both cases, the blades were hafted with the pointed end in. Lithic examples of this blade shape are known from Onondaga sites, but to date no copper examples have been reported.

34. Conical projectile points of copper have been found at both the Chase and Dwyer sites. Beauchamp reports three unperforated triangular copper points from the Sheldon site (1902b:Figures #50, 113 and 164). While small awls—hafted slivers of sheet metal—have yet to be reported from Onondaga sites, they have been recovered from Seneca sites. An example is RMSC29/41 from the Cameron site, now in the collection of the Rochester Museum and Science Center.

35. There is one additional factor of importance bearing on the question of when and how copper working was revived in Onondaga. As discussed in Chapter 2, there was a long hiatus—most of the Late Woodland stage—during which the use of copper ceased in Central New York. It is quite possible that the groups antecedent to the Onondaga may have lost their metal-working skills during the period. Among other Iroquoian groups, however, especially the Ontario Iroquois, the tradition of working copper continued throughout the Late Woodland (McPherron 1967:164–75; Finlayson, personal communication). Though less

well documented, native copper was apparently used by the St. Lawrence Iroquois as well (Pendergast and Trigger 1972:149–50). It is possible that the impetus, and perhaps expertise, for the revival in copper-working are further aspects of the northern influence discussed in the text above.

36. This paralleling of bone and copper beads is most clearly evident in two size groups. On the earlier protohistoric sites, the small copper beads—those 3–5mm in diameter and 5–10mm in length—are very similar to the small bone beads from late Garoga phase and early protohistoric sites. On the later protohistoric sites, the larger copper beads—those about 10mm in diameter and from 20 to 40mm in length—closely parallel the beads made from the long bones of wild turkey *(Meleagris gallopavo)* common on late Garoga and early protohistoric sites. With larger samples, it should be possible to demonstrate these clusterings statistically.

37. Beauchamp describes this as a "quadrangular steel [sic] blade" (1902b:75 and Figure 126). A small piece of iron (wire?) was recovered from a disturbed midden by Ted Whitney and Stan Gibson (see Bradley 1979:117). Because of the questionable provenience, this piece is not included in the discussion of protohistoric iron artifacts.

38. During the protohistoric period, lithic celts occur into two distinct groups. While the general form is the same for both groups—rectangular or trapezoidal—the size and thickness are significantly different. The larger group ranges from 110–180mm in length, 50–60mm wide at the bit, 20–40mm thick, and generally ovoid in section. The smaller group ranges from 40–50mm in length, 20–30mm wide, 5–10mm thick, and is usually rectangular in section. The protohistoric iron celts from Onondaga parallel these smaller lithic celts quite closely. While these iron implements are referred to here as celts, it is unclear whether they were hafted and used as celts, adzes, or both.

39 Jan Piet Puype, personal communication. This highly distinctive form of cutlery is also described in detail by Blair (1974:175–81), who illustrates four additional examples.

40. These beads, which have been referred to as Early Blue beads, have been recovered from early protohistoric Seneca sites as well as Susquehannock sites (Wray and Schoff 1953:55; Stewart 1973:4–6; Kent 1984:213). They are also common on sixteenth-century native sites in the southeastern portion of North America, early seventeenth-century French sites such as St. Croix Island (1604), and early seventeenth-century English sites in New England (Smith 1983:150; Bradley 1983:35, 38; Pendery 1984:43–51).

3. Processing the Protohistoric

1. Although this interpretation of Iroquois origins is no longer considered accurate by most scholars, a curious vestige does persist. This is the notion that the Iroquois were in an embattled and defensive position during the late sixteenth and early seventeenth centuries (Trigger 1976, 1:223–24; 1978:346–47; Jennings 1984:43).

2. The best, albeit brief, review is Pendergast 1975. The section on "St Lawrence Iroquoians" in Volume 15 of the Smithsonian Institution *Handbook* is rather limited and focuses only on those groups identified in the historical record (Trigger and Pendergast 1978:357–61). Most of the available literature is in the form of individual site reports, particularly those in southern Ontario (Wintemberg 1936; Pendergast 1966, 1973, 1981a, 1984; and Pendergast and Trigger 1972).

3. While a great deal of excavation has taken place on these sites, few synthetic works (and not even many site reports) have been produced. Available summaries include Skinner 1921 and Harrington 1922. Among current researchers who have considerable expertise in this area are Peter and Marjorie Pratt and Earl Sidler. The present discussion of site sequences and chronology is based on conversations with Sidler and with Ed Kondratowitz of Pulaski, New York.

4. The Jayne/LaPoint site (PLI 1-3) is a multicomponent fishing station located on the eastern shore of Lake Ontario near the mouth of the Salmon River. Although most of the ceramics appear to be of St. Lawrence Iroquois origin, some show strong similarities with late Chance and Garoga phase Onondaga pottery. This area (known as "La Famine" by the French) is well documented as a seasonal fishing area used by the Onondaga during the seventeenth century (note 9, chapter 4 below).

5. Pendergast 1968:16; 1973:67; Pendergast and Trigger 1972:198, 284. Interestingly enough, the St. Lawrence Iroquois ceramics from Draper correspond most closely with those from the Dawson site, although the two sites are a considerable distance apart (Pendergast 1981b). Despite its reputation as Cartier's "Hochelaga," the Dawson may well be a pre-contact site. None of the European materials recovered are diagnostically sixteenth century, and serious questions as to the reliability of their provenience have been raised (Kidd, in Pendergast and Trigger 1972:330-32; Bruce G. Trigger, personal communication).

6. While no European materials have been recovered from Glenbrook, Pendergast considers the site to be protohistoric and dates it to the mid-sixteenth century (1981a:37).

7. The marine shell found on Late Woodland stage sites in the Northeast comes primarily from three genera: *Busycon*, *Mercenaria*, and *Prunum*. Several species of *Busycon* appear to have been utilized most frequently. These include *B. canaliculatum* (channeled whelk), and *B. carcia* (knobby whelk). The range of both species extends from Massachusetts to Florida (Morris 1975: 213-15). An additional species, *B. contrarium* (lightning whelk), was also used, although its range is more restricted, from Cape Hatteras to Florida (ibid.:215-16). Occasionally these large whelks are referred to by their family name, conch *(Melongenidae)*. It should be noted that species identification is possible only with complete shells; columella can only be ascribed to family or perhaps genus. *Mercenaria mercenaria*, or quahog, is a medium sized, hard shelled clam. It is found from the Gulf of St. Lawrence to Florida. Notable characteristics include a dark violet border, closely spaced concentric growth lines, and fine serations along the ventral margin (ibid.:59). *Prunum apicinum*, or common marginella, is a small gastropod which occurs from North Carolina to Florida (ibid.:232).

8. Several Shenks Ferry sites have produced a wide range of marine shell ornaments. Among them are Murray (Kinsey and Graybill 1971:20-21, 42), Shenks Ferry (Heisey and Witmer 1964:15-18), and Locust Grove (Kent 1974:2-3). Marine shell is a frequent occurrence on Monongahela sites as well (Davis 1984:4-5; James Herbstritt, personal communication). On sites of the McFate-Quiggle complex such as Kalgren, marine shell is fairly common and occurs in a pattern similar to that on Monongahela sites (James Herbstritt, personal communication). For marine shell on the Parker site (Wyoming Valley complex) see Smith 1973:29. While marine shell is generally scarce on Five Nations Iroquois sites, examples are known from the Mohawk Elwood site (Dean Snow, personal communication), the Oneida Nichols Pond and Olcott sites (Pratt 1976:201, Plate 10, #1; 1963:78, 80), the Onondaga Barnes site (Bradley 1979:68-69), and the Seneca California Ranch site (Collections of the Rochester Museum and Science Center). Marine shell from the Wenro-related Alhart site is discussed by Hamell 1982. Marine shell ornaments have been reported from St. Lawrence Iroquois sites in Jefferson County, New York, by Harrington (Parker 1920:337) and Skinner 1921:163, 170. Among the St. Lawrence Iroquois sites in Ontario which have produced marine shell are Beckstead (Pendergast 1984:49, Plate 14c) and Roebuck (Wintemberg 1936:63). On Huron sites, shell has been reported from Draper (William Finlayson, personal communication) and Black Creek (Prevec and Noble 1983:49). Marine shell has been reported from Neutral sites, although specific details are not available (Fitzgerald 1982:290).

9. The case for shell artifacts of *Busycon* or *Mercenaria* is less clear-cut than that for marginella because the distribution of these species is much broader. Nonetheless, a strong case can be argued that artifacts made from these species also originated from the mid-Atlantic coast rather than New England or coastal New York. In general, there is little evidence for the ornamental use of shell on Late Woodland sites in New England (Willoughby 1935:264-65). Where shell ornaments have been recovered, the pattern appears to be one of limited and localized use (Bruce Bourque, Paul Robinson, David Poirier, and Kevin McBride, personal communications). Lynn Ceci has observed a similar dearth of pre-contact shell beads

on coastal New York (1977:19–20). In contrast, shell ornaments found on Late Woodland sites along the mid-Atlantic coast (Phelps 1983:39, 44) parallel quite closely those which occur in the Northeast.

10. The occurrence of shell and a brass spiral at the Shenks Ferry site are described by Cadzow 1936:51, 58. During the 1985 field season, fragments of three copper beads were also found (Barry Kent, personal communication). Virtually all the shell and European material recovered from early Schultz stage Susquehannock sites has come from burials. These sites include Englebert (Stewart 1973:11), Pumpelly Creek (Dolores Elliott, Richard McCracken, personal communications), Ellis Creek (Lucy 1950:57–58), Murray Garden (Parker 1938:47–49; Wren 1909), and Overpeck (Forks of the Delaware Chapter 1980:16–17, 19–21). Among the mid-sixteenth century Iroquois sites with marine shell and European materials are the Mohawk Garoga site (Wayne Lenig, personal communication), the Oneida Vaillancourt site (Pratt 1976:117, 273–74, 278–79), the Onondaga Temperance House and Atwell sites (see Chapter 2 above), and the Seneca Richmond Mills and Culbertson sites (Collections of the Rochester Museum and Science Center; Charles F. Wray, personal communication; Bradley 1979:383). While European materials have been reported from protohistoric Huron sites such as Parsons and Benson, no information is available on the occurrence of shell (Ramsden 1977a:68, 72–73). At the Trent site, European materials were recovered, but no shell was found (Peter Pratt, personal communication). Both marine shell and European material have been recovered from the Neutral Cleveland site (Fitzgerald 1982:295; Prevec and Noble 1983:47–49).

11. A cache of 76 *Mercenaria* "blanks" were recovered at the Ellis Creek site (Lucy 1950:57–58). At the Overpeck site, a cache of approximately a dozen large, unmodified columella were reported (Forks of the Delaware Chapter 1980:16–17, 19). Both European materials and Susquehannock ceramics were found in related contexts on both sites.

12. It should be noted that both spiral ornaments and hoops are considered together in this discussion. Both forms appear to have a similar spatial and chronological distribution, and it is often not possible to determine from a fragment which form the original was. Spirals have been reported from only two Iroquois sites which date from the mid-sixteenth century or earlier. These are Richmond Mills (RMSC60/101) and Culbertson (RMSC33/182). The fragmentary example from Richmond Mills was recovered from a midden context. It was tested by x-ray flourescence to determine composition in April, 1979, at Syracuse University. Results indicated a copper alloy with approximately 5% tin and a trace of zinc.

While spirals never become common on Iroquois sites, they do occur more frequently on sites of the last half of the sixteenth century. These include the Mohawk Smith-Pagerie and England's Woods sites (Wayne Lenig, personal communication), the Oneida Diable site (Pratt 1976:277), the Onondaga Dwyer and Brewerton sites (see Chapter 2), and the Seneca Tram and Cameron sites (RMSC collections). At present, no spirals or hoops have been reported from protohistoric Huron or Neutral sites. In contrast, the Susquehannock Schultz site has produced numerous examples. Over two dozen have been recovered from burial excavations (Kent 1984:331) and many more have been found on the village site itself.

13. This increase can be seen in the difference between Cemetery I and Cemetery II at the Schultz site (Kent 1984:330–31). On late sixteenth-century Iroquois sites such as Chase and Dwyer, European materials seem to be in the range of 1 to 3% of the total material assemblage. The frequency on Neutral sites appears to be somewhat lower (Fitzgerald 1982:243).

14. While sizable amounts of shell and European goods occur on virtually all early seventeenth-century Iroquoian sites in the Northeast, the distribution is neither uniform nor equal. The largest concentrations still appear on Susquehannock sites (terminal Schultz/early Washington Boro stage). The quantities that occur on Five Nations Iroquois sites seem slightly less. What is more striking is the continued similarity of European materials across Iroquoia. In both volume and kind, the same basic assemblage occurs on the following sites: the Mohawk Rice's Woods and Wagners Hollow sites (New York State Museum collection and Robert Funk, personal communication; Lenig 1977:78); the Oneida Cameron site (Pratt 1976:121–24; Bennett 1978; 1981); the Onondaga Pompey Center site (Bradley 1977; 1979:192–224); the Cayuga Genoa Fort site (DeOrio 1978); and the Seneca Dutch Hollow

and Factory Hollow sites (Wray and Schoff 1953:54–55; Ritchie 1954; Parker 1919). While larger amounts of shell and European material also occur on comparable Neutral (Fonger and Christianson) and Huron (Ball) sites, the increases definitely seem smaller (Fitzgerald 1982:243; Knight 1978).

15. At least five examples of white quartz and two of smoky gray ("Broad Run") chalcedony have been recovered from the Pompey Center site. Projectile points of these two materials are common on protohistoric and early historic Susquehannock sites (Barry C. Kent, personal communication).

A comparable pattern of Susquehannock-related lithics and ceramic traits also occurs on late sixteenth- and early seventeenth-century Oneida sites. White quartz points have been reported from the Diable and Cameron sites (Pratt 1976:254; Bennett 1978:16). At Diable, Pratt typed 3.1% of the pottery as Genoa Frilled and 1.6% as Ithaca Linear. At Cameron these percentages increase to 19.1% for Genoa Frilled and 6.5% for Ithaca Linear (Pratt 1976:175). The similarities between Susquehannock sites and Seneca/Cayuga sites are even stronger. The relationship among these three Iroquoian groups remains a critical area for future research.

16. Smith's description has also been used, mistakenly, as evidence that French trade in the St. Lawrence reached as far as the Susquehannocks during the early seventeenth century (Jennings 1984:115; Brasser 1978:81). The cause for confusion is a series of poorly utilized pronouns in Smith's account: "many descriptions and discourses they [Susquehannocks] made us of Atquanahucke, Massawomecke, and other people, signifying *they* inhabit the river of Cannida, and from the French to have *their* hatchets, and such like tools by trade, / *these* knowe no more of the territories of Powhatan than his name, and he as little of *them*" (Barbour 1969 2:408–9) [emphasis added]. It is quite clear that the emphasized they/their/these and them refer to the "other people," not the Susquehannocks. It is likely that these "other people" were Ontario Iroquois, possibly Neutral or Huron.

17. Most of the recent scholarly work on the sixteenth century continues to emphasize that the St. Lawrence was the only source of the European materials which reached Iroquoia (Trigger 1976, 1:220–24; 1978:345–46; Lenig 1977:73, 77). This assessment, in turn, has been cited by other authors and has become an accepted part of the literature (Fisher and Hartgen 1983:51; Jennings 1984:75; Curtin 1984:214–16).

18. As discussed in note 5 above, the evidence for European contact at the Dawson site is now considered to be equivocal. Others who have remarked on this scarcity of contact sites include Kenneth Kidd (1972:331) and Donald Lenig (1977:75).

19. Earl Sidler, personal communication. One possible exception is a copper bead from the Morse site. Unfortunately, this bead (never tested for composition) has apparently been lost.

20. A more comprehensive assessment of native American-European interaction during the sixteenth century is currently being conducted by James Pendergast. For a preliminary attempt, see Bradley 1979:367–73.

21. The exception to this is the Cayuga, whose protohistoric sequence at present is poorly understood. See Niemczycki 1984 for the most current assessment.

22. Examples include the Taiping Revolution in China, ca. 1850–65, and the Sudanese Mahdi, ca. 1880–98. The English Civil War, particularly Cromwell's rise, and the French Revolution, its aftermath, and the emergence of Napoleon demonstrate that fulminant revitalization movements are not restricted to non-Western societies.

23. The word "power" as used in this study is a shorthand for the complex set of relationships that defined how and why the Onondaga valued certain substances. Hamell has discussed the issue in detail (1985); this note is intended as a brief summary of that work to assist the reader. The essence of understanding these substances can be summarized in the equation, "power" = "wealth" = "well-being" (spiritual, physical, and social). Shell, native copper (and other free-state metals), and crystal (including white siliceous rock), as well as their European analogs, were perceived as substances which had the potential to bring or promote "well-being" (that is, long life, good health, success/luck). While this "power"

was inherent, it was also latent and was only activated when the substance(s) was consecrated for ritual purposes. In this sense, these substances functioned as a "medicine." By acquiring and possessing these substances, one accumulated "wealth," or the "power" to assure and insure "well-being." I have chosen to use the word power rather than wealth in order to emphasize the ideological rather than the materialistic importance of these substances.

24. This model is drawn from several sources, primarily Hamell 1985 and personal communication; Burridge 1960:28–29; and Wallace 1956.

25. See pages 88–89 above. While the middleman model (Ray 1978) works well for the historic period, it is less applicable to the protohistoric. One problem is that in order to have a middleman, there must first be a fixed point of trade or contact. Until the establishment of regularly occupied European settlements, this was rarely the case. Contact and trade were largely opportunistic and the resulting fluidity was not conducive to the formation of middleman trade zones. Directly related to this was the high degree of mobility exercised by many native groups. Whoever the Massawomekes were, they were certainly not content to allow the Susquehannocks to serve as their middlemen. Finally, a middleman analysis presumes a utilitarian orientation to European goods on the part of native people. While this may be correct for the seventeenth and eighteenth centuries, it is less useful in understanding native motivation in the sixteenth century.

26. Much of the credit for this observation belongs to George Hamell, whose pioneering work has begun to make it possible to understand the Contact period from a native point of view.

4. The Historic Onondaga 1600–1656

1. Juet observed that the natives had both "yellow Copper," probably brass, and "red Copper Tobacco pipes, and other things of copper they did weare about their neckes" (Purchas 1906, 13:363, 364). The red copper was probably smelted copper or a copper alloy. Given the extent of protohistoric contact along the coast, it is not surprising that natives in the area would already have received a substantial amount of European material.

2. There would appear to be some convergence between Champlain's account of the "Carantouanais," who were allied with the Huron and also at war with the Iroquois (Biggar 1922–36, 3:53–55), and John Smith's description of the Susquehannocks and their Massawomeke oppressors.

3. Considerable debate has occurred over the location and identification of the "fort" which Champlain's party attacked. See Pratt 1976:61–68 for a review of the contending locations. Contrary to Trigger's claim (1976, 1:311), Biggar's identification of the Entonhonoron as Onondaga was warranted. Archaeological evidence not available to Biggar now tends to confirm his assessment (see note 8 below). Conversely, in identifying Nichols Pond in Madison County as the site of Champlain's battle, Beauchamp made one of his few errors (Beauchamp 1900:88–89; Pratt 1976:87–93, 148).

4. Jameson 1909:137–57. A new translation by Charles Gehring with commentary by William Starna enhances the utility of this remarkable document even further (Gehring and Starna n.d.).

5. LeMoine's journal to Onondaga is recounted in the Jesuit Relation of 1653–54 (Thwaites 1896–1901, 41:91–129). Dablon's journal is in the Relation of 1655–56 (ibid., 42:127–85). For a recent summary of documentary and archaeological research of Ste. Marie, see Connors, DeAngelo, and Pratt 1980.

6. The archaeological record for historic Onondaga sites, like that for the protohistoric, is based largely on amateur excavation and avocational collecting. Brief summaries of some of these sites are presented by Beauchamp (1900) and Tuck (1971). The most detailed review is Bradley 1979. The data presented in Tables 12–24 are compiled from the available published sources as well as examination of all available collections. Important individual collections now in institutions include: Warren G. Haberle (formerly at the Onondaga Historical As-

sociation, currently at the Seneca Iroquois National Museum), Robert Hill and William Ennis (RMSC), and Herbert Bigford, Jr. (Colgate University). Private collections include: Albert D. LaFrance, Ferdinand LaFrance, Dr. A. Gregory Sohrweide, Tyree Tanner, and material in the author's possession.

7. Beauchamp mentions several small sites and weirs along the Oneida River between Brewerton (Tethiroquen) and Three Rivers (1900:117, #33 and 133, #9). For the native origin of Te-thir-o-quen, see Beauchamp 1907:142. Caughdenoy is derived from the Iroquois name meaning "where the eel is lying down"; it was still considered a good place to catch eel in Beauchamp's day (ibid.:142). Another important fishing station was located on the Oswego River at Phoenix (Beauchamp 1900:133, #10). These sites appear to correlate with the fishing camps described by Le Moine and Dablon as they traveled to and from Onondaga (Thwaites 1896–1901, 41:97–99, 125; 42:75, 81–83).

8. Another fishing village was located near the head of Onondaga Lake within the last westward meander of Onondaga Creek before it entered the lake. Beauchamp mentions the site briefly and notes that artifacts from several occupation periods have been found in the vicinity (1900:116, #32). The most available information on this site is a historical marker located just north of Hiawatha Boulevard, east of the Barge Canal Bridge. This marker in part reads: "KA-NE-EN-DA The only pre-colonial Iroquois village site on Onondaga lake. Located on lake front north of this place. Iroquois pottery with human faces, 1570–1620, found here but not elsewhere around Onondaga lake." This information was based on the research of Dr. William G. Hinsdale of Syracuse, an amateur archaeologist and associate of Beauchamp. Hinsdale was the only person who had an opportunity to collect systematically on the site. The area "was only plowed one year [1893] and after that the City of Syracuse began to use it as a dump . . . now it is covered with [the] Solvay refuse discharge, which is generally about the lake" (Letter of June 20, 1933, Onondaga Historical Association). During that year, however, Hinsdale found "large quantities of Iroquois pottery in fragment form, upon some of which are human faces." Also recovered were "pieces of scrap copper and other articles of European origin" (Beauchamp 1900:116, #32). In a letter to Beauchamp, Hinsdale described in greater detail his first recoveries from Ka-ne-en-da: "I found net sinkers, flakes, split bones of deer, cracked stones, a few wrought flints and many fragments of pottery. These latter are very interesting in that they resemble in the ornamentation and the representation of a human face . . . those from the Delphi group of sites [Chase and Dwyer] dating from about A.D. 1600 (Beauchamp n.d., 6:79–80).

While Hinsdale collected, Beauchamp recorded the information into his notebooks. This included illustrations of many of the artifacts which Hinsdale found. With this surviving inventory, it is possible to draw some conclusions about Ka-ne-en-da and its relationship to the other Onondaga sites.

The "Iroquois pottery" that Hinsdale found is generally medium to low collar in height and appears to be mostly biconcave or concave in profile. Most of the collar bases are notched, while the decorative motifs are broadly incised (ibid.:52, 163–64, 166e, 167a, b, and d, 210–15, 299, 302–4, 414). Included in the sample are four applied face effigies, all small and stylized, and part of an applied figure effigy (ibid.:30, 157, 444, 670, 294). Among the other artifacts are a few native pipe fragments, finely flaked triangular projectile points, many net sinkers, and several partial bone awls and needles (for pipe fragments, see ibid.:156, 251, and 8:662; for points, ibid., 6:243; for net sinkers, ibid.:248; for bone awls and needles, ibid.:159, 160, 178). In addition, shell beads and some European artifacts were illustrated by Beauchamp. These include two glass beads and a tubular brass bead (for shell beads, see ibid.:162, 855; for glass beads, ibid.:426 [round, dark blue] and 854 [tubular, light blue]; for tubular brass beads, ibid.:682). One other piece of European material, a small rectangular piece of utilized scrap brass, was also found on the site by another collector. These artifacts bear out Hinsdale's initial observation. The artifacts from Ka-ne-en-da do closely resemble those from the late sixteenth- or early seventeenth-century Onondaga sites in Pompey.

For a discussion of Ka-ne-en-da as the site of Champlain's 1615 attack, see Bradley 1979:311–13. Ka-ne-en-da is not, itself, a native place name but appears to be an Anglicism of Ga-nuu-ta-ah, Onondaga Lake (Beauchamp 1907:146).

9. Beauchamp notes this site briefly (1900:132, #1) and discusses both its native and French appellations (1907:171–72). The area was mentioned several times by mid-seventeenth century French travelers and identified specifically as the site of an Onondaga village and a "greatly renowned" fishing site (Thwaites 1896–1901, 41:97; 42:71–73; and 43:145). During the fall of 1971, a seventeenth-century burial was discovered at the Jayne/LaPoint site (PLI 1–3), located along the beach of Selkirk Shores State Park. Salvage excavations revealed the flexed, young adult female buried with two brass kettles, two carved wooden ladles, numerous duck vertebrae, and an iron axe resting on the cranium (Harris 1972, 2(4):1). While this burial cannot be considered diagnostically Onondaga, it does document mid-seventeenth century use of the area.

10. Radisson mentions "French corne" and "tournaps" as well as "hoggs" and "fowles" (Scull 1885:118). Other accounts describe the planting of "French grain and other legumes" (O'Callaghan 1853–1887, 9:380). I would like to thank Jon Anderson, site manager at Ste. Marie, for discussing his ongoing research into seventeenth-century French food ways with me.

11. To state this another way, by the middle of the seventeenth century Onondaga pottery had ceased to function as a stylistic marker of tribal identity. While small amounts of native pottery continue to occur on Onondaga sites until the end of the century, they are more a reflection of the ceramic traditions of assimilated people than of the Onondaga.

12. For comparable examples from the Neutral Hamilton site, see Lennox 1981:295, Figure 21. Lennox lists three collared bowls and twenty-four flared bowls with a pattern of incised horizontal lines. These compare closely with the example from the Carley site illustrated in Figure 10. The second rimless trumpet pipe from the Carley site, one with a motif of opposed triangles, is also similar to other collared and flared bowl pipes from the Hamilton site (ibid.:389, Figure 42, #18 and #22).

13. Archaeological examples of turtle-shell rattles appear to have been made from Box Turtle (Terrapene carolina). Although complex elaborate forms such as figures and combs are more common on historic Onondaga sites than on protohistoric ones, this pattern is less clear on Onondaga than other comparable Iroquois sites. For examples from Oneida and Seneca sites, see Pratt 1976:214, Plate 23; 219, Plate 28; 220, Plate 29; 228, Plate 37; Ritchie 1954:25, Plate 9 #23–26; 29, Plate 11.

14. These discoidal and small tubular forms appear to correspond to the seventeenth-century terms "roanoke" and "peake" (Miller et al. 1983:139). Peake was also called "wampumpeag" or just "wampum." Given sampling problems, it is difficult to reliably quantify the changing ratio of occurrence for these forms. At Pompey Center, the ratio is approximately 5:1 discoidal to wampum (sample of 52). At the Carley site, the ratio has shifted to 20:1 wampum to discoidal (sample of 126).

15. The common forms for these later seventeenth-century shell effigies include turtles, fish, birds, and other zoomorphic shapes with long bodies and/or tails. For examples from Onondaga, see Beauchamp 1901:Plate 6. Many of these same forms occur elsewhere in the Northeast. For Susquehannock examples, see Kent 1970; 1984:173–74. For Delaware examples, see Heye and Pepper 1915:37–43. Some of these effigy forms have been recovered as far west as Michigan (Cleland 1971:35–39).

16. While no examples of rolled copper pipes are currently known from Onondaga sites, several have been reported from other second quarter seventeenth century Iroquois sites. These include Mohawk sites Briggs (Beauchamp 1902b:57 and Plate 19, #80) and Oak Hill (Hagerty 1975:Plate 13B) and the Oneida sites Thurston (Pratt 1976:130 and Plate 34, #4) and Quarry (Hagerty 1975:Plate 13C). Examples of flanged copper liners have been reported from the Seneca Dutch Hollow site (Ritchie 1954:32, Plate 12, #6) and the Oneida Thurston site (Pratt 1976:133, Plate 34, #1)

17. The remaining two copper implements from the Lot 18 site are an L-shaped vent pick and an unbarbed fish hook or gaff.

18. These bells are the same as the variety which Ian Brown has described as "flush-edge, flush loop" (1979:201–2). The majority of these bells are small (12mm in diameter).

On the Lot 18 site, however, two larger sizes—16mm and 22mm in diameter—also occur. Sheet metal bells have been recovered from several of the Dutch colonial sites described by Paul Huey (1984). These include Fort Orange, Beverwyck, Van Buren, and Schuyler Flatts (Paul Huey, personal communication).

19. Similar thimbles have been recovered from Fort Orange (Huey, personal communication). Comparable seventeenth-century examples from Amsterdam are illustrated by Baart et al. (1977:146). The two cast buttons from the Lot 18 site compare with those described by Baart et al. (1974:37, #39 [plain] and 42, #57 [cross hatched motif]).

20. Jan Baart, personal communication. This style of marked brass mouth harp first occurs on the Carley site. Examples have been reported on all subsequent Onondaga sites up through the early eighteenth-century Sevier site. The examples from Sevier appear to be roughly contemporary with those from Fort Michilimackinac, Michigan, which Stone has described as type SA,T2 (Stone 1974:141–45). Although the chronological range of these R-marked mouth harps extends into the early eighteenth century, the most frequent occurrences appear to be on mid-seventeenth century sites. Examples are known from several Mohawk sites (Rumrill 1985:20–23, 26), Seneca sites (Wray 1985:104, 106–7), and Fort Corchaug, Long Island (Solecki 1950:30 and Figure 18y). The Dutch origin of these mouth harps is underscored by their presence on Dutch colonial sites, among them Schuyler Flatts and Fort Orange (Paul Huey, personal communication). For a more general review on mouth harps, see Ypey 1976.

21. Six of the twelve rings have the letters IHS with the cross above. All are of fairly crude manufacture, what Wood has termed "IHS motif 1" (Wood 1974:86). Four of the remaining rings have an L-Heart motif. While the variation of motif does not correspond exactly to those proposed by Wood, the four could be classified as follows: two examples—motif II, one example—motif IV, and one example—motif VII (ibid.:84–85). The last two rings differ from those illustrated by Wood, but belong in the category of incised abstract rings (ibid.:94–95).

22. Jameson 1909:141, retranslated by Charles Gehring (Gehring and Starna n.d.).

23. The relative absence of knives with a tapered tang in Ontario led Garrad to a similar conclusion (1960:11). To date, only a few knives intact enough for identification have been recovered from Dutch colonial sites. These include a tapered tang knife with a thin collar from the Van Buren site and a tapered tang knife with a cylindrical collar from Fort Orange (Paul Huey 1984, personal communication). Although knives with both flat and tapered tangs were used in Amsterdam from the beginning of the fourteenth century on, the tapered tang varieties from Onondaga sites are comparable to excavated seventeenth-century Dutch examples (Baart et al. 1977:325–37; personal communication).

24. The prevalence of flat-tanged knives as well as those with folding blades on early seventeenth-century sites in Ontario has been discussed by Garrad 1969. That this is a reflection of French influence is suggested by a comparable pattern on French sites, such as Ste. Marie aux Hurons (Kidd 1949:10 and Plate XLII), and more recently reported Ontario Iroquois sites, including Hamilton (Lennox 1981:331) and Walker (Wright 1981:107 and Figure 60). The association of clasp (folding blade) knives with the French is also supported by documentary evidence which indicates that small pocket knives, or "jambettes," were among the preferred items of trade (Thwaites 1896–1901, 12:119–21; 15:159). The extensive occurrence of French clasp knives on sites of the late seventeenth and early to mid-eighteenth centuries is discussed in detail by Stone 1974:263–65.

25. Even though they may have been functionally equivalent, native-made awls, whether produced from kettle bails, nails, or other iron objects, are not included in this discussion. They are discussed separately in the section on native reuse of iron.

26. Type I awls only occur on the early seventeenth-century Pompey Center site. Similar examples of curved or crooked awls, apparently related to shoe and saddle making, have been recovered from late sixteenth- and early seventeenth-century contexts in Amsterdam (Baart et al. 1977:136–37 and Figures 128, 129). The pattern for Type II and Type III awls

is less clear. Based on feature association, however, these forms appear to correlate with the French occupation at Fort Michilimackinac (Stone 1974:157–59).

27. While the accusations of supplying guns to the natives were both contradictory and shrill, the reality was quite straightforward. No one, either in New France or New Netherlands, was supposed to give or trade firearms to the natives. When it suited their purposes, however, almost everyone did. The most common rationale was that "good" Indians could have guns. For the French, "good" Indians usually meant Christianized ones. As Barthelemy Vimont, superior of the Jesuit missions in New France, observed in an unguarded moment: "The use of arquebuses, refused to the Infidels by Monsieur the Governor, and granted to the Christian neophytes, is a powerful attraction to win them" (Thwaites 1896–1901, 25:27). For the Dutch, "good" Indians were their trading partners, the Five Nations, especially the Mohawk. At times, however, the expediency of using firearms as gifts supplanted even deeply ingrained fears. In the summer of 1654, when the French colonists from Ste. Marie de Gannentaha came to Onontaque for council, their presents included "arquebuses, powder and lead" in addition to the usual hatchets and kettles (ibid., 43:171).

28. See Kist et al. 1974 for a review of comparable Dutch firearms in Europe. I would like to thank J. P. Puype for his permission to cite his findings (Puype 1985).

29. Examples of these scraping tools have been recovered from most of the seventeenth-century Onondaga sites from Shurtleff through Jamesville. Barka describes and illustrates several comparable examples from the site of Fort LaTour, St. John, New Brunswick (ca. 1640–1645) and notes that numerous others have been found on Micmac sites throughout Acadia (1965:249–50 and Plate 62). William Fitzgerald has observed that these implements are also a frequent occurrence on seventeenth-century Huron sites (personal communication). Another form of French-related ironwork designed for trade is the long-tanged arrowhead, often mentioned in lists of trade merchandise (Thwaites 1896–1901, 4:207; 11:227). Beauchamp illustrates examples from two seventeenth-century Iroquois sites and describes the form as "frequent and widespread" (1902b:76, Plate 28, Figures 119, 121). Comparable examples have been recovered from several French sites, including: St. Croix Island, Maine, 1604; Fort Pentagoet, Castine, Maine, 1635–1654 (Alaric Faulkner, personal communication); and Ste. Marie aux Hurons, Midland, Ontario, 1639–1649 (Kidd 1949:126, Plate 49A and B).

30. The dimensions of these lead bars appear to be quite standardized; trapezoidal in section, they are 25mm across the top, 35mm across the bottom, and 15mm in height. It is likely that this form of bar lead is Dutch; one example was recovered during excavations at Fort Orange (Paul Huey, personal communication). Although this form of lead bar is by far the most common, other forms also occur. These include a roughly rectangular shaped bar 9 × 14mm (two examples from Shurtleff) and a single specimen of a triangular shaped bar from the Lot 18 site.

31. Pewter spoons have been recovered from the Shurtleff and Lot 18 sites. Both have fig-shaped rather than round bowls and a stalk that is hexagonal in cross section. While this style was common across northern Europe, the Onondaga examples appear most similar to Dutch examples (Baart et al. 1977:299). A pewter basin recovered from the Lot 18 site is described in greater detail in Bradley 1979:289 and Figure 17D.

32. Pewter pipes without effigies have been recovered from seventeenth-century contexts in Amsterdam (Jan Baart, personal communication). Beauchamp discusses several examples of pewter pipes from Iroquois sites, including one recovered from the north side of the Oneida River, Town of Schroeppel, another traditional Onondaga fishing area (1902b:56–59, Plate 29, Figure 130). For other published examples of pewter pipes with effigies, see Heye and Pepper 1915:50–54; Witthoft and Kinsey 1959:145, Figure 230; Kent 1984:288; Rumrill 1985:28 and Figure 8.

33. Six examples of Weser slipware have been recovered from the Pompey Center site. All appear to be from a pot or pipkin (Bradley and Bennett 1984). For a discussion of Weser slipware in Amsterdam, see Baart 1981. The four pieces of majolica from Pompey Center all appear to be from a polychrome ointment jar (zalfpot) or albarello. Another comparable

example is illustrated by Korf 1981:139, #348. For additional information on Dutch majolica, see Willcoxen 1982.

34. Of the six pieces of Weser slipware found on the Oneida Cameron site, two had been ground into discs (Bennett 1981:16 and Plate 15, Figures 5 and 7). Similar discs from Seneca sites are reported by Wray 1985:109, Plate 10 b, d. Hamell has suggested that native people could easily have interpreted these glazed ceramics as "crystal," a traditional substance often associated with dream guessing and divination (1983:20, passim).

35. These pipe marks and their distribution on seventeenth-century Onondaga sites are discussed in detail in Bradley and DeAngelo 1981. Unfortunately, several errors appear therein. The following comments are intended to correct those errors: (a) The summary on the Indian Castle site (top p. 124) belongs at the top of p. 126. In other words, the list of pipes on p. 124 accompanies the Carley site summary (p. 123). The Lot 18 site summary and list of pipe marks is correct, although a redundant set of headings beginning with "Stem marks" appears two-thirds of the way down p. 125. The Indian Castle site summary should then follow and introduce the list of pipes that follows on p. 126; (b) Two pipes were omitted from the list of Indian Hill site marks. These should have been the first two heelmarks listed from the site:

EB, type I   Figure 2a   medium heel   1 example   8/64 stem bore
EB, type I   Figure 2a   flush heel   1 example   9/64 stem bore

(c) The group of heelmarks that begins halfway down p. 127 is the start of the list for the Bloody Hill II site, not a part of the Indian Hill list. Unfortunately, the list of pipe marks for the Bloody Hill II site appears to begin on p. 128. The site summary for Bloody Hill II is out of place, however, and the marks on p. 128 are a continuation of the list that began on p. 127.

36. Published reports on glass beads from these sites include: Bradley 1977 (Pompey Center), Bradley 1984 (Shurtleff and Carley), and Bradley 1976 and Tanner 1978 (Lot 18).

37. Baart et al. 1977:183; personal communication. Black glass buttons have also been recovered from sites related to other Dutch exploratory ventures such as the camp of Willem Barentsz's 1596 expedition to Nova Zembla (Baart et al. 1974:28).

38. Information on glass beads from Fort Orange is taken from Huey 1983:87-90 with two modifications. One is the addition of black glass buttons to the bead sample. The second is the grouping of specific bead varieties in order to minimize artificial distinctions which often arise when different individuals "type" specimen. Examples of bead varieties lumped together include IV a11/13, IIa31/36/40, and IIb56/57. The beads from Fort Orange have been examined by the author through the courtesy of Paul Huey.

39. For information on glass bead production in Amsterdam, see Karklins 1974, 1983, 1985b, and Baart n.d. While most of these beads appear to have been made for export, many also have been recovered from domestic cesspits (Karklins 1985a). It is unclear whether these beads reflect home manufacture or a previously undocumented use of beads by the Dutch for adornment.

5. Accommodating Change

1. This interpretation stresses the functional and/or aesthetic value of European goods to native people. Ritchie's description of native preference for "toil alleviating tools" and "ego-enhancing" ornaments is an example (Ritchie 1954:1-2, 24). For other examples of this interpretation, see Hunt 1940:19; Trelease 1960:viii, 28-29, 48; Pratt 1976:145; and Trigger 1976, 1:409-13.

2. The difference between these criteria can be a subtle one. The point of discrimination is whether the substance was consecrated for ritual purposes or not. See Hamell 1985 for a more detailed discussion of this point. The distinction is not always apparent in the archaeological record.

3. Relevant here is a principle that Hockett and Ascher (1964) termed Romer's Rule. This principle states that "The initial survival value of a favorable innovation is conservative, in that it renders possible the maintenance of a traditional way of life in the face of changed circumstances. Later on, of course, the innovation may allow the exploitation of some . . . niche not available . . . before the change; but this is a consequence [of the innovation] not a cause" (137). This principle, initially offered as an "antidote for the improper use of keen hindsight" (ibid.), exemplifies why acculturation cannot be examined satisfactorily through the direct historical approach.

4. The fact that this new form with its integral hafting survives better archaeologically also makes the degree of change seem more dramatic than it really was.

5. As nearly as can be ascertained from the available ethnohistorical and archaeological data, kettles were used in the same manner as pots. In contrast to the Micmac (Martin 1975), there was no major change in Onondaga settlement or subsistence patterns as a result of this substitution.

6. The crooked knife is a good case in point. The evolution of this distinctive native implement has yet to be fully documented. Nevertheless, the Onondaga evidence suggests that broken knives were reground and used in place of traditional woodworking tools such as a hafted beaver incisor. The example from the Pompey Center site (Figure 17b) appears to predate any direct Onondaga exposure to European tools, aside from the stock trade items, and is morphologically identical to the crooked knives that occur more frequently on Onondaga sites after 1655. See Tuck 1971:179, Plate 40, #10 for an example. This evidence argues that the crooked knife was a native innovation and not copied from the farrier's knife or other European forms (Prisch 1982:5).

7. Brief discussions of the condolence ritual are presented by Fenton 1978:316–19 and Tooker 1978:437–44. Both Hamell (n.d.) and Ceci (1982) review the relationship between wampum and the condolence ceremony as part of the larger issue of why wampum (shell) had value to the Iroquois.

8. It was Hiawatha who discovered wampum while grieving over his daughter's death, and who subsequently introduced it as part of the condolence ritual (Parker 1916:20–21, 116–17). Different versions of the origin myth attribute the discovery of wampum to different places. Most frequently mentioned are the Tully Lakes south of Syracuse (ibid.; Beauchamp 1900:339). Other sources suggest Oneida Lake (Converse 1908:139–40).

9. Ceci 1977:191–276; 1980. Also see William Bradford's telling assessment of the Dutch incorporation of wampum into their commercial system (Bradford 1952:203).

10. For a more detailed discussion, see Lenig 1977:80 and Trigger 1976, 2:463–64.

11. Thwaits 1896–1901, 21:41, 49. The attackers were probably Mohawk, who had sworn unending hatred for the Algonquin (ibid.:37).

12. Webb traces in detail both Garacontié's life and role in formulating the Covenant Chain (1984:251–302). Garacontié is a figure worthy of the attention. In both his personal life and his role as a League sachem he sought to reconcile Iroquois traditions with the new trans-cultural realities. In many ways he personified the acculturative process during the third quarter of the seventeenth century.

Bibliography

Abler, Thomas S. 1980. Iroquois cannibalism: Fact not fiction. *Ethnohistory* 27(4):309–16.

Alexander, Maurice M. 1976. *The ecology of Onondaga County and vicinity.* Syracuse: State University of New York, College of Environment Science and Forestry.

Baart, Jan M. n.d. Seventeenth century glass bead sites in Amsterdam. *Historical Archaeology.* Forthcoming.

———. 1981. Weserware in Amsterdam. In *Coppengrave Studien zur Töpferei des 13 bis 19. Jahrhunderts in Nordwestdeutschland,* ed. Hans-George Stephan, 138–41. Verlag August Lax Hildesheim.

Baart, Jan M., W. Krook, A.C. Lagerweij, C.A. Ockers, and G.W. Stouthart. 1974. *Opgravingen in Amsterdam.* Amsterdam: Amsterdams Historisch Museum.

Baart, Jan, Wiard Krook, Ab Lagerweij, Nina Ockers, Hans Van Regteren Altena, Tuuk Stam, Henk Stoepker, Gerald Stouthart, and Monika Van Der Zwan. 1977. Knopenaan het Hollandse Kostuum uit de zestiende en zeventiende eeuw. *Antiek* 9(1):17–49.

Barbour, Philip L., ed. 1969. *The Jamestown voyages under the first charter 1606–1609.* 2 vols. Published for the Hakluyt Society. Cambridge: The University Press.

Barka, Norman F. 1965. Historic sites archaeology at Portland Point, New Brunswick, Canada—1631–c.1850 A.D. Ph.D diss., Department of Anthropology, Harvard University, Cambridge, Mass.

Beauchamp, William M. 1907. *Aboriginal place names of New York.* New York State Museum Bulletin, no. 108 (Archaeology no. 12). Albany: New York State Education Department.

———. 1905a. *A history of the New York Iroquois.* New York State Museum Bulletin, no. 78. Albany: University of the State of New York.

———. 1905b. *Perch Lake mounds with notes on other New York mounds, and some accounts of Indian trails.* New York State Museum Bulletin, no. 87. Albany: New York State Education Department.

———. 1905c. *Aboriginal use of wood in New York.* New York State Museum Bulletin, no. 89. Albany: New York State Education Department.

————. 1903. *Metallic ornaments of the New York Indians.* New York State Museum Bulletin, no. 73. Albany: New York State Education Department.

————. 1902a. *Horn and bone implements of the New York aborigines.* New York State Museum Bulletin, no. 50. Albany: University of the State of New York.

————. 1902b. *Metallic implements of the New York Indians.* New York State Museum Bulletin, no. 55. Albany: University of the State of New York.

————. 1901. *Wampum and shell articles used by the New York Indians.* New York State Museum Bulletin, no. 41. Albany: University of the State of New York.

————. 1900. *Aboriginal occupation of New York.* New York State Museum Bulletin, no. 32. Albany: University of the State of New York.

————. 1898. *Earthenware of the New York aborigines.* New York State Museum Bulletin, no. 22. Albany: University of the State of New York.

————. 1897. *Polished stone articles used by the New York aborigines before and during European occupation.* New York State Museum Bulletin, no. 18. Albany: University of the State of New York.

————. n.d. Antiquities of Onondaga. 10 vols. Unpublished. New York State Museum, Albany.

Bennett, Monte. 1978. Recent excavations on the Cameron site (OND 8-4). *Bulletin.* Chenango Chapter, New York State Archaeological Association 17(4):1-36.

————. 1981. A longhouse pattern on the Cameron site (OND 8-4). *Bulletin.* Chenango Chapter, New York State Archaeological Association 19(2):1-23.

Berry, John W. 1980. Acculturation as varieties of adaptation. In *Acculturation Theory, Models and Some New Findings,* ed. Amado M. Padilla, 9-25. AAAS Selected Symposium 39. Boulder, Colorado: Westview Press.

Biggar, Henry P. [1901] 1965. *The early trading companies of New France: A contribution to the history of commerce and discovery in North America.* New York: Argonaut Press.

Biggar, Henry Percival., ed. 1922-1936. *The works of Samuel de Champlain.* 6 vols. Toronto: The Champlain Society.

Biggar, Henry P., ed. 1924. *The voyages of Jacques Cartier.* Publications of the Public Archives of Canada, Ottawa, no. 11.

Blair, Claude. 1974. *Arms, armour and base metal work [from] the James A. de Rothschild collection at Waddesdon Manor.* London: The National Trust for Places of Historic Interest or Natural Beauty.

Blau, Harold, Jack Campisi, and Elisabeth Tooker. 1976. Onondaga. In *Northeast,* vol. 15 of *Handbook of North American Indians,* ed. Bruce G. Trigger, 491-99. Washington, D.C.: Smithsonian Institution.

Bradford, William. 1952. *Of Plymouth Plantation, 1620-1647.* New York: Alfred A. Knopf.

Bradley, James W. 1984. Glass beads from two early 17th century Onondaga Iroquois sites. *Bulletin.* William M. Beauchamp Chapter, New York State Archaeological Association 4(1):141-48.

————. 1983. Blue crystals and other trinkets: Glass beads from 16th and early 17th century New England. In *Proceedings of the 1982 Glass Trade Bead Conference,* ed. Charles F. Hayes III. Research Records, no. 16:29-39.

————. 1980a. Ironwork in Onondaga, 1550-1650. In *Studies in Iroquoian culture,* ed. Nancy Bonvillain, 109-17. Occasional Publications in Northeastern Anthropology, no. 6. Rindge, N.H.: Department of Anthropology, Franklin Pierce College.

————. 1980b. Dutch bale seals from 17th century Onondaga Iroquois sites in New York State. *Post-Medieval Archaeology* 14:197–200.

————. 1979. The Onondaga Iroquois: 1500–1655. A study in acculturative change and its consequences. Ph.D. diss., Interdisciplinary Program in Social Science, Syracuse University, Syracuse, N.Y.

————. 1977. The Pompey Center site: The impact of European trade goods, 1600–1620. *Bulletin.* William M. Beauchamp Chapter, New York State Archaeological Association 2(1):1–23.

————. 1976. Report on European glass beads from the Lot 18 site, 1650–1655. *Bulletin.* William M. Beauchamp Chapter, New York State Archaeological Association 1:34–36.

Bradley, James W. and Monte Bennett. 1984. Two occurrences of Weser slipware from early 17th century Iroquois sites in New York State. *Post-Medieval Archaeology* 18:301–5.

Bradley, James W. and Gordon DeAngelo. 1981. European clay pipe marks from 17th century Onondaga Iroquois sites. *Archaeology of Eastern North America* 9:109–33.

Brain, Jeffrey P. 1979. *Tunica treasure.* A joint publication of the Peabody Museum, Harvard University, and the Peabody Museum of Salem. Papers of the Peabody Museum of Archaeology and Ethnology, vol. 71. Cambridge: Harvard University and the Peabody Museum of Salem.

Brasser, T. J. 1978. Early Indian-European contacts. In *Northeast,* vol. 15 of *Handbook of North American Indians,* ed. Bruce G. Trigger, 78–88. Washington, D.C.: Smithsonian Institution.

Braudel, Fernand. 1984. *The perspective of the world. Civilization and capitalism, 15th–18th century.* Vol. 3. New York: Harper and Row.

Brawer, Catherine C., ed. 1983. *Many trails: Indians of the lower Hudson valley.* Katonah, N.Y.: The Katonah Gallery.

Brown, Ian W. 1979. Bells. In *Tunica treasure* by Jeffrey Brain, 197–205. Papers of the Peabody Museum of Archaeology and Ethnology, vol. 71. Cambridge: Harvard University and the Peabody Museum of Salem.

Brown, M. L. 1980. *Firearms in colonial America.* Washington, D.C.: Smithsonian Press.

Burger, Marjorie K. and Peter P. Pratt. 1973. SUNY-Oswego excavations in Ontario relating to the disappearance of the St. Lawrence Iroquois. Proceedings of the annual meeting, Eastern States Archaeological Federation *Bulletin,* no. 32 (July):14–15.

Burridge, Kenelm. 1960. *Mambu: A Melanesian millennium.* London: Methuen and Co., Ltd.

Cadzow, Donald A. 1936. *Archaeological studies of the Susquehannock Indians of Pennsylvania.* Harrisburg: Publications of the Pennsylvania Historical Commission.

Carpenter, Edmund. 1942. Iroquoian figures. *American Antiquity* 8(1):105–13.

Ceci, Lynn. 1982. The value of wampum among the New York Iroquois: A case study in artifact analysis. *Journal of Anthropological Research* 38(1):97–107.

————. 1980. The first fiscal crisis in New York. *Economic Development and Cultural Change* 28(4). Reprinted in *The second coastal archaeology reader: 1900 to the present,* ed. James E. Truex. Lexington: Ginn Custom Publishing.

————. 1977. The effect of European contact and trade on the settlement pattern of Indians in coastal New York, 1524–1665: The archaeological and documentary evidence. Ph.D. diss., Department of Anthropology, The City University of New York, New York.

Clark, Joshua V. H. 1849. *Onondaga; or reminiscences of earlier and later times.* . . . 2 vols. Syracuse: Stoddard & Babcock.

Clarke, John M. 1915. *Eleventh report of the director of the State Museum and Science Department.* University of the State of New York Bulletin, no. 601. Albany: University of the State of New York.

Cleland, Charles E., ed. 1971. *The Lasanen site, An historic burial locality in Mackinac County, Michigan.* Publications of the Museum, Michigan State University, Anthropological Series, vol. 1, no. 1. Ann Arbor: Lithocrafters.

———. 1982. The inland shore fishery of the northern Great Lakes: Its development and importance in prehistory. *American Antiquity* 47 (October):761–84.

Connors, Dennis J., Gordon DeAngelo and Peter P. Pratt. 1980. *The search for the Jesuit mission of Ste. Marie de Gannentaha.* Liverpool, N.Y.: Office of Museums and Historical Sites, County of Onondaga Department of Parks and Recreation.

Converse, Harriet Maxwell. 1908. *Myths and legends of the New York State Iroquois.* Ed. Arthur C. Parker. New York State Museum Bulletin, no. 125. Albany: University of the State of New York.

Cox, Donald D. 1959. *Some postglacial forests in central and eastern New York State as determined by the method of pollen analysis.* New York State Museum and Science Service Bulletin, no. 377. Albany: University of the State of New York.

Coyne, James H., trans., ed. 1903. *Galinee's narrative and map.* Ontario Historical Society, Papers and Records. Vol. 4. Toronto: Ontario Historical Society.

Curtin, Philip D. 1984. *Cross-cultural trade in world history.* Cambridge: Cambridge University Press.

Davis, Christine. 1984. A mortuary pattern for Monongahela. *Pennsylvania Archaeologist* 54(1–2):3–11.

Denys, Nicolas. [1672] 1908. *The description and natural history of the coasts of North America (Acadia).* 2 vols. Edited and translated by William F. Ganong. Toronto: The Champlain Society.

DeOrio, Robert N. 1978. A preliminary sequence of the historic Cayuga Nation within the traditional area, 1600–1740. William Beauchamp Chapter, New York State Archaeological Association *Newsletter* 9(4):2–7.

DePratter, Chester B. and Marvin T. Smith. 1980. Sixteenth century European trade in the southeastern United States: Evidence from the Juan Pardo expeditions (1566–1568). In *Spanish colonial frontier research*, ed. Henry Dobyns, 57–77, Albuquerque: Center for Anthropological Studies.

Dunbar, Helene R. and Katherine C. Ruhl. 1974. Copper artifacts from the Engelbert site. *Bulletin*, New York State Archaeological Association 61:1–10.

Endrei, Walter and Geoff Egan. 1982. The sealing of cloth in Europe, with special reference to the English evidence. *Textile History* 13(1):47–75.

Engelbrecht, William. 1974. Cluster analysis: A method for studying Iroquois prehistory. *Man in the Northeast* 7:57–70.

———. 1972. The reflection of patterned behavior in Iroquois pottery decoration. *Pennsylvania Archaeologist* 42(3):1–15.

Fenton, William N. 1978. Northern Iroquoian cultural patterns. In *Northeast*, vol. 15 of *Handbook of North American Indians*, ed. Bruce G. Trigger, 296–321. Washington, D.C.: Smithsonian Institution.

———. 1975. The lore of the longhouse: Myth, ritual and red power. *Anthropological Quarterly* 48 (no. 3):131–47.

———. 1940. Problems arising from the historic Northeastern position of the Iroquois. In *Essays in historical anthropology of North America.* Smithsonian Miscellaneous Collections, vol. 100, pp. 159–251. Washington, D.C.: Smithsonian Institution.

Finlayson, William. 1985. *The 1975 and 1978 rescue excavations at the Draper site: Introduction and settlement patterns.* Paper no. 130, Mercury Series, Archaeological Survey of Canada. Ottawa: National Museum of Man.

Finlayson, William D. And Robert H. Pihl. 1980. Some implications for the attribute analysis of rim sherds from the Draper site. In *Proceedings of the 1979 Iroquois pottery conference,* ed. Charles F. Hayes III, 113–29. Rochester: Rochester Museum and Science Center.

Fisher, Charles and Karen Hartgen. 1983. Glass trade beads from Waterford, New York. *Pennsylvania Archaeologist* 53(1–2):47–52.

Fitzgerald, William A. 1982. *Lest the beaver run loose: The early 17th century Christianson site and trends in historic Neutral archaeology.* Paper no. 111, Mercury Series, Archaeological Survey of Canada. Ottawa: National Museum of Man.

Forks of the Delaware Chapter. 1980. The Overpeck site (36 BU5). *Pennsylvania Archaeologist* 50(3):1–46.

Foster, George M. 1960. *Culture and conquest: America's Spanish heritage.* Viking Fund Publications in Anthropology, no. 27. New York: Wenner-Gren Foundation for Anthropological Research, Inc.

Funk, Robert E. and Bruce E. Rippenteau. 1977. *Adaptation, continuity and change in upper Susquehanna prehistory.* Occasional Publications in Northeastern Anthropology, no. 3. George's Mills, N.H.: Man in the Northeast, Inc.

Garrad, Charles. 1969. Iron trade knives on historic Petun sites. *Ontario Archaeology* 13:3–15.

Gehring, Charles and William Starna. n.d. A journey into Mohawk and Oneida country: The journal of Harmen Meyndertsz van den Bogart. Unpublished manuscript.

Gibson, Stanford. 1968. The Oran-Barnes site. *Bulletin,* Chenango Chapter, New York State Archaeological Association 10 (August):1–22.

Griffin, James B., ed. 1961. *Lake Superior copper and the Indians: Miscellaneous studies of Great Lakes prehistory.* Anthropology Papers, no. 17. Ann Arbor: Museum of Anthropology, University of Michigan.

Guilday, John E. 1963. The cup-and-pin game. *Pennsylvania Archaeologist* 33(4):159–63.

Hagerty, Gilbert. 1975. Oneida miscellany. *Bulletin,* Chenango Chapter, New York State Archaeological Association 16(1):1–31.

———. 1963. The iron trade knife in Oneida territory. *Pennsylvania Archaeologist* 33(1–2):93–114.

Hamell, George R. n.d. Life's immortal shell: Wampum among the Iroquois. Unpublished manuscript.

———. 1985. Under(water) world wealth and European trade goods: Mythical realities and European contact in the Northeast during the 16th–17th centuries. Paper presented at the 5th North American Fur Trade Conference, McGill University, Montreal.

———. 1983. Trading in metaphors: The magic of beads. In *Proceedings of the 1982 glass trade bead conference*, ed. Charles F. Hayes III, 5–28. Research Records, no. 16. Rochester: Rochester Museum and Science Center.

———. 1982. Some thoughts on Wenro-Seneca relationships: An archaeological perspective. Paper presented at the Annual Conference on Iroquois Research, Rensselaerville, N.Y.

———. 1978. Wooden smoking pipes of the Seneca Iroquois of western New York State: Sixteenth and seventeenth centuries. Unpublished manuscript.

Hamilton, T.M. 1968. *Early Indian trade guns, 1625–1775*. Contributions of the Museum of the Great Plains, no. 3. Lawton, Oklahoma.

———. 1980. *Colonial frontier guns*. Chadron, Nebraska: The Fur Press.

Harington, C. Richard. 1981. Whales and seals of the Champlain Sea. *Trail & Landscape* 15(1):32–47.

Harrington, M. R. 1922. Prehistoric Iroquois sites in northern New York. Report of Peabody Museum Expedition, 1906. In *The Archaeological History of New York* by Arthur C. Parker, 1922: 315–39.

Harris, Barbara. 1972. Intrusive burial at Jayne/LaPoint (PLI 1–3). *Newsletter*, William M. Beauchamp Chapter, New York State Archaeological Association 2(4):1.

Hart, Simon. 1959. *The prehistory of the New Netherland Company*. Amsterdam: City of Amsterdam Press.

Hasenstab, Robert J. 1985. Pits, palisades, and longhouses: An hypothesis for the development of agriculture, warfare, and tribalization among the Iroquois of New York State. Diss. prospectus, Department of Anthropology, University of Massachusetts, Amherst.

Hayes, Charles F. III, ed. 1983. *Proceedings of the 1982 glass trade bead conference*. Research Records, no. 16. Rochester: Rochester Museum and Science Center.

———, ed. 1981. *The Iroquois in the American Revolution. 1976 conference proceedings*. Research Records, no. 14. Rochester: Rochester Museum and Science Center.

———, ed. 1980. *Proceedings of the 1979 Iroquois pottery conference*. Research Records, no. 13. Rochester: Rochester Museum and Science Center.

Heisey, Henry W. and J. Paul Witmer. 1962. Historic Susquehannock cemeteries. *Pennsylvania Archaeologist* 32(3–4):99–130.

———. 1964. The Shenks Ferry people: A site and some generalities. *Pennsylvania Archaeologist*. 34(1):8–34.

Hewitt, John N. B. 1928. *Iroquoian cosmology*, second part. Annual Report of the Bureau of American Ethnology, Smithsonian Institution 43(1925–1926).

Heye, George G. and George H. Pepper. 1915. Exploration of a Munsee cemetery near Montague, New Jersey. *Contributions from the Museum of the American Indian*, Heye Foundation, vol. 2:1–78. New York: Museum of the American Indian.

Hinsdale, William G. 1927. Old Iroquois needles of brass. *Indian Notes* 4(2):174–76.

Hockett, Charles and Robert Ascher. 1964. The human revolution. *Current Archaeology* 5(3):135–68.

Huey, Paul R. 1985. Archaeological excavations in the site of Fort Orange, a Dutch West India Company trading fort built in 1624. *Bulletin KNOB* Jaargang 84(2/3):68–79.

———. 1984. Dutch sites of the 17th century in Rensselaerswyck. In *The scope of historical archaeology: Essays in honor of John L. Cotter*, ed. David G. Orr and Daniel G. Crozier, 63–85. Occasional Publication. Philadelphia: Department of Anthropology, Temple University.

———. 1983. Glass beads from Fort Orange (1625–1676), Albany, New York. In *Proceedings of the 1982 glass trade bead conference*, ed. Charles F. Hayes III, 83–110. Research Records, no. 16. Rochester: Rochester Museum and Science Center.

Hunt, George T. [1940] 1960. *The wars of the Iroquois.* Madison: University of Wisconsin Press.

Hutton, Frank Z., Jr. and C. Edwin Rice. 1977. *Soil survey of Onondaga County, New York.* Washington, D.C.: United States Department of Agriculture Soil Conservation Service and Cornell University Agricultural Experimental Station.

Innis, Harold A. 1956. *The fur trade in Canada.* Rev. ed. Toronto: University of Toronto Press.

Jaenen, Cornelius J. 1976. *Friend and foe. Aspects of French-American cultural contact in the sixteenth and seventeenth centuries.* New York: Columbia University Press.

Jameson, John Franklin, ed. 1909. *Narratives of New Netherland, 1609–1664.* New York: Charles Scribner and Sons.

Jennings, Francis. 1984. *The ambiguous Iroquois empire. The convenant chain confederation of Indian tribes with English colonies from its beginnings to the Lancaster Treaty of 1744.* New York: W. W. Norton and Company.

Johnson, Marion. 1970. The cowrie currencies of West Africa. Part 1. *Journal of African History* 11(1):17–49.

Juet, Robert. 1841. Extract from the journal of the voyage of the Half-Moon . . . in the year 1609. *Collections of the New York Historical Society*, 2d series, vol. 1:320–32.

Karklins, Karlis. 1985a. Towards a chronology for Dutch trade beads. Paper presented at the Society for Historical Archaeology annual meeting, Boston, Mass.

———. 1985b. Early Amsterdam trade beads. *Ornament* 9(2):36–41.

———. 1983. Dutch trade beads in North America. In *Proceedings of the 1982 glass trade bead conference*, ed. Charles F. Hayes III, 111–26. Research Records, no. 16. Rochester: Rochester Museum and Science Center.

———. 1974. Seventeenth century Dutch beads. *Historical Archaeology* 8:64–82.

Kent, Barry C. 1984. *Susquehanna's Indians.* Anthropological Series, no. 6. Harrisburg: Pennsylvania Historical and Museum Commission.

———. 1983. More on gunflints. *Historical Archaeology* 17(2):27–40.

———. 1980. An update on Susquehanna Iroquoian pottery. In *Proceedings of the 1979 Iroquois pottery conference*, ed. Charles F. Hayes III, 99–103. Research Records, no. 13. Rochester: Rochester Museum and Science Center.

———. 1974. Locust Grove pottery: A new Late Woodland variety. *Pennsylvania Archaeologist* 44(4):1–5.

———. 1970. An unusual cache from the Wyoming Valley, Pennsylvania. *American Antiquity* 35(2):185–93.

Kenyon, Ian and William Fitzgerald. 1986. Dutch glass beads in the Northeast: An Ontario perspective. *Man in the Northeast* 32:1–34.

Kenyon, Walter A. 1982. *The Grimsby site: A historic Neutral cemetery.* Publications in Archaeology. Toronto: Royal Ontario Museum.

———. 1968. *The Miller site*, Occasional Paper, 14, Art and Archaeology, Royal Ontario Museum, University of Toronto. Toronto: The Bryant Press.

Kidd, Kenneth E. 1972. Contact material from the Dawson site. In *Cartier's Hochelaga and the Dawson site* ed. James F. Pendergast and Bruce G. Trigger, 327–32. Montreal: McGill-Queen's University Press.

————. 1955. A statistical analysis of trade axes. *Bulletin*, New York State Archaeological Association 5(5):6.

————. 1949. *The excavation of Sainte-Marie I.* Toronto: University of Toronto Press.

Kidd, Kenneth E. and Martha Ann Kidd. 1970. A classification system for glass beads for the use of field archaeologists. *Canadian historic sites: Occasional papers in archaeology and history*, no. 1:45–89. Ottawa: Maracle Press, Limited.

Kinsey, W. Fred, III and Jeffrey R. Graybill. 1971. Murry site and its role in Lancaster and Funk phases of Shenks Ferry culture. *Pennsylvania Archaeologist* 41(4):7–43.

Kist, J. B., J. P. Puype and R. B. F. Van der Sloot. 1974. *Dutch muskets and pistols: An illustrated history of seventeenth century gunmaking in the Low Countries.* York, Penn.: George Shumway.

Knight, Dean. 1978. The Ball site: A preliminary statement. *Ontario Archaeology* 29:53–63.

Korf, Dingeman. 1981. *Nederlandse majolica.* Haarlem: DeHaan.

Kraft, Herbert C. 1975. *The archaeology of the Tocks Island area.* South Orange: Seton Hall Archaeological Museum.

LaFrance, Albert D. 1984. The Christopher site (TLY 7-2). *Bulletin*, William Beauchamp Chapter, New York State Archaeological Association 4(1):149–68.

————, 1980. Onondaga Chance phase ceramic trends: An attribute approach. In *Proceedings of the 1979 Iroquois pottery conference*, ed. Charles F. Hayes III, 51–63. Research Records, no. 13. Rochester: Rochester Museum and Science Center.

————. 1977. The Chase site, CZA 5-3. *Bulletin*, William Beauchamp Chapter, New York State Archaeological Association 2(1):35–46.

————. n.d. The Burke II site. Unpublished manuscript.

LaFrance, Albert D. and Ferdinand LaFrance. 1976. An Onondaga Chance phase site: Carley II. *Bulletin*, William Beauchamp Chapter, New York State Archaeological Association 1:1–24.

LaFrance, Ferdinand. 1977. The application of Tuck's attribute percentages to unrecorded Onondaga prehistoric sites. *Bulletin*, William Beauchamp Chapter, New York State Archaeological Association 2(1):32–34.

Lenig, Donald. 1977. Of Dutchmen, beaver hats and Iroquois. In *Current perspectives in northeastern prehistory*, ed. Charles Hayes and Robert Funk. *Researches and Transactions of the New York State Archaeological Association* 17(1):71–84. Buffalo: New York State Archaeological Association.

————. 1965. *The Oak Hill horizon and its relationship to the development of Five Nations Iroquius culture. Researches and Transactions of the New York State Archaeological Association* 15(1):1–114 Buffalo: New York State Archaeological Association.

Lennox, Paul A. 1981. *The Hamilton site: A late historic Neutral town.* Paper no. 103, Mercury Series, Archaeological Survey of Canada. Ottawa: National Museum of Man.

Lindner, Christopher. 1983. Evidence against prehistoric digging tools of sandstone in central New York State. *Man in the Northeast* 26:55–73.

Linton, Ralph, ed. 1940. *Acculturation in seven American Indian tribes.* New York: Appleton-Century Company.

Lucy, Charles L. 1950. Notes on a small Andaste burial site and Andaste archaeology. *Pennsylvania Archaeologist* 20(3–4):55–62.

Lurie, Nancy O. 1959. Indian cultural adjustment to European civilization. In *Seventeenth Century America*, ed. James M. Smith, 33–60. Chapel Hill: University of North Carolina Press.

MacNeish, Richard S. 1952. *Iroquois pottery types*. National Museum of Canada Bulletin, no. 124. Ottawa: National Museum of Canada.

Martin, Calvin. 1978. *Keepers of the game. Indian animal relationships and the fur trade.* Berkeley: University of California Press.

—————. 1975. The four lives of a Micmac copper pot. *Ethnohistory* 22(2):111–33.

Mathews, Zena Pearlstone. 1982. On dreams and journeys: Iroquoian boat pipes. *American Indian Art Magazine* 7(3):46–51, 80.

—————. 1981a. Janus and other multiple-image Iroquoian pipes. *Ontario Archaeology* 35:3–22.

—————. 1981b. The identification of animals on Ontario Iroquoian pipes. *Canadian Journal of Archaeology* 5:31–47.

—————. 1978. *The relation of Seneca false face masks to Seneca and Ontario archaeology.* New York: Garland Publishing, Inc.

—————. 1976. Huron pipes and Iroquoian shamanism. *Man in the Northeast* 12:15–31.

Mayer, Joseph. 1943. *Flintlocks of the Iroquois, 1620–1687.* Research Records, no. 6. Rochester: Rochester Museum of Arts and Sciences.

McCashion, John H. 1975. The clay tobacco pipes of New York State, part one: Caughnawaga 1667–1693. *Bulletin*, New York State Archaeological Association 65:1–19.

McDowell-Loudan, Ellis E., ed. 1984. Reports and comments on Indian Hill II (CZA 8–1): Reputed site of a trenched wall longhouse with multiple components. *Bulletin*, William Beauchamp Chapter, New York State Archaeological Association 4(1):1–139.

McPherron, Alan. 1967. *The Juntunen site and the Late Woodland prehistory of the upper Great Lakes area.* Anthropology Papers no. 30. Ann Arbor: Museum of Anthropology, University of Michigan.

Miller, Henry M., Dennis J. Pogue, and Michael A. Smolek. 1983. Beads from the seventeenth century Chesapeake. *Proceedings of the 1982 glass bead conference*, ed. Charles F. Hayes III, 127–44. Research Records, no. 16. Rochester: Rochester Museum and Science Center.

Morgan, Lewis Henry. [1851] 1962. *League of the HO-DE'-NO-SAU-NEE, Iroquois.* New York: Corinth Books.

Morris, Percy A. 1975. *A field guide to shells of the Atlantic and Gulf coasts and the West Indies.* 3rd ed. Boston, Mass.: Houghton Mifflin Co.

Niemczycki, Mary Ann. 1984. *The origin and development of the Seneca and Cayuga tribes of New York State.* Research Records, no. 17. Rochester: Rochester Museum and Science Center.

Noble, William C. 1979. Ontario Iroquois effigy pipes. *Canadian Journal of Archaeology* 3:69–89.

—————. 1975. Corn, and the development of village life in southern Ontario. *Ontario Archaeology* 25:37–46.

—————. 1971. The Sopher celt: An indicator of early prehistoric trade in Huronia. *Ontario Archaeology* 16:42–47.

O'Callaghan, Edmund B., ed. 1853–1887. *Documents relative to the colonial history of the state of New York; procured in Holland, England and France by John R. Brodhead.* 15 vols. Albany: Weed, Parsons and Company.

Parker, Arthur C. 1922. *The archaeological history of New York.* New York State Museum Bulletin, nos. 235–38. Albany: University of the State of New York.

———. 1919. A Contact period Seneca site situated at Factory Hollow, Ontario County, N.Y. *Researches and Transactions of the New York State Archaeological Association* 1(2). Rochester: Lewis H. Morgan Chapter.

———. 1916. *The constitution of the five nations.* New York State Museum Bulletin, no. 184. Albany: University of the State of New York.

Parker, Arthur C., ed. 1938. *A report of the Susquehanna River expedition sponsored in 1916 by the Museum of the American Indian,* comp. and ann. by Warren K. Moorehead. Andover, Mass.: The Andover Press.

Parkman, Francis. [1867] 1895. *The Jesuits in North America in the seventeenth century.* Boston: Little, Brown and Company.

Pendergast, James F. 1984. *The Beckstead site—1977.* Paper No. 123, Mercury Series, Archaeological Survey of Canada. Ottawa: National Museum of Man.

———. 1982. Significance of a Huron archaeological presence in Jefferson County, New York. Paper presented at the McMaster University Symposium, "The Ontario Iroquois Tradition Revisited."

———. 1981a. *The Glenbrook Village site: A late St. Lawrence Iroquoian component in Glengarry County, Ontario.* Paper no. 100, Mercury Series, Archaeological Survey of Canada. Ottawa: National Museum of Man.

———. 1981b. Origins of the St. Lawrence Iroquoian pottery on the Draper site. Unpublished manuscript.

———. 1975. An in situ hypothesis to explain the origin of the St. Lawrence Iroquoians. *Ontario Archaeology* 25:47–55.

———. 1973. *The Roebuck prehistoric village site rim sherds—An attribute analysis.* Paper no. 8, Mercury Series, Archaeological Survey of Canada. Ottawa: National Museum of Man.

———. 1968. *The Summerstown Station site.* Anthropology Papers, no. 18 (September). Ottawa: National Museum of Canada.

———. 1966. *Three prehistoric Iroquois components in eastern Ontario: The Salem, Grays Creek, and Beckstead sites.* National Museum of Canada Bulletin, no. 208, Anthropological Series, no. 73. Ottawa: National Museum of Man.

Pendergast, James F. and Bruce G. Trigger. 1972. *Cartier's Hochelaga and the Dawson site.* Montreal: McGill-Queen's University Press.

Pendery, Stephen. 1984. Final report, Phase III Chelsea-Water Streets Connector Project, Charlestown, Massachusetts. Excavation at the Wapping Street and Maudlin Street archaeological districts. Cambridge: Peabody Museum, Harvard University.

Phelps, David Sutton. 1983. Archaeology of the North Carolina coast and coastal plain: Problems and hypotheses. In *The prehistory of North Carolina,* ed. M. A. Mathis and J. J. Crow, 1–51. Raleigh: North Carolina Division of Archives and History.

Potter, Stephen R. 1984. Baubles and burials: An analysis of nineteenth-century archaeological discoveries in the vicinity of Potomac Creek, Virginia. Paper presented at the Middle Atlantic Archaeological Conference, Rehoboth Beach, Delaware, April 13–15, 1984.

———. 1982. An analysis of Chicacoan settlement patterns. Ph.D. diss., Department of Anthropology, University of North Carolina at Chapel Hill.

Pratt, Peter P. n.d. *Onondaga Iroquois acculturation at the time of Frontenac's invasion of 1696.* Forthcoming.

————. 1977. A perspective on Oneida archaeology. In *Current perspectives in Northeastern Archaeology, Essays in Honor of William A. Ritchie,* ed. Robert E. Funk and Charles F. Hayes, III. *Researches and Transactions of the New York State Archaeological Association* 17(1):51–69.Rochester and Albany.

————. 1976. *Archaeology of the Oneida Iroquois: Vol. 1.* Occasional Papers in Northeast Archaeology, no. 1. George's Mills, N.H.: Man in the Northeast, Inc.

————. 1963. A heavily stockaded late prehistoric Oneida Iroquois settlement. *Pennsylvania Archaeologist.* 33(1–2):56–92.

————. 1961. *Oneida Iroquois glass trade bead sequence, 1585–1745.* Syracuse: Onondaga Printing Co.

Prevec, Rosemary and William C. Noble. 1983. Historic Neutral Iroquois faunal utilization. *Ontario Archaeology* 39:41–56.

Prisch, Betty C. 1982. *Aspects of change in Seneca Iroquois ladles A. D. 1600–1900.* Research Records, no. 15. Rochester: Rochester Museum and Science Center.

Purchas, Samuel. 1906. *Hakluytus posthumus, or Purchas his pilgrimes.* 20 vols. Glasgow: James MacLetiose and Sons.

Puype, Jan Piet. 1985. Dutch and other flintlocks from 17th century Iroquois sites. *Proceedings of the 1984 trade gun conference.* Research Records, no. 18, Part 1. Rochester, N.Y.: Rochester Museum and Science Center.

Ramsden Peter G. 1977a. *A refinement of some aspects of Huron ceramic analysis.* Paper 63, Mercury Series, Archaeological Survey of Canada. Ottawa: National Museum of Man.

————. 1977b. Current Iroquoian research in the upper Trent Valley, Province of Ontario. *Proceedings of the annual meeting, Eastern States Archaeological Federation.* Bulletin, nos. 35–36 (September):20.

Ray, Arthur J. 1978. History and archaeology of the northern fur trade. *American Antiquity* 43(1):26–34.

Ricklis, Robert. 1967. Excavation of a probable late prehistoric Onondaga house site. *Bulletin,* New York State Archaeological Association 39:15–17.

————. 1966. A preliminary report on some late prehistoric and early historic Onondaga sites near Syracuse, New York. *Newsletter,* Morgan Chapter, New York State Archaeological Association 6:1–13.

————. 1963. Excavations at the Atwell Fort site, Madison County, New York. *Bulletin,* New York State Archaeological Association 28:2–5.

Ritchie, William A. 1969. *The archaeology of New York State.* Rev. ed. Garden City: Natural History Press.

————. 1961. *A typology and nomenclature for New York projectile points.* New York State Museum and Science Service Bulletin, no. 384. Albany: University of the State of New York.

————. 1954. *Dutch Hollow, an early historic period Seneca site in Livingston County, New York.* Research Records, no. 10. Rochester: Rochester Museum of Arts and Sciences.

————. 1952. *The Chance horizon, an early stage of Mohawk Iroquois cultural development.* New York State Museum Circular, no. 29. Albany: University of the State of New York.

————. 1946. *A stratified prehistoric site at Brewerton, New York.* Research Records of the Rochester Museum of Arts and Sciences, no. 8. Rochester: Rochester Museum of Arts and Sciences.

———. 1944. *The pre-Iroquoian occupations of New York State.* Rochester Museum of Arts and Sciences, Memoir, no. 1. Rochester: Rochester Museum of Arts and Sciences.

———. 1936. *A prehistoric fortified village site at Camandaigua, Ontario County, New York.* Research Records of the Rochester Museum of Arts and Sciences, no.3. Rochester: Rochester Museum of Arts and Sciences.

Ritchie, William A. and Richard S. MacNeish. 1949. The pre-Iroquoian pottery of New York State. *American Antiquity* 15 (October):97–124.

Ritchie, William A. and Robert E. Funk. 1973. *Aboriginal settlement patterns in the Northeast.* New York State Museum and Science Service, Memoir, no. 20. Albany: University of the State of New York.

Rumrill, Donald A. 1985. An interpretation and analysis of the seventeenth century Mohawk nation: Its chronology and movements. *Bulletin and Journal of Archaeology for New York State* 90:1–39.

Russell, Carl P. 1967. *Firearms, traps, and tools of the mountain men.* New York: Alfred A. Knopf.

Ryder, A. F. C. 1965. Dutch trade on the Nigerian coast during the seventeenth century. *Journal of the Historical Society of Nigeria* 3(2):195–210.

Saraydar, Stephen and Izumi Shimada. 1971. A quantitative comparison of efficiency between a stone axe and a steel axe. *American Antiquity* 36(2):216–17.

Sassi, Anthony L., Jr. n.d. *Notes on the Amerind manufacture of smoking devices as artistic expression in northeastern Iroquois.* Private printing, n.p.

Scammell, G. V. 1981. *The world encompassed: The first European maritime empire c. 800–1650.* Berkeley: University of California Press.

Schroeder, D. L. and K. C. Ruhl. 1968. Metallurgical characteristics of North American prehistoric copper work. *American Antiquity* 33:162–69.

Scull, Gideon D., ed. 1885. *Voyages of Pierre Esprit Radisson, being an account of his travels and experiences among the North American Indians from 1652–1684.* Boston: The Prince Society.

Sheldon, R. E. 1952. Pollen analysis of central New York bogs. Ph.D. diss., Department of Forestry, Syracuse University.

Sidler, Earl R., III. 1971. The Durham site: A prehistoric Iroquois component in Jefferson County, New York. Master's thesis, Department of Anthropology, State University of New York at Buffalo.

Skinner, Alanson. 1921. *Notes on Iroquois archaeology.* New York: Museum of the American Indian, Heye Foundation.

Slotkin, J. S. and Karl Schmitt. 1949. Studies of wampum. *American Anthropologist* 51:223–36.

Smith, Ira F., III. 1973. The Parker site: A manifestation of the Wyoming Valley culture. *Pennsylvania Archaeologist* 43(3–4):1–56.

Smith, Ira F., III, and Jeffrey C. Graybill. 1977. A report on the Shenks Ferry and Susquehannock components at the Funk site, Lancaster County, Pennsylvania. *Man in the Northeast.* 11:45–65.

Smith, Marvin T. 1984. Depopulation and culture change in the early historic period interior southwest. Ph.D. diss., Department of Anthropology, University of Florida, Gainesville.

———. 1983. Chronology from glass beads: The Spanish period in the Southeast, 1513–1670. In *Proceedings of the 1982 glass trade bead conference,* ed. Charles

F. Hayes III, 147–58. Research Records, no. 16. Rochester: Rochester Museum and Science Center.

————. 1975. European materials from the King site. *Southeastern Archaeological Conference, Bulletin* 18:63–66.

Smith, Marvin T. and Mary Elizabeth Good. 1982. *Early sixteenth century glass beads in the Spanish colonial trade.* Greenwood, Miss.: Cottonlandia Museum Publications.

Social Science Research Council, Summer Seminar on Acculturation, 1953. 1954. Acculturation: An exploratory formulation. *American Anthropologist* 56(6):973–1000.

Sohrweide, Anton W. 1963. The Oak Orchard pot. *Pennsylvania Archaeologist* 33(1–2):51–53.

Solecki, Ralph. 1950. The archaeological position of historic Fort Corchang, L. I., and its relation to contemporary forts. *Bulletin, Archaeological Society of Connecticut* 24:3–40.

Spicer, Edward H. 1962. *Cycles of conquest. The impact of Spain, Mexico, and the United States on the Indians of the Southwest, 1533–1960.* Tucson: University of Arizona Press.

Starna, William A., George R. Hamell and William L. Butts. 1984. Northern Iroquois horticulture and insect infestation: A cause for village removal. *Ethnohistory* 31(3):197–207.

Stewart, Julian. 1942. The direct historical approach to archaeology. *American Antiquity* 7:337–43.

Stewart, Marilyn C. 1973. A proto-historic Susquehannock cemetery near Nichols, Tioga County, New York. *Bulletin, New York State Archaeological Association* 58:1–21.

Stone, Lyle M. 1974. *Fort Michilimackinac 1715–1781. An archeological perspective on the Revolutionary frontier.* East Lansing: Publications of the Museum, Michigan State University, in cooperation with the Mackinac Island State Park Commission.

Storey, Mike. 1977. *Heartland: A natural history of Onondaga County, New York.* Syracuse: Onondaga Audubon Society, Inc.

Sturtevant, William C., gen. ed. 1978. *Handbook of North American Indians.* Vol. 15, *Northeast,* ed. Bruce G. Trigger. Washington, D.C.: Smithsonian Institution.

Tanner, Tyree. 1978. The Lot 18 site. *Bulletin, William Beauchamp Chapter, New York State Archaeological Association* 3:1–10.

Thwaites, Reuben Gold. 1896–1901. *The Jesuit relations and allied documents.* 73 vols. Cleveland: The Burrows Brothers Co.

Tooker, Elisabeth. 1981. Eighteenth century political affairs and the Iroquois league. In *The Iroquois in the American Revolution,* ed. Charles F. Hayes, III, 1–12. Rochester: Rochester Museum and Science Center.

————. 1978. The league of the Iroquois: Its history, politics, and ritual. In *Northeast,* vol. 15 of *Handbook of North American Indians,* ed. Bruce G. Trigger, 418–41. Washington, D.C.: Smithsonian Institution.

Trelease, Allen. [1960] 1971. *Indian affairs in colonial New York: The seventeenth century.* Port Washington, N.Y.: Kennikat Press.

Trigger, Bruce G. 1983. American archaeology as native history: A review essay. *The William and Mary Quarterly* 40 (3rd series): 413–52.

————. 1978. Early Iroquoian contacts with Europeans. In *Northeast*, vol. 15 of *Handbook of North American Indians*, ed. Bruce G. Trigger, 344–56. Washington, D.C.: Smithsonian Institution.

————. 1976. *The children of Aataentsic: A history of the Huron people to 1660.* 2 vols. Montreal: McGill-Queen's University Press.

Trigger, Bruce G., ed. 1978. *Northeast*. Vol. 15 of *Handbook of North American Indians*. Washington, D.C.: Smithsonian Institution.

Trigger, Bruce G. and James F. Pendergast. 1978. Saint Lawrence Iroquoians. In *Northeast*, vol. 15 of *Handbook of North American Indians*, ed. Bruce G. Trigger, 357–61. Washington, D.C.: Smithsonian Institution.

Trudel, Marcel. 1973. *The beginnings of New France, 1524–1663*, trans. Patricia Claxton. Toronto: McClelland and Stewart, Ltd.

Tuck, James A. 1978. *Northern Iroquoian prehistory*. In *Northeast*, vol. 15 of *Handbook of North American Indians*, ed. Bruce G. Trigger, 322–33. Washington, D.C.: Smithsonian Institution.

————. 1971. *Onondaga Iroquois prehistory a study in settlement archaeology*. Syracuse: Syracuse University Press.

————. 1969. Iroquoian cultural development in central New York. Ph.D. diss., Department of Anthropology, Syracuse University, Syracuse, N.Y.

Van Laer, Arnold J. F., ed. 1908. *Van Rensselaer Bowier manuscripts, being the letters of Kiliaen Van Rensselaer, 1630–1643, and other documents relating to the colony of Rensselaerswyck.* Albany: University of the State of New York.

Wallace, Anthony F. C. 1972. *The death and rebirth of the Seneca*. New York: Vintage Books.

————. 1958. The Dekanawideh myth analyzed as the record of a revitalization movement. *Ethnohistory* 5(2):118–30.

————. 1956. Revitalization movements: Some theoretical considerations for their comparative study. *American Anthropologist* 58(2):264–81.

Webb, Stephen S. 1984. *1676, the end of American independence*. New York: Alfred A. Knopf.

Weber, Joann Cynthia. 1970. Types and attributes in the study of Iroquois pipes. Ph.D. diss., Department of Anthropology, Harvard University, Cambridge, Mass.

Weinman, Paul L. and Thomas P. Weinman. 1982. The Conway site. On the way to Onondaga. *Bulletin and Journal of Archaeology for New York State* 83:7–15.

Wells, Peter S. 1980. *Culture contact and culture change: Early Iron Age central Europe and the Mediterranean world.* Cambridge: Cambridge University Press.

Willcoxen, Charlotte. 1982. Dutch majolica of the seventeenth century. *American Ceramic Circle Bulletin* 3:17–28.

Willoughby, Charles C. 1935. *Antiquities of the New England Indians*. Cambridge, Mass.: Cosmos Press.

Wintemberg, W. J. [1936] 1972. *Roebuck prehistoric village site, Greenville County, Ontario*. National Museum of Canada Bulletin, no. 83. Ottawa: National Museum of Canada.

Witthoft, John and W. Fred Kinsey, eds. [1959] 1969. *Susquehannock miscellany*. Harrisburg: Pennsylvania Historical and Museum Commission.

Witthoft, John and S. S. Farver. 1952. Two Shenks Ferry sites in Lebanon County, Pennsylvania. *Pennsylvania Archaeologist* 22(1):3–32.

Wolf, Eric R. 1982. *Europe and the people without history*. Berkeley: University of California Press.

Wood, Alice S. 1974. A catalogue of Jesuit and ornamental rings from western New York State. *Historical Archaeology* 8:83–104.

Worsley, Peter. 1968. *The Trumpet shall sound: A study of "cargo" cults in Melanesia.* Second augmented edition. New York: Schocken Books.

Wray, Charles F. 1985. The volume of Dutch trade goods received by the Seneca Iroquois, 1600–1687 A.D. *New Netherland Studies Bulletin KNOB* Jaargang 84(2–3):100–12.

———. 1978. Varieties and sources of flint found in New York State. *Pennsylvania Archaeologist* 18(nos. 1–2):25–45.

———. 1973. *Manual for Seneca Iroquois archeology.* Honeoye Falls, N.Y.: Cultures Primitive, Inc.

———. 1948. Varieties and sources of flint found in New York State. *Pennsylvania Archaeologist* 18(1–2):25–45.

Wray, Charles F. and Harry Schoff. 1953. A preliminary report on the Seneca sequence in western New York. *Pennsylvania Archaeologist* 23(2):53–61.

Wren, Christopher. 1914. *A study of North Appalachian Indian pottery.* Wilkes-Barre: E. B. Yordy Company.

———. 1909. Turtle shell rattles and other implements from Indian graves at Athens, Pennsylvania. *Wyoming Historical and Geological Society Publications* 13:194–210.

Wright, James V. [1966] 1973. *The Ontario Iroquois tradition.* National Museum of Canada Bulletin, no. 210. Ottawa: National Museum of Canada.

Wright, Milton J. 1981. *The Walker site.* Paper no. 103:vi–209, Mercury Series, Archaeological Survey of Canada. Ottawa: National Museum of Man.

Yeager, Donald. 1969. A pollen profile from Kennedy's Bog in Mendon Ponds Park. *Proceedings,* Rochester Academy of Science 12 (October):24–45.

Ypey, J. 1976. Mondharpen. *Antiek* 11(3):209–31.

Index

EVOLUTION OF THE ONONDAGA IROQUOIS

was composed in 10 on 13 Trump Mediaeval on a Malibu Autologic
by Williams Press, Inc.;
with display type set in Bernhard Gothic by Typotronics Inc.;
printed by sheet-fed offset on 50-pound, acid-free Glatfelter Natural Hi-Bulk,
Smyth sewn and bound over binder's boards in Holliston Roxite C,
by Braun-Brumfield, Inc.;
with dust jackets printed in two colors
by Braun-Brumfield, Inc.;
and published by

SYRACUSE UNIVERSITY PRESS
SYRACUSE, NEW YORK 13244–5160